Machine Learning and Deep Learning Driven Techniques for Multimodal Data Security in the Internet of Multimedia Things

Other related titles:

You may also like

- PBSE031 | Srivastava | Intelligence-driven Smart Technologies for Multimedia and Multimodal Data Security (Multimedia book series) | under development
- PBSE032 | Ur Rehman| AI and Post-Quantum Approaches for Multimedia Security: Foundations, protocols, and applications (Multimedia book series) | under development
- PBPC082 | Dalal | Generative AI in Multimedia Content Processing: Security and privacy perspectives (Multimedia book series) | 2026
- PBSE030 | Deb | Fortressing: Information security for images, videos, audio and beyond (Multimedia book series) | 2026

We also publish a wide range of books on the following topics:
Agricultural Engineering and Technology
Applied Physics
Built Environment
Computing and Networks
Control, Robotics and Sensors
Electrical Regulations
Electromagnetics and Radar
Energy Engineering
Healthcare Technologies
History and Management of Technology
IET Codes and Guidance
Materials, Circuits and Devices
Model Forms
Nanomaterials and Nanotechnologies
Production, Design and Manufacturing
Security
Telecommunications
Transportation

All books are available in print via https://shop.theiet.org or as eBooks via our Digital Library https://digital-library.theiet.org.

IET SECURITY SERIES 29

The IET International Book Series on Multimedia Information Processing and Security

Call for author's page

Multimedia data (and more generally multimodal data) stands as one of the most demanding and exciting aspects of the information era. The processing of multimedia has been an active research area with applications in secure multimedia contents on social networks, digital forensic, digital cinema, education, secured e-voting systems, smart healthcare, automotive applications, the military, insurance and more. The advent of the internet of things (IoT), big data, cyber-physical systems (CPSs), robotics as well as personal and wearable devices now provide many opportunities for the multimedia community to reach out and develop synergies.

This book series comprehensively defines the current trends and technological aspects of multimedia research with a particular emphasis on interdisciplinary approaches. The authors will review a broad scope to identify challenges, solutions and new directions The published books can be used as references by practicing engineers, scientists, researchers, practitioners and technology professionals from academia, government and Industry working on state-of-the-art multimedia processing, analysis, search, mining, management and security solutions for practical applications. It will also be useful to senior undergraduate and graduate students.

This book series comprehensively defines the current trends and technological aspects of multimedia research with a particular emphasis on interdisciplinary approaches. The authors will review a broad scope to identify challenges, solutions and new directions The published books can be used as references by practicing engineers, scientists, researchers, practitioners and technology professionals from academia, government and Industry working on state-of-the-art multimedia processing, analysis, search, mining, management and security solutions for practical applications. It will also be useful to senior undergraduate and graduate students.

- Dr. Amit Kumar Singh, Department of Computer Science & Engineering, National Institute of Technology Patna, India; Emails: amit_245singh@yahoo.com; amit.singh@nitp.ac.in
- Prof. Stefano Berretti, Media Integration and Communication Center (MICC) & Department of Information Engineering (DINFO), University of Florence, Italy; E-mail: stefano.berretti@unifi.it

Machine Learning and Deep Learning Driven Techniques for Multimodal Data Security in the Internet of Multimedia Things

Sita Rani and Sachin Kumar

The Institution of Engineering and Technology

About the IET

This book is published by the Institution of Engineering and Technology (The IET).

We inspire, inform and influence the global engineering community to engineer a better world. As a diverse home across engineering and technology, we share knowledge that helps make better sense of the world, to accelerate innovation and solve the global challenges that matter.

The IET is a not-for-profit organisation. The surplus we make from our books is used to support activities and products for the engineering community and promote the positive role of science, engineering and technology in the world. This includes education resources and outreach, scholarships and awards, events and courses, publications, professional development and mentoring, and advocacy to governments.

To discover more about the IET, please visit https://www.theiet.org/.

About IET books

The IET publishes books across many engineering and technology disciplines. Our authors and editors offer fresh perspectives from universities and industry. Within our subject areas, we have several book series steered by editorial boards made up of leading subject experts.

We peer review each book at the proposal stage to ensure the quality and relevance of our publications.

Get involved

If you are interested in becoming an author, editor, series advisor, or peer reviewer please visit https://www.theiet.org/publishing/publishing-with-iet-books/ or contact author_support@theiet.org.

Discovering our electronic content

All of our books are available online via the IET's Digital Library. Our Digital Library is the home of technical documents, eBooks, conference publications, real-life case studies and journal articles. To find out more, please visit https://digital-library.theiet.org.

In collaboration with the United Nations and the International Publishers Association, the IET is a Signatory member of the SDG Publishers Compact. The Compact aims to accelerate progress to achieve the Sustainable Development Goals (SDGs) by 2030. Signatories aspire to develop sustainable practices and act as champions of the SDGs during the Decade of Action (2020–30), publishing books and journals that will help inform, develop, and inspire action in that direction.

In line with our sustainable goals, our UK printing partner has FSC accreditation, which is reducing our environmental impact to the planet. We use a print-on-demand model to further reduce our carbon footprint.

Published by The Institution of Engineering and Technology, London, United Kingdom

The Institution of Engineering and Technology (the "**Publisher**") is registered as a Charity in England & Wales (no. 211014) and Scotland (no. SC038698).

Published: 2026

The Institution of Engineering and Technology
Futures Place,
Kings Way,
Stevenage,
Herts, SG1 2UA,
United Kingdom

www.theiet.org

British Library Cataloguing in Publication Data
A catalogue record for this product is available from the British Library

ISBN 978-1-83724-135-4 (hardback)
ISBN 978-1-83724-136-1 (PDF)
ISBN 978-1-80705-349-9 (ePub3)

Typeset in India by MPS Limited

Cover image credit: andresr/E+ via Getty Images

Contents

Foreword

Multimedia (and more generally multimodal data) stands as one of the most demanding and exciting aspects of the information era. The processing of multimedia has been an active research area with applications in secure multimedia content on social networks, digital forensics, digital cinema, education, secured e-voting systems, smart healthcare, automotive applications, the military, finance, insurance, and more. The advent of the Internet of Things (IoT), cyber–physical systems (CPSs) and robotics as well as personal and wearable devices now provide many opportunities for the multimedia community to reach out and develop synergies.

Our book series comprehensively defines the current trends and technological aspects of multimedia research with a particular emphasis on interdisciplinary approaches. The authors will review a broad scope to identify challenges, solutions, and new directions. The published books can be used as references by practicing engineers, scientists, researchers, practitioners, and technology professionals from academia, government, and industry working on state-of-the-art multimedia processing and security in Industry 5.0 applications. It will also be useful to senior undergraduate and graduate students as well as PhD students and Postdoc researchers.

The book titled "*Machine Learning and Deep Learning Driven Techniques for Multimodal Data Security in the Internet of Multimedia Things*" focuses on advanced artificial intelligence methods to protect multimedia data such as images, videos, audio, and sensor data in interconnected smart systems. The book explains how machine learning (ML) and deep learning (DL) techniques can enhance privacy, authentication, encryption, and intrusion detection in the Internet of Multimedia Things (IoMT) in diverse application domains. It highlights the importance of multimodal data fusion, where information from different sources is combined to improve security accuracy and decision-making. The text also discusses real-world applications in healthcare, smart cities, surveillance, and communication networks. Emphasis is placed on emerging technologies such as federated learning, blockchain, and neural networks to address modern cyber threats. Overall, the book serves as a useful reference for researchers and students working in AI-driven cybersecurity and multimedia data protection.

We hope the readers will find this book of great value in its visionary words.

Dr. Amit Kumar Singh, Book Series Editor
Department of Computer Science and Engineering
National Institute of Technology, Patna 800005, India

Prof. Stefano Berretti, Book Series Editor
Department of Information Engineering
University of Florence, Florence 50139, Italy

About the authors

Sita Rani is a postdoctoral research scientist at the University of South Florida, USA, and also serves at Guru Nanak Dev Engineering College, Ludhiana, India. She earned her PhD in Computer Science and Engineering from I.K. Gujral Punjab Technical University, India, in 2018 and completed her postdoctoral research at South Ural State University, Russia (2022–23). She also holds a PG certificate in Data Science and Machine Learning from IIT Roorkee.

With over 23 years of academic and research experience, she has been recognized among Stanford University's Top 2% Scientists (2024, 2025). She has received the ISTE Best Teacher Award (2020) and the International Young Scientist Award (2021). Her work includes SCIE/Scopus publications, patents, books, and contributions to AI, data science, healthcare, and sustainability.

Sachin Kumar is an associate professor and researcher in the Akian College of Science and Engineering at the American University of Armenia (AUA), Yerevan, Armenia, since July 2024, and is currently serving as vice chair of IEEE Armenia subsection. He is a senior member of the Institute of Electrical and Electronics Engineers (IEEE), a life member of the International Association of Engineers (IAENG), and a member of the Association for Computing Machinery (ACM). He is an associate editor of various indexed journals published by the IET, Wiley, Elsevier, and Nature. His research interests include AI and its applications to smart environments, Internet of Things, natural language processing, and cognitive sciences. He is the author of 90+ scientific articles published in peer-reviewed journals indexed in Web of Science (WoS) and Scopus. He earned his PhD degree in Data Mining from IIT Roorkee, India.

Glossary

A

Access Control	Restricting and managing who can view, use, or modify resources or information
Accuracy	The proportion of correct predictions made by the model out of all predictions
Adversarial Attacks	Adversarial attacks are deliberate manipulations of input data designed to trick machine learning models into making incorrect predictions
Annotation	The process of labeling or tagging data (text, images, audio, etc.) to make it understandable for machine learning models
Asymmetric Encryption	A cryptographic method that uses two different keys – a public key for encryption and a private key for decryption
Attack Vectors	The methods used by attackers to gain unauthorized access to a system or data
Authentication	The process of verifying the identity of a user, device, or system before granting access
Autoencoders	Neural network models that learn to compress data into a lower-dimensional representation and then reconstruct the original data
Autonomous Systems	Systems that can operate and make decisions independently without human intervention

B

Big Data	Extremely large and complex datasets that require advanced tools and techniques for storage, processing, and analysis
Big Data Analytics	The process of analyzing large and complex datasets to discover patterns, trends, and useful insights
Blockchain	A decentralized digital ledger that securely records transactions in linked blocks across multiple computers

C

Compression Tools	Software or algorithms used to reduce the size of data for efficient storage and transmission
Computational Cost	The amount of time, memory, and processing power required to run an algorithm or model

Convolutional Neural Networks (CNNs)	Deep learning models designed to automatically extract features from images and spatial data
Cross-Modal Representations	Data representations that integrate information from multiple modalities such as text, image, audio, or video
Collaborative Intelligence	An approach where humans and AI systems work together to improve decision-making and problem-solving
Cross-Modality Attacks	Cyberattacks that exploit relationships between different data types (e.g., image and text) to mislead AI models
Cryptographic Techniques	Mathematical methods used to secure data through encryption, hashing, and digital signatures
Cybersecurity	The practice of protecting systems, networks, and data from digital attacks and unauthorized access

D

Data Alignment	The process of matching and synchronizing data from different sources or modalities to ensure consistency
Distributed Computing	A computing method where multiple interconnected computers share tasks to improve performance and efficiency
Distributed Denial-of-Service (DDoS)	A cyberattack in which multiple systems flood a server or network to make it unavailable to users
Data Cleaning	The process of detecting and correcting errors, missing values, or inconsistencies in a dataset
Dimensionality	The presence of many features or variables in multimodal data, increasing complexity for analysis
Data Lifecycle	The complete sequence of stages a dataset goes through, from creation and storage to processing, sharing, and deletion
Data Labeling	The process of assigning meaningful tags or categories to data for training machine learning models
Data Modality	The type or form of data such as text, image, audio, video, or sensor data
Data Ownership	The legal rights and control over the collection, use, and distribution of data
Data Poisoning	A cyberattack where malicious or manipulated data is inserted into a dataset to corrupt machine learning model performance
Data Preprocessing	The set of steps applied to raw data to prepare it for analysis or machine learning, such as normalization and cleaning
Data Privacy	The protection of personal or sensitive data from unauthorized access or misuse

Data Breaches	Sensitive multimedia data (e.g., medical videos, images) intercepted during transmission or stored insecurely
Data Scalability	The ability of a system to handle increasing volumes of data efficiently without performance loss
Data Visualization	Interactive charts, graphs, and dashboards to support data-driven decision-making
Denial-of-Service (DoS)	Overloading networks to degrade multimedia service availability
Deep Learning	A subset of machine learning that uses multilayer neural networks to learn complex patterns from large datasets
Descriptive Analytics	The analysis of historical data to understand past trends and patterns
Differential Privacy	A privacy-preserving technique that protects individual data by adding controlled noise while allowing useful analysis

E

Encryption	The process of converting data into a coded form to prevent unauthorized access
Early Fusion	A technique that combines data from multiple modalities at the input stage before model processing
End-to-End Encryption	A security method where data is encrypted on the sender's device and decrypted only on the receiver's device
Electronic Health Records (EHRs)	Digital versions of patients' medical history, diagnoses, treatments, and health information
Explainable AI	AI methods that provide understandable explanations for how models make decisions
Exploratory Analytics	The process of analyzing data to discover patterns, relationships, or insights without predefined assumptions
Edge Computing	A computing approach where data processing occurs near the data source instead of a centralized cloud
Educational IoT	IoT-based smart devices and systems used to enhance teaching, learning, and campus management
Energy-Efficient Computing	Designing computing systems and algorithms that consume less power while maintaining performance

F

F1 Score	A performance metric that balances precision and recall, used to evaluate classification models, especially with imbalanced data
Federated Learning	A machine learning approach where models are trained across multiple devices or servers without sharing raw data, ensuring privacy

Feature Engineering	The process of selecting, transforming, and creating input variables (features) to improve machine learning model performance
Fusion	The integration of data from multiple sources (e.g., sensors, datasets) to produce more accurate and reliable information
Fog Computing	A decentralized computing approach that processes data closer to the source (between cloud and devices) to reduce latency and bandwidth use

G

Gated Recurrent Unit (GRU)	A type of recurrent neural network that captures sequence patterns efficiently using gates
Graph Learning	Machine learning techniques that analyze data represented as nodes and connections
Graph Neural Networks (GNNs)	Neural networks designed to learn from graph-structured data
Geospatial Data	Data that contains location information such as coordinates, maps, or regions

H

Hadoop	An open-source framework for storing and processing large datasets across distributed computers
Hadoop Distributed File System (HDFS)	A distributed storage system in Hadoop that stores big data across multiple machines
Heterogeneity	Diversity in data types, formats, structures, or statistical properties across different sources/modalities
Homomorphic Encryption (HE)	An encryption method that allows computations to be performed on encrypted data without decrypting it
Hybrid Fusion	A method that combines multiple fusion approaches (e.g., data, feature, decision) to improve accuracy

I

Identity Theft	Unauthorized use of someone's personal information for fraud
Internet of Multimedia Things (IoMT)	Network of devices that capture, process, and share multimedia data (audio, video, images)
Internet of Things (IoT)	Network of connected physical devices that collect and exchange data via the Internet
Industrial IoT	Use of IoT technologies in industries for monitoring, control, and automation
Integrity Risks	Threats that may alter or damage data accuracy or reliability

Industrial Automation Use of control systems and machines to operate industrial processes with minimal human intervention

Interactive Storytelling Multimedia-based platforms for creating interactive movies, web series, and choose-your-own-adventure experiences

L

Late Fusion Combining results from multiple models or data sources at the decision stage

Lightweight Cryptography Encryption methods designed for devices with limited power, memory, or processing capacity

M

MapReduce A programming model for processing large datasets in parallel across distributed systems

Machine Learning A method where computers learn patterns from data to make predictions or decisions

Modality-Specific Attacks Attacks targeting a particular data type such as image, text, or audio

Multimodal AI AI systems that process and integrate multiple types of data (e.g., text, image, audio)

Multimodal Data Data from different formats such as text, images, audio, video, or sensors

Multimodal Data Analytics Analysis of data from multiple modalities to extract useful insights

Multimodal Datasets Collections of data containing multiple data types or modalities

Multimodal Databases Databases designed to store and manage multiple types of data formats

Multimodal Environments Systems or settings where multiple data types are generated and used

Multimedia Formats File formats used to store media such as images, audio, and video (e.g., JPEG, MP3, MP4)

Multimedia Systems Computer systems designed to process, store, and transmit multimedia content

Multimodal Security Security methods that protect systems handling multiple types of data

Multimedia Technologies Technologies used to create, process, and deliver multimedia content

Multimodal Fusion Networks Neural networks that combine information from multiple data modalities for better predictions

N

Networking Components	Hardware or software elements (e.g., router, switch, server) used to connect and manage networks
Noise	Unwanted or irrelevant data that reduces the accuracy or quality of information
NoSQL	Non-relational databases designed to store and manage large, unstructured, or flexible data

P

Physical Attacks	Tampering with or stealing IoMT devices
Precision Agriculture	Use of sensors, data, and technology to optimize farming and improve crop yield
Privacy	Protection of personal or sensitive information from unauthorized access
Predictive Modeling	Using data and algorithms to forecast future outcomes
Precision (ML models)	The proportion of correctly predicted positive results among all predicted positives
Privacy-Preserving Machine Learning (PPML)	ML methods that protect sensitive data while training models

R

RFID (Radio Frequency Identification)	Technology that uses radio waves to automatically identify and track tagged objects
Rehabilitation	Use of interactive games or apps to support physical and cognitive therapy recovery
Real-Time Analytics	Immediate analysis of data as soon as it is generated
Recurrent Neural Networks (RNNs)	Neural networks designed to process sequential data such as text or time series
Recall	The proportion of actual positive cases correctly identified by a model
Redundancy	Presence of overlapping or repeated information across multiple data sources/modalities
Recurrent Neural Networks (RNNs)	A deep learning model that captures patterns in sequential or time-dependent data

S

Sensor Data	Data collected from sensors measuring physical conditions like temperature, motion, or pressure
Social Media Data	Information generated from social platforms such as posts, images, videos, and interactions
Secure Communication	Exchange of information protected from unauthorized access using security methods
Secure Multi-Party Computation (SMPC)	A method that allows multiple parties to jointly compute results without sharing their private data
Security Systems	Technologies designed to protect data, devices, or infrastructure from threats
Split Learning	A machine learning approach where model training is divided between devices to enhance data privacy
Smart Contract	A self-executing digital contract with rules stored on a blockchain
Surgical Simulation	Use of VR/AR technology to train and practice surgical procedures safely
Supply Chain Management	Management of the flow of goods, information, and resources from production to delivery
Symmetric Encryption	Encryption method where the same key is used for both encryption and decryption

T

Threat Landscape	Overview of current and emerging cybersecurity threats and risks
Transformers	Deep learning models that use attention mechanisms to process sequential data like text or images efficiently

V

Variational Autoencoders (VAEs)	Generative neural networks that learn data patterns and create new, similar data samples
Virtual and Augmented Reality (VR/AR)	Immersive environments for gaming, simulations, and interactive storytelling using headsets and real-time rendering
Virtual Reality Therapy	Uses VR to treat psychological conditions like phobias and PTSD through controlled exposure

Z

Zigbee	A low-power wireless communication technology used for short-range data transfer in IoT and smart devices

Chapter 1
Introduction to multimodal data

Abstract

Multimodal data combines numerous forms of data, including text, images, audio, and sensor inputs, among others, to gain deeper understanding than can be acquired through unimodal data. This chapter presents the concept of multimodal data and pays attention to its significance in modern practice, including multimedia analysis, autonomous systems, and medicine. It explains significant methods of fusion and representation learning and attracts attention to the challenges associated with the accumulation, coordination, and processing of multiple streams of data. Readers are introduced to foundational concepts, typical sources of data, and real-world applications to demonstrate the power and complexity of multimodal systems. This chapter sets the foundation for discussing more intricate topics in multimodal learning, integration, and applications as the role of multimodal data is clearly defined.

Keywords: data preprocessing; early fusion; late fusion; multimodal; Internet of Multimedia Things (IoMT)

1.1 Overview of multimodal data

We have entered the era of data-driven life, whereby massive amounts of digital data are created, collected, and processed on a daily basis. The advancements in technology have made it possible to use this data to innovate, automate, and make informed decisions that have transformed the behavior and interactions of people, organizations, and governments in different areas. The information obtained in different sources is in diverse modalities or forms and these are: text, images, audio, video, and sensor data. The different modalities offer different and complementary views on the same topic or event. As an illustration, in a healthcare setting, the record of a patient can contain clinical notes, medical images, or physiological signals. Combining these various types of data makes the analysis more comprehensive and allows for a better understanding. The multimodal data processing needs special methods to match and integrate various formats. It is an important component of artificial intelligence applications such as medical diagnosis, autonomous systems, emotion recognition, and human–computer interaction, where a more detailed, more precise understanding is needed [1].

1.1.1 Definition and scope

Multimodal data is information collected via multiple types or sources of signals, such as text, photos, audio, video, sensor measurements, and so on. Each modality captures different aspects or perspectives of the same phenomenon, which provides additional data which, when combined, allows a deeper and more comprehensive understanding. Multimodal data deals with a broad scope of areas, which include robotics, healthcare, artificial intelligence, multimedia, and human–computer interaction. Improving such operations as pattern recognition, decision-making, and prediction involves compiling, matching, integrating, and evaluating numerous types of data. Through the use of complementary information in modalities, multimodal data will enable the development of more robust, accurate, and context-driven systems, enhancing uses such as augmented reality, medical diagnostics, autonomous driving, and sentiment analysis.

1.1.2 Examples and sources on the Internet of Multimedia Things (IoMT)

Multimodal data is provided by a variety of networked sensors and devices in the Internet of Multimedia Things (IoMT), whose collection of numerous types of data is used to create a complete image of user states and the environment. One of the primary sources is video and picture streams of cameras utilized in smart cities, smart homes, and medical facilities. As medical apparatus such as MRI scanners and X-ray machines generate high-resolution images to be used in telemedicine and remote diagnoses, surveillance cameras, such as the ones used in security surveillance, provide 24/7 video to be used in security measures. Audio data is another critical IoMT modality that is collected by microphones installed in wearables and smart devices. This will incorporate voice commands in smart assistants and background noise to monitor the noise levels in the city or detect an event, like falls or emergencies, in healthcare facilities. Also, various sensors employ embedded Internet of Things sensors or wearable health sensors to log environmental and physiological data, such as motion, temperature, humidity, and heart rate. The use of GPS and accelerometer information provided by mobile smartphones is the basis of location and movement tracking that is necessary in applications like patient monitoring and tracking of assets. Textual data, which is also highly significant, is formed by logs generated by IoMT systems, by the input of the user, and by electronic health records. Social media messages and material can be used to enhance contextual awareness. The combination of various multimodal sources of data can help to supply more accurate and real-time information provided by IoMT applications, which will improve interactive multimedia services, security, and patient care.

1.2 Types of modalities

The general data modalities are text (documents, social media), images (photos, medical scans), audio (speech, music), video (surveillance, movies), sensor data (wearables, Internet of Things (IoT) devices), and numerical data (statistics, financial records) [2]. A combination of these modalities improves analysis and decision-making in a wide variety of fields [3]. Figure 1.1 gives various data modalities and their uses.

1.2.1 Visual data

Visual data is the information presented in the form of pictures or films so that people and machines can understand and analyze the visual data. This comprises pictures, movies, graphs, charts, satellite images, medical scans (e.g., MRIs, CT scans, and X-rays), and videos. Visual data is invaluable in such areas as entertainment, security, health care, and remote sensing since it offers contextual and geographical information that cannot be offered by numbers or texts alone. The recent advances in computer vision and deep learning have greatly enhanced the capability of automatic interpretation of visual input. It has resulted in the use of autonomous vehicles, object detection, medical diagnosis, and facial recognition, which enhance automation and decision-making [4].

1.2.2 Audio data

Audio data is sound information stored digitally or analogously, either as speech, music, ambient noise, or other auditory signals. It is used in sound monitoring, music analysis, speech-to-text, and voice recognition. Audio processing involves signal processing, feature extraction, and machine learning to decode and classify sounds. The use of audio-based diagnostics, transcription software, and voice assistants has become more functional due to recent advances in natural language processing and deep learning. Audio data is also mandatory in the fields of surveillance, accessibility technologies, and human–computer interaction, as it gives information to supplement written and visual data [5].

1.2.3 Textual data

Textual data is information that is provided in a written format, which includes emails, reports, articles, social media posts, and documents. It has wide application in natural language processing (NLP) applications such as chatbots, machine translation, sentiment analysis, and information retrieval. The methods, such as tokenization, parsing, and semantic analysis, are applied when handling textual data to locate significant trends and insights. Advances in the field of deep learning, especially transformer-based models, have enhanced human language generation and understanding to a great extent. Given that text data transforms unstructured text into usable, useful data, it is essential to knowledge management, decision-making, and customer service [5].

1.2.4 Sensor and IoT signals

IoT and sensor signals are data streams generated by equipment that monitors variables that are biological, environmental, or physical. Sensors measure such

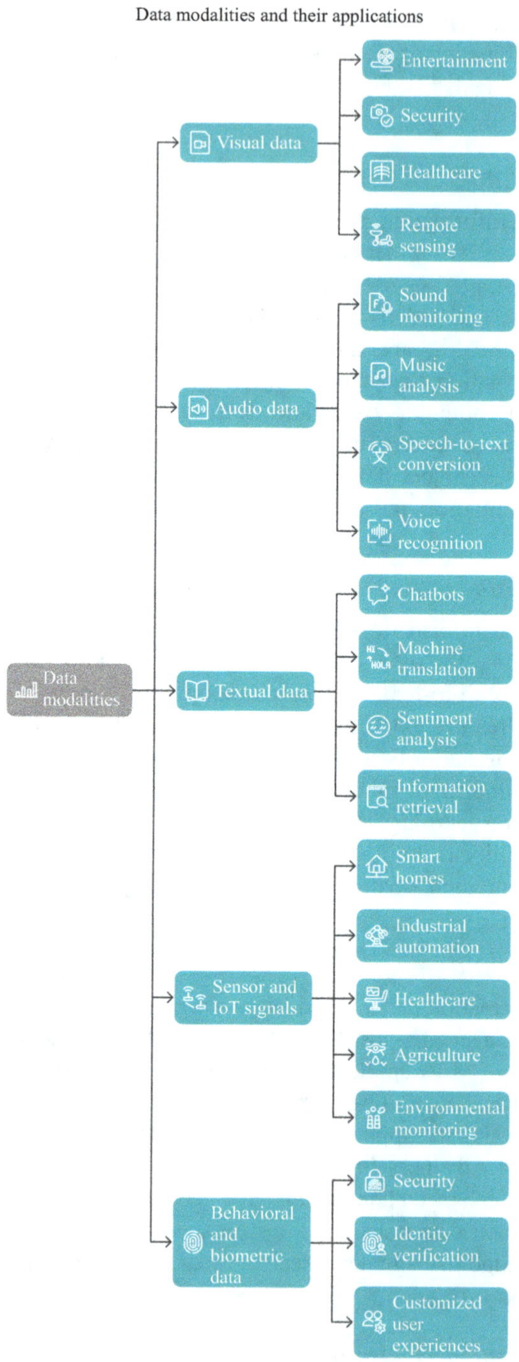

Figure 1.1 Data modalities and respective applications

things as temperature, humidity, motion, heart rate, and air quality, and IoT (Internet of Things) devices connect these sensors to networks to allow transmitting and analyzing data in real time. These signals make it possible to have smart homes, industrial automation, healthcare, agriculture, and environmental monitoring. To detect anomalies, to optimize systems, and to facilitate the decision-making process, sensor and Internet of Things data will have to be processed through filtering, pattern recognition, and machine learning. The combination of these signals makes it easy to predict maintenance, enhance automation, and make various industries more efficient.

1.2.5 Behavioral and biometric data

Biometric and behavioral data capture different patterns in regard to the actions and physical appearance of a person. Data on the behavior of individuals in their use of gadgets are known as behavioral data, e.g., the way individuals type, the movements of their mouse, or how they browse. Physical characteristics like voice patterns, heart rate, iris scan, fingerprints, and facial recognition are all biometric data that can be measured. There are many uses of this type of data such as security, identity authentication, and personalized user experiences. Biometric and behavioral data analysis enhances monitoring of healthcare and increases access control and fraud detection. The precision and reliability of systems that use such data have been enhanced with the advancement of machine learning, which makes interaction with them safer and smoother. Table 1.1 summarizes various data modalities, their sources, and applications.

Table 1.1 Data, sources, and uses

Data modality	**Sources**	**Applications**
Text data	Books, emails, social media, websites	Sentiment analysis, language translation, chatbots
Image data	Cameras, satellites, medical imaging devices	Object detection, medical diagnosis, surveillance
Audio data	Microphones, voice recordings, music files	Speech recognition, music recommendation, voice assistants
Video data	CCTV cameras, smartphones, streaming platforms	Video surveillance, autonomous vehicles, video analytics
Sensor data	IoT devices, wearables, environmental sensors	Health tracking, smart cities, industrial automation
Numerical data	Financial records, sensor readings, surveys	Statistical analysis, forecasting, business intelligence
Behavioral data	Website clicks, app usage, user interactions	User profiling, recommendation systems, fraud detection
Biometric data	Fingerprints, facial recognition, iris scans	Security authentication, access control, identity verification

1.3 Characteristics and challenges

Multimodal data is data that includes a combination of various types of data (e.g., text, images, audio), which provides more comprehensive and deeper insights. Its peculiarities are high dimensions, heterogeneity, and different formats. The issues include data fusion, synchronization, and missing or noisy modalities. The processing of a wide range of sources will demand sophisticated algorithms to identify significant correlations and be readable. The complexity of computations and data quality between modalities are major challenges to successful multimodal analysis, as well [6].

1.3.1 Heterogeneity and dimensionality

Heterogeneity and dimensionality are two critical characteristics and challenges of multimodal data processing. Heterogeneity is the term used to refer to the diversity of data kinds, which are utilized, such as text, photo, audio, and sensor signals, all of which possess distinct forms, structures, and statistical features. This diversity presents a challenge to the task of data integration since different modalities often require different preprocessing, feature extraction, and modeling methods. Heterogeneous data have to be brought into one representation with complex algorithms that are capable of bridging modality gaps without losing key information. In the combination of multiple modalities, the term dimensionality is used to mean the richness of characteristics or variables. High-dimensional data can cause computational problems including increased processing time, increased memory usage, and overfitting of machine learning models. It complicates interpretation and visualization as well. This complexity requires the application of good dimensionality reduction and feature selection methods to ensure that very important information is not lost. Heterogeneity and dimensionality, as they are put together, pose big challenges to creating reliable, effective, and interpretable multimodal systems [7,8].

1.3.2 Synchronization and alignment

Synchronization and alignment are two important points and characteristics of multimodal data. Multimodal fusion needs the signals of multiple modalities (text, audio, and video) to be coherent in time, which synchronization ensures. The synchronization would, however, be hard because of the differences in sample rates, device latencies, and signal drift, which influence audiovisual speech acknowledgment activities. It is necessary to align information across modalities to a common reference to understand cross-modal interactions, including relating spoken words to facial expressions, since this is a fundamental aspect of understanding cross-modal interactions. The dissimilarity of modalities in terms of structure and semantics, however, complicates the alignment process and requires either manual annotation or complicated models such as attention mechanisms. All these problems are caused by the inherent heterogeneity of multimodal data, whereas asynchrony and structural differences should be considered to support logical analysis. Some of the solutions include joint embedding technique, dynamic time warping, and hardware synchronization. These issues are vital to multimodal systems to make them reliable and comprehensible.

1.3.3 Noise and redundancy

Two major characteristics and challenges of multimodal data are redundancy and noise. Irrelevant or distorted signals may be caused by environmental factors, faulty sensors, or modality-specific artifacts (including motion blur in video or background noise in audio) and are known as noise. It is a fact in real-world data, but it raises issues where important information is not obtained due to noise that covers the relevant details. The background noise can be a nuisance to voice recognition, e.g., whereas occlusions can affect visual analysis. Redundancy, on the other hand, refers to information that is repeated or that cuts across modalities, e.g., voice and lip movements that carry the same semantic information. Redundancy may help enhance robustness because the data that has been lost in one modality may be accessible in another modality, yet it may also complicate learning by introducing bias or overfitting. Models can be disoriented by conflicting duplicate cues or oversensitized to one modality and neglect to take into account complementary information. Multimodal learning involves the need to deal with redundancy and noise. Noise is minimized and redundancy can be controlled by weighting more reliable signals and eliminating spurious signals by using modality dropout, denoising autoencoders, and attention mechanisms. Finally, effective multimodal data fusion and interpretation require finding a balance between the two characteristics [9,10].

Various characteristics and challenges of multimodal data are summarized in Table 1.2.

1.4 Importance in security applications

Multimodal data is necessary in security applications as it enhances accuracy and reliability. With audio, video, and sensor data, systems are more able to detect abnormalities, authenticate users, and track suspicious activity. To illustrate, a combination of video feed and motion sensors can be used to improve situational awareness, whereas facial recognition and speech verification should be combined to increase identification confirmation. This synergy enhances threat detection and decision-making to make the security systems more resilient and intelligent [11,12].

1.4.1 Enhancing authentication and identification

Multimodal information is necessary in enhancing identity and authentication because it integrates various sources of data, such as fingerprints, voice recognition, face recognition, and behavioral patterns, in order to create a more reliable and

Table 1.2 Multimodal data: characteristics and challenges

Aspect	Description	Key challenges	Typical solutions
Multimodal data (General)	Combination of multiple data types (text, image, audio, video, sensors) for richer insights	Data fusion, synchronization, missing or noisy modalities, high computational complexity, data quality variation	Advanced fusion models, robust preprocessing, scalable algorithms
Heterogeneity	Diversity in data formats, structures, and statistical properties across modalities	Difficult integration, modality-specific preprocessing and modeling, loss of information during fusion	Unified representations, cross-modal embeddings, modality-aware models
Dimensionality	High number of features due to multiple modalities	High computation cost, memory usage, overfitting, poor interpretability	Dimensionality reduction, feature selection, representation learning
Synchronization	Temporal coherence across modalities (e.g., audio–video alignment)	Different sampling rates, device latency, signal drift	Hardware synchronization, dynamic time warping, temporal modeling
Alignment	Mapping semantic and structural information across modalities	Structural and semantic mismatch, need for annotations	Attention mechanisms, joint embedding spaces
Noise	Distortions from environment, sensors, or modality-specific artifacts	Masking of relevant information, degraded model performance	Denoising autoencoders, filtering, attention-based weighting
Redundancy	Overlapping or repeated information across modalities	Bias, overfitting, modality dominance	Modality dropout, redundancy-aware fusion, reliability weighting

secure system. Although using a single modality (e.g., speech or face) may be vulnerable to noise in the background, occlusions, or spoofing, using a high number of modalities enhances resilience to attacks. As an example, voice or fingerprint input at the same time reduces the possibility of an unauthorized access attempt that may succeed, even when a face recognition system is spoofing a photograph. Multimodal systems can also make a dynamic trade-off between different modalities based on the situation, prioritizing one modality when another is impaired (e.g., low light to scan faces). They also make users more comfortable by allowing smooth and continuous authentication via organic interactions. Taking everything into account, multimodal methods enhance reliability, accuracy, and usability of identity and authentication systems, which are the key to modern security applications [13].

1.4.2 Context-aware threat detection

The multimodal data significantly enhances the context-sensitive threat detection through the integration of multiple information streams, such as motion sensors, audio, video, and textual data, to bring about a more comprehensive image of potential threats. By combining these modalities, systems are able to detect anomalies that a single source of data may not be able to detect. An example here is that audio might indicate that there are voices that are getting higher or alarms, whereas video might indicate suspicious actions (loitering or unusual movements). Adding environmental context (e.g., a sudden movement of the device or being near a sensitive area) can add more data to sensors (e.g., proximity detectors or accelerometers) to enhance detection further. Due to this fusion, systems are able to understand complex situations, distinguish between suspicious and benign activity, and reduce false alerts. Moreover, multimodal models can adapt to the changing environment by using contextual signals in order to improve situational awareness. Everything said and done, multimodal data allows the threat detection systems to be more accurate, flexible, and sensitive to emerging security threats.

1.4.3 Privacy preservation concerns

Despite the fact that multimodal data enhances the performance of the system, it has severe privacy preservation problems. Combining numerous types of data, audio, photos, biometric signals, and behavioral patterns can reveal very personal information about individuals, e.g., their whereabouts, identity, and habits. This fusion allows profiling users more easily, and this fact makes it more likely that the data may become exploited and illegally spied on. An illustration is that when camera shots, audio, and sensor data are combined, even when only one source is utilized, then private conversations or activities can be shown. Moreover, linking multiple modalities often requires the exchange and storage of a lot of data, which enlarges the attack space of potential security violations. Overcoming these challenges can be achieved by privacy-sensitive algorithms like secure multiparty computation, federated learning, and differential privacy to process the data without revealing personally identifying information. A balance needs to be struck between privacy and usefulness; systems should have user consent, only data should be collected when it is needed, and the use of strong encryption and anonymization strategies. Thus, despite the possible benefits of multimodal data in enhancing the work of the system, it will require extensive privacy measures to maintain user trust and comply with legal standards. Multimodal data integration incorporates more accurate and robust data integration with context awareness in applications, such as authentication and threat detection.

It also brings about the issue of privacy, though, which requires very high protection. Finally, multimodal systems provide better decision-making and security; however, they need to be balanced between benefits and privacy concerns to guarantee trust and adherence.

1.5 Multimodal data processing pipeline

A common multimodal data processing pipeline includes the following steps (Figure 1.2 shown): data acquisition, the step of collecting data through multiple sensors; preprocessing, the step of synchronization and noise removal; feature extraction, the step of transforming raw data into useful representations; fusion, the step of combining modalities by joint embeddings, concatenation, or attention; and decision-making, the step of using models to analyze fused data with the aim of performing tasks such as detection, classification, or prediction. With the help of this pipeline, various sources of data are ensured to effectively add to the overall functioning and knowledge of the system [14,15].

1.5.1 Data collection and preprocessing

Within a multimodal data processing pipeline, data collection involves the acquisition of different streams of data acquired by different means such as textual databases, cameras, microphones, and sensors. Every modality captures free information. As an example, contextual or biological data, audio records, speech and surrounding noise, and video records images are all possible sensors. This step requires careful equipment calibration to ensure that data is collected accurately and in time. Dealing with different sample rates (e.g., audio 16 kHz, video 30 fps), synchronization, and device drift, leading to misalignments between modalities, are

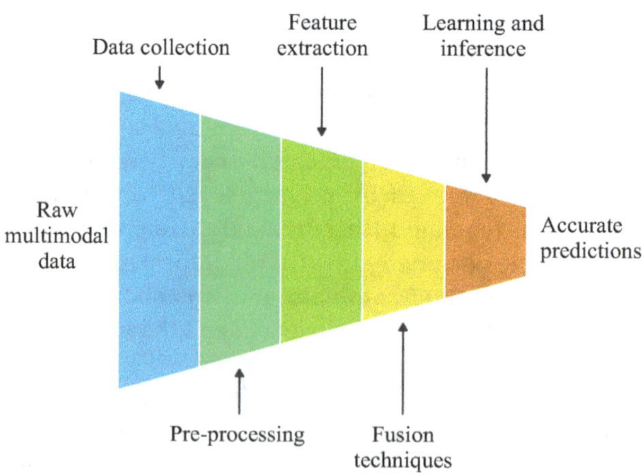

Figure 1.2 Steps of multimodal data processing pipeline

some of the challenges. This raw data needs cleaning and harmonization before it can be further investigated. This step consists of temporal alignment to bring different streams of data into time, normalization to put different modalities of data into a common form, and noise removal (e.g., removing background noise in audio or deblurring of photos). This may include language preparation and tokenization of text. Due to the fact that different sensors can sometimes fail or produce incomplete results, it is also important to deal with missing data (interpolation or imputation). Segmentation can also be required to isolate relevant events (e.g., isolating relevant frames in video or isolating speech and silence in audio). In multimodal analysis, effective preprocessing has ensured that the information is uniform, clean, and ready to be extracted as reliable features and further fused [16].

1.5.2 Feature extraction and fusion techniques

The raw data in each modality is converted into useful forms through feature extraction so that they can be analyzed and combined. This can be required to extract spectrograms or Mel-frequency cepstral coefficients (MFCCs) in order to obtain pitch, tone, and timbre in audio. Video uses convolutional neural networks (CNNs) commonly to derive time-dependent and location-dependent features, including the emotion on a face or the motion of an object. To extract semantic meaning, text data is tokenized and embedded with word2vec, BERT, or GPT embeddings. Significant patterns, such as movement dynamics or physiological indicators, may be derived from sensor data by applying statistical or deep learning-based techniques. The modalities of each modality are then normalized to ensure that fusion scales are the same. Since it retains discriminative information and reduces the dimension of the data as well as provides an effective fusion of the data with other modalities, feature extraction is necessary. Finally, a powerful feature extraction enhances the ability of the system to incorporate multimodal signals and perform specific functions such as detection, classification, and identification.

Fusion techniques (indicated in Figure 1.3) are necessary in a multimodal data processing pipeline to combine data in multiple modalities, such as text, audio, video, and sensor data, to enhance the understanding and decision-making capabilities of the system. Fusion strategies can be classified into three general categories, including early, intermediate, and late fusion. Early fusion enables the model to acquire joint representations through the combination of low-level or raw data in each modality at the input phase. In spite of the fact that such an approach captures fine-grained interactions, it might not be practical with different data formats and sampling rates. In intermediate fusion, known also as joint or hybrid fusion, the modality-specific features are gained by processing the two modalities separately. These characteristics are subsequently merged in an underlying layer with the use of neural structures like transformers, concatenation, or attention systems. This retains some processing that is modality-specific and allows model learning of complex cross-modal interactions. In late fusion, each modality is first processed independently, and the end results are fused, often through a voting or

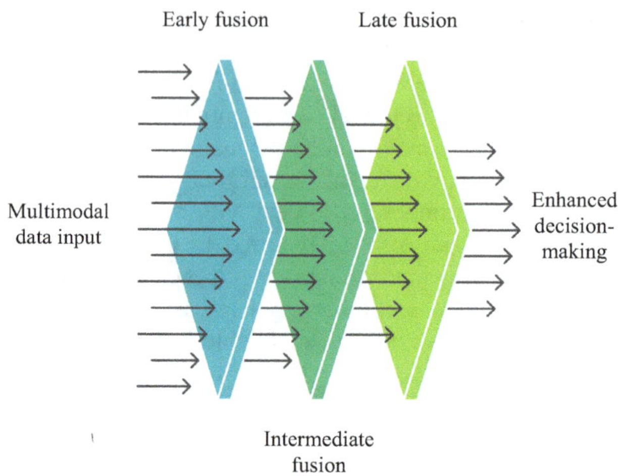

Figure 1.3 Multimodal data: fusion techniques

weighted averaging process. It is more resilient to missing modalities, and it is easier to implement deeper cross-modal linkages, which are missed [17].

The selected fusion approach is dependent on the job, accessible data, and computational abilities. The effective compromise between computational efficiency and cross-modal synergy achieved through successful fusion, is better in the overall performance of the system in activities like detecting activities, recognizing emotions, and detecting danger contextually.

1.5.3 Learning and inference

This phase is a part of a multimodal data processing pipeline where fused features are trained in models to perform such tasks as prediction, detection, and classification. Joint representations learned by probabilistic models, transformers, or deep neural networks represent both modality-specific and cross-modal interactions. Such techniques as contrastive learning and multitask learning enhance generalization and robustness. During inference, the trained model takes in other multimodal inputs and processes them through the fusion layers and produces outputs (e.g., labels, probabilities, or decisions). Inference requires strong methods, like modality dropout or attention mechanisms, to handle issues, such as noise and missing modalities. Learning and inference should collaborate in order to enable multimodal systems to perceive, judge, and respond to complex real-world contexts.

1.6 Role of machine learning and deep learning

To process multimodal data, machine learning and deep learning are necessary since they can acquire complex correlations and representations among different modalities. Machine learning methods like random forests and support vector machines allow basic fusion and classification and may combine information obtained in one or more modalities. Deep learning (especially CNNs, RNNs, and transformers) does not achieve intra- and inter-modal relationships and joint representations through hierarchical feature extraction and attention. These methods significantly enhance the features of multimodal systems by dealing with challenges such as heterogeneity, noise, and time alignment. This facilitates the identification of emotions, detection of risks with respect to context, and robust authentication [18,19].

1.6.1 Traditional ML approaches

Before the widespread application of deep learning, the classical ML methods played a major role in the processing of multimodal data. In such techniques, different sources of information are typically fused together through feature concatenation or vector fusion once features have been extracted in each of the modalities. Some of the commonly used methods are decision trees, random forests, support vector machines (SVMs), and ensemble methods, such as bagging or boosting. In order to match modalities, these models require careful feature engineering and heavily depend on hand-crafted features (e.g., MFCCs on audio, HOG or SIFT on images). Traditional machine learning also uses late fusion methods, where each of the modalities is modeled independently and the outputs are combined by voting or averaging. Sequential data may be modeled using conditional random fields (CRFs) and hidden Markov models (HMMs) but are often difficult to apply to complex, high-dimensional multimodal inputs. These methods are successful when dealing with simpler tasks, but fail to represent complex cross-modal interactions and require much manual labor to formulate features and align them. Nonetheless, during the early work in multimodal research, they laid the groundwork for more advanced deep learning-based fusion systems, which provided stable and interpretable solutions to structured multimodal problems [20].

1.6.2 Deep learning architectures for multimodal data

Multimodal data processing with deep learning architectures has transformed the way in which joint representations are learned and by which multimodal interactions can be learned. Key architectures include:

- **The Convolutional Neural Networks (CNNs)**
  CNNs are used in the second category of neural networks. CNNs are mainly applied to space features in images and video. CNNs are used in combination with other networks to combine the visual data with text or audio.
- **LSTMs and Recurrent Neural Networks (RNNs)**
  Applicable to the modeling of the temporal sequences such as speech, video frames, or text, modeling long-term dependencies and temporal alignments.

- **Transformers**
  Excellent at modeling sequences, particularly when attention is needed to multiple modalities (e.g., VisualBERT, ViLBERT, LXMERT). The self-attention of transformers is effective in context and relations between modalities.
- **Autoencoders**
  These models train on an auto-encoded architecture, where the encoder is responsible for producing the representation of the data being encoded.
- **Autoencoders and Variational Autoencoders (VAEs)**
  These models are trained on an autoencoder model, where the encoder performs the task of generating the representation of the data being encoded. Learn joint, compressed representations through reconstruction of inputs, which is beneficial to denoising and dimensionality reduction.
- **Multimodal fusion networks**
  The Multimodal Compact Bilinear Pooling (MCB), Low-rank Multimodal Fusion (LMF), and cross-modal attention networks are architectures that are successful in combining modalities. All these architectures improve such tasks as emotion recognition, context-aware threat detection, and multimodal reasoning, which make multimodal AI systems robust and adaptable.

1.7 Emerging trends and future directions

To enhance the decision-making process and to make machine learning models more expressive, a new stream of multimodal data focuses on integrating multiple types of data, such as text, pictures, audio, and others. The strategies, such as knowledge graphs, multimodal transformers, and contrastive learning, make more cross-modal understanding and advanced performance possible. Some of the challenges are managing data heterogeneity, ensuring fairness, and harmonization modalities. Future research will focus on powerful generalization between tasks, explainability, and real-time fusion. Context-aware AI is finding its way in more complex applications in human–computer interaction, health care, and autonomous systems. Data privacy, ethical AI, and sustainable architectures should be prioritized in order to ethically use multimodal data in the creation of intelligent systems.

1.7.1 Multimodal foundation models

Being able to compute and reason with many data modalities, such as text, graphics, audio, and even video, in one and the same fully integrated architecture, multimodal foundation models represent a significant advancement in artificial intelligence. Since they are founded on transformer-based architectures (e.g., GPT-4, Flamingo, Gemini), they use large datasets to learn cross-modal representations; they can create, categorize, and understand complex multimodal information. The ability of these models to match and integrate information from multiple sources, including the multifaceted contextual connections that may be missed by traditional single-modality models, is one of their key strengths. In order to achieve high integration, cross-modal attention and contrastive learning strategies are commonly employed. Indicatively, text, image, and audio input models such as GPT-4o can be used to generate smooth, multimodal outputs through the combination of text, image, and audio inputs, whereas CLIP can use joint vision-language embeddings to perform powerful zero-shot learning. The applications are many and they comprise video comprehension, autonomous robotics, multimodal communication, visual question answering, and picture captioning. However, problems that still exist include the management of high computational costs, scalability, fairness, and interpretability. Following the advancement in research, the focus is shifting toward developing more efficient, versatile, and ethically viable models that may understand and reason about the world in many different ways, and this has introduced new possibilities to artificial intelligence.

1.7.2 Federated and privacy-preserving learning

Federated and privacy-preserving learning is a possible future direction of multimodal data, where cooperative model training is made possible even without sharing data centrally. In federated learning, devices or organizations generate their own multimodal data, e.g., text, photos, or sensor measurements, and train local models. They just update the models and not the raw data. This approach reduces the chances of data leakage, and it ensures privacy of data. In large, heterogeneous multimodal systems, the confidentiality of the data is ensured by integrating federated learning with privacy-preserving methods such as secure multiparty computation and differential privacy, which protect against reverse engineering the updates to the model shared. Due to the frequent spread of sensitive multimodal data (patient records, medical images, sensor data) across multiple organizations, this paradigm is particularly relevant to the applications of the healthcare, financial, and Internet of Things domains. The process of matching the multimodal data formats of different clients, ensuring that communication is effective, and equity across the different devices with varying capacities a remains challenging task. Some of the future research directions are to develop lightweight multimodal fusion algorithms to operate at federated systems, reduce communication costs, and ensure that they generalize well to unseen multimodal situations. Our approach to cooperation, where data ownership is not compromised, is ethically compliant with AI standards and safe and practical; multimodal AI opens the potential.

1.7.3 Ethical and regulatory considerations

Multimodal data regulatory and ethical focus is on enhancing the transparency of AI systems by ensuring data justice and protecting the privacy of individuals. Multimodal datasets often contain sensitive information that can disclose personal identities or behavioral patterns, e.g., text, speech, photos, or biometric data. To prevent misuse, there is a need to have strict data protection measures such as anonymization, permission management, and differential privacy. As the multimodal models that are trained on skewed or nonrepresentative data sets can perpetuate bias along social, racial, or gender-based lines, bias and fairness are essential factors. Regulatory frameworks such as the CCPA, GDPR, and upcoming AI acts have placed a greater emphasis on accountability and require clear explanations of why models are selected and how they will use the data. Explainability and transparency mechanisms (feature attribution or interpretable multimodal attention) are also involved in the development of user and regulatory confidence. It is also important to define clear ownership, rights, and responsibilities, which is referred to as data governance, particularly when integrating data of multiple sources. To detect and decrease biases, ethical principles suggest continuous performance monitoring of the models alongside stakeholder interaction to ensure that the use of AI is maintained at the societal standards. The interdisciplinary collaboration of engineers, ethicists, and legislators will be essential as multimodal AI evolves to be able to cross those complex ethical and legal spaces accordingly.

1.8 Conclusions

Multimodal data is a revolutionary concept in data science that can include multiple sources of information, such as text, images, audio, and sensor data, and analyze them. The main concepts were introduced in this chapter, and the importance of multimodal data in enhancing modeling and decision-making was highlighted as a means of more refined and complementary perspectives on complex phenomena. We discussed the principal challenges that should be addressed to enable the adequate use of multimodal systems, including heterogeneity of data, alignment, fusion, and interpretability. New methods of deep learning, such as transformers and contrastive learning, are successfully solving these challenges. Finally, the concept of multimodal data understanding and use is a significant advance to more intelligent, context-sensitive technologies and should be the key to the creation of applications in fields like healthcare, autonomous systems, and human–computer interaction.

References

[1] F. Zhao, C. Zhang, and B. Geng, "Deep multimodal data fusion," *ACM Computing Surveys*, vol. 56, no. 9, pp. 1–36, 2024.

[2] S. Kumar, S. Rani, S. Sharma, and H. Min, "Multimodality fusion aspects of medical diagnosis: a comprehensive review," *Bioengineering*, vol. 11, no. 12, p. 1233, 2024.

[3] P. Kumar, S. Srivastava, and R. Srivastava, "Basic understanding of medical imaging modalities," in *High-Performance Medical Image Processing*. Apple Academic Press, 2022, pp. 1–17.

[4] J. Shin, N. Hassan, A. S. M. Miah, and S. Nishimura, "A comprehensive methodological survey of human activity recognition across diverse data modalities," *Sensors*, vol. 25, no. 13, p. 4028, 2025.

[5] S. Sysko-Romańczuk, P. Zaborek, A. Wróblewska, J. Dąbrowski, and S. Tkachuk, "Data modalities, consumer attributes and recommendation performance in the fashion industry," *Electronic Markets*, vol. 32, no. 3, pp. 1279–1292, 2022.

[6] Martin Wagner, Johanna M. Brandenburg, Sebastian Bodenstedt, *et al.*, "Surgomics: personalized prediction of morbidity, mortality and long-term outcome in surgery using machine learning on multimodal data," *Surgical Endoscopy*, vol. 36, no. 11, pp. 8568–8591, 2022.

[7] A. Nunes, T. Trappenberg, and M. Alda, "The definition and measurement of heterogeneity," *Translational Psychiatry*, vol. 10, no. 1, p. 299, 2020.

[8] Yang Yang, Hongjian Sun, Yu Zhang, *et al.*, "Dimensionality reduction by UMAP reinforces sample heterogeneity analysis in bulk transcriptomic data," *Cell Reports*, vol. 36, no. 4, p. 109442, 2021.

[9] J.-L. Yin, B.-H. Chen, and Y. Li, "Highly accurate image reconstruction for multimodal noise suppression using semisupervised learning on big data," *IEEE Transactions on Multimedia*, vol. 20, no. 11, pp. 3045–3056, 2018.

[10] M. Chen, J. Yao, L. Xing, Y. Wang, Y. Zhang, and Y. Wang, "Redundancy-adaptive multimodal learning for imperfect data," *Neural Networks*, vol. 191, p. 107821, 2025.

[11] V. Kolluri, S. Jain, M. Malaga, and J. Das, "Advancing biometric security through AI and ML: a comprehensive analysis of neural network architectures for multimodal authentication systems," *International Journal of Communication Networks and Information Security*, vol. 16, no. 5, pp. 487–505, 2024.

[12] E. P. Nittala, "Secure data warehousing in ERP environments: an AI-based multimodal threat detection framework," *International Journal of Emerging Trends in Computer Science and Information Technology*, vol. 5, no. 3, pp. 111–121, 2024.

[13] S. Vatchala, C. Yogesh, Yeshwanth Govindarajan, *et al.*, "Multi-modal biometric authentication: leveraging shared layer architectures for enhanced security," *IEEE Access*, vol. 13, pp. 28029–28041, 2025.

[14] O. Solomentsev, M. Zaliskyi, D. I. Bakhtiiarov, and B. S. Chumachenko, "Data processing method for multimodal distribution parameters estimation," *in CS&SE@ SW*, 2023, pp. 144–154.

[15] S. Jia, "Research and application of multimodal data fusion technology for oil and gas pipelines," *in 2024 IEEE 2nd International Conference on Control, Electronics and Computer Technology (ICCECT)*. IEEE, 2024, pp. 1093–1097.

[16] S. Chaabene, A. Boudaya, B. Bouaziz, and L. Chaari, "An overview of methods and techniques in multimodal data fusion with application to healthcare," *International Journal of Data Science and Analytics*, pp. 1–25, 2025.

[17] D. Wang, Y. Li, L. Jia, Y. Song, and Y. Liu, "Novel three-stage feature fusion method of multimodal data for bearing fault diagnosis," *IEEE Transactions on Instrumentation and Measurement*, vol. 70, pp. 1–10, 2021.

[18] Paul Pu Liang, Yiwei Lyu, Xiang Fan, *et al.*, "Multibench: multiscale benchmarks for multimodal representation learning," *Advances in Neural Information Processing Systems*, vol. 2021, no. DB1, p. 1, 2021.

[19] X. Chen, "Multimodal systems of natural language processing based on deep learning," *in 2024 International Conference on Data Science and Network Security (ICDSNS)*. IEEE, 2024, pp. 1–5.

[20] K. Sharma and M. Giannakos, "Multimodal data capabilities for learning: what can multimodal data tell us about learning?," *British Journal of Educational Technology*, vol. 51, no. 5, pp. 1450–1484, 2020.

Chapter 2

Role of multimedia systems and tools in diversified domains

Abstract

The multimedia tools and systems are increasingly finding significance in diverse businesses and are changing the way information is developed, shared, and stored. In this chapter, their disruptive nature in areas such as business, entertainment, healthcare, education, and industrial applications are discussed. It discusses the key multimedia components, namely, text, pictures, sound, and video, and their integration to enhance communication and user experiences. The chapter identifies the use of multimedia in digital marketing, telemedicine, interactive learning, remote collaboration, and process automation through case studies. It also talks about the technical basis of multimedia systems like streaming, data compression, and real-time processing. This chapter demonstrates the ways multimedia systems can be used to make a number of sectors creative and efficient, providing a comprehensive description of the field, preconditioning the further evolution.

Keywords: education; healthcare; multimedia systems; scientific research; cultural heritage; tourism

2.1 Introduction

The multimedia technologies and systems have become fundamental in most areas and they have transformed how individuals associate, interact, and learn [1]. They deftly integrate text, photos, music, video, and interactive elements to enhance user experiences and facilitate efficient information sharing. Multimedia increases classroom learning through e-learning platforms and simulations. It supports patient education, telemedicine, and diagnostics in the field of medicine. Although the leisure industry depends on immersive media such as games and movies, multimedia is applied in business marketing, training, and teamwork. Moreover, advanced visualization and interactive technologies are beneficial to scientific research, cultural heritage, and tourism, which demonstrates the extensive impact of multimedia.

2.1.1 Overview of multimedia systems and tools

Multimedia systems and tools entail the integration of various media functions such as text, images, music, video, and animations into coherent and interactive experiences. Such systems are effective in processing, managing, and distributing multimedia content through the use of specialized hardware and software platforms. Information capture, handling, storage, and compression, as well as synchronization, are critical components that enable various forms of media to be delivered dynamically. The number of video editors, audio processors, 3D modeling tools, and virtual reality environments is only a few of the tools that allow users to create rich, engaging content to use in business, education, and other applications. The development of multimedia systems has revolutionized communication, which has led to digital marketing, telemedicine, interactive entertainment, and e-learning systems. They promote innovation in the areas such as tourism, cultural heritage, and scientific research through real-time collaboration, visualization, and simulation. The future potential of multimedia is further improved by the emergence of new technologies such as AI, augmented reality (AR), and virtual reality (VR), which make the use of technology and information more immersive, contextual, and personalized, changing the way we use technology and information [2,3].

2.1.2 Evolution and growth of multimedia technologies

The manner in which we create, share, and consume information has been transformed due to the invention of multimedia technology since the first digital computers were invented in the 1980s; multimedia was restricted to text and graphics. This, however, changed with the inclusion of audio, video, and interactive features. The development of sound cards, high-resolution displays, and graphical user interfaces (GUIs) allowed creation of more complex multimedia systems. The internet also increased growth as it enabled web-based applications and streaming media. Due to the arrival of social media, cloud computing, and mobile devices during the 2000s, multimedia content became more interactive and more accessible than ever. Nowadays, multimedia systems are being transformed because of technologies such as artificial intelligence (AI), augmented reality (AR), and virtual reality (VR) that enable personalized interaction, immersive experiences, and the creation of content in real time. Multimedia growth is supported by the current advancement in technology, software, and connectivity, which affects scientific research, business, healthcare, education, and entertainment around the world [4].

2.1.3 Importance of multimedia in modern society

Multimedia has greatly influenced modern culture and has altered our way of communicating, learning, and entertaining ourselves. Its ability to combine text, images, audio, video, and interactive features generates unique and engaging experiences that enhance better understanding and recall of information. Multimedia in education facilitates interactive learning by use of digital classrooms, simulations, and e-learning platforms. It assists in the medical sphere in the field of patient education, telemedicine, and diagnostics. Gaming, streaming, and the immersive aspect of entertainment are driven by multimedia and marketing, training, and collaborative efforts in business. Digital storytelling and the capacity of social media sites to interact and reach people globally would not be possible without multimedia. Moreover, multimedia promotes scientific research, tourism, and cultural conservation due to advanced visualization and interactive technologies. The prospects of multimedia are also extended to the new technologies, such as AR, VR, and AI, which can offer a personalized and context-related experience. Everything said and done, multimedia is an essential element of the digital era, which promotes innovation, creativity, and global connectivity in every aspect of life.

2.2 Fundamentals of multimedia systems

Multimedia systems bring together numerous elements such as text, audio, video, graphics, and animation to create fascinating and interactive digital experiences. These systems depend on several technologies and components to be able to manage and distribute multimedia material such as networking, storage, input/output devices, and compression. Compression, synchronization, and digitization are the important elements that facilitate smooth playback and transmission. The aspects are interactivity, flexibility, and real-time streaming. Multimedia system applications can be used in communication, education, entertainment, and healthcare, and this has transformed the manner in which individuals obtain and communicate information. One has to understand their design concepts, standards, and architecture to develop multimedia solutions that are functional [5].

2.2.1 Components of multimedia systems

A multimedia system consists of a combination of interrelated elements that facilitate the smooth generation, processing, storing, and presentation of the different elements of media (as illustrated in Figure 2.1). Input devices such as cameras, scanners, and microphones can be used to digitize real-world signals to be further processed by recording audio, video, and photos. Storage devices, including hard drives, SSDs, optical discs, and cloud storage facilities, are effective at handling large volumes of multimedia data. The processing units (such as CPUs, GPUs, DSPs, etc.) are the central part of the system that takes care of the calculation, rendering, and signal processing tasks required to manipulate the multimedia information. While sound output devices such as speakers and headphones are used to create an immersive sound, display devices, such as monitors, projectors, and VR headsets, are used to make visual information come alive. Compression and decompression methods are used to reduce files using codecs such as MP3 and H.264 to ensure that files are stored and streamed effectively, to ensure smooth playback. Software components that facilitate easier creation, editing, and presentation of information include multimedia players, editing programs, and

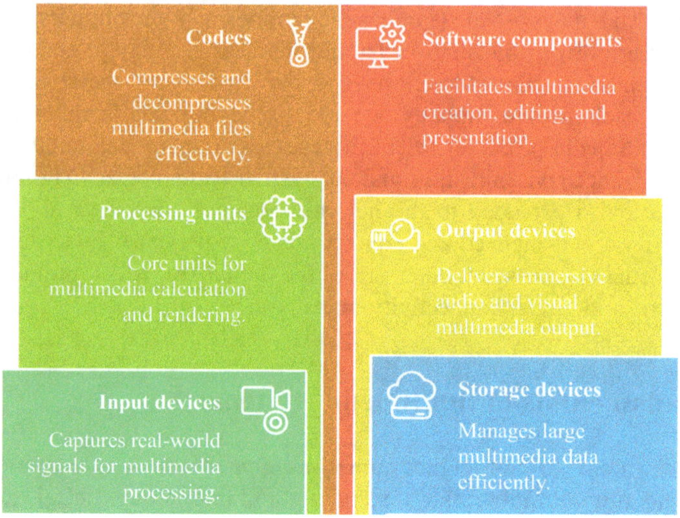

Figure 2.1 Multimedia system architecture: connected components and layers

Table 2.1 Example multimedia components

Component	Details/Examples
Input devices	Microphones, cameras, scanners, graphic tablets, sensors
Storage	Hard drives/SSDs, optical media, cloud storage, databases
Processing units	CPU, GPU, DSPs, multimedia accelerators
Display devices	Monitors, projectors, HMDs, mobile displays
Audio output	Speakers, headphones/earphones, audio interfaces
Compression tools	Codecs (MP3, AAC, H.264), decompression
Software components	Authoring tools, editing software, players, CMS
Networking components	Routers/switches, streaming servers, protocols, cloud

authoring tools. Finally, networking elements such as routers, streaming servers, and communication protocols are necessary to provide the sharing, distribution, and real-time transmission of multimedia material over networks. These aspects are complementary to each other in terms of offering the immersive and interactive experiences that define modern multimedia systems. Combined, these aspects enable the capture, processing, storage, transmission, and presentation of multimedia content to provide immersive and interactive experiences in a broad range of applications: virtual reality and medical care, education, and entertainment [6,7]. Table 2.1 summarizes various example multimedia components.

2.2.2 Hardware and software considerations

Multimedia systems require a balanced hardware and software solution to create high-quality and immersive experiences. One of the hardware issues to consider is the selection of powerful CPUs and GPUs to undertake real-time graphics, video, and audio processing. Examples of high-capacity storage devices include large hard drives or SSDs, which are required to deal with the huge volumes of data that are associated with multimedia files. In the case of multimedia content recording and presentation, input and output devices like cameras, microphones, speakers, and high-resolution screens are necessary. Network equipment, including streaming servers and routers, ensures real-time streaming and continuous multimedia transmission. Content development and editing require specialized software such as video editing suites, graphic design software, and audio production applications. Multimedia players and real-time streaming software handle playback and delivery, often with compression codecs to optimize storage and bandwidth. Moreover, middleware and multimedia frameworks (e.g., DirectX, OpenGL, or HTML5 APIs) allow the smooth integration of hardware and application software, and stable operating systems and device drivers are needed to manage hardware resources. These software and hardware components collaborate to offer a smooth environment that ensures scalability, interoperability, and performance in modern multimedia systems.

2.2.3 Multimedia formats and standards

Multimedia formats and standards are important to compatibility, interoperability, and effective transmission of different types of media between platforms and devices. Sound is digitized, compressed, and stored based on audio formats such as MP3, AAC, and WAV, which are balanced in file size and quality. Video codecs such as MPEG-4, H.264, and AVI determine the encoding and compression of moving pictures, thus supporting smooth playback and streaming. Image formats like JPEG, PNG, and GIF support the use of different levels of compression and transparency in the creation of static images. Textual content is organized and presented in text formats like HTML, RTF, and plain text. Multimedia standards, such as HTML5 to integrate multimedia in the web, JPEG to compress images, and MPEG (Moving Picture Experts Group) to compress audio and video, enable multimedia systems to work perfectly on most platforms due to their promotion of uniformity. These standards also facilitate streaming and content sharing as well as cross-platform communication in order to ensure a consistent user experience. When multimedia formats and standards are adhered to, compatibility problems are eliminated and ensure that producers, developers, and users efficiently create, share, and enjoy rich interactive multimedia content [8,9].

2.3 Applications in education

Multimedia tools and systems have a groundbreaking effect on modern learning by enhancing the opportunities of learning, promoting engagement, and supporting

Table 2.2 Multimedia applications in education

Application	Description
Interactive presentations	Integrate text, images, audio, and video for engaging lectures.
Simulations and virtual labs	Enable safe, cost-effective exploration of experiments or scenarios.
E-learning platforms	Combine videos, quizzes, and animations for self-paced learning.
Educational games	Use interactive, game-based learning for motivation and engagement.
VR/AR experiences	Immerse students in 3D environments to visualize complex concepts.
Accessibility tools	Include captions, audio descriptions, and adaptive interfaces to support diverse learners.

different learning styles. Interactive presentations are brief in explaining complex concepts compared to normal lectures because of the combination of text, graphics, audio, and video. Simulations and virtual laboratories allow students to explore historical events or scientific experiments in a very safe and cost-effective way. E-learning systems incorporate videos, tests, and animations to create dynamic, self-paced learning materials that can be accessed anywhere [10]. Educational games are motivating and interactive through interactive tutorials and multimedia-based games. Virtual reality headgear and augmented reality programs can help students feel the abstract concepts by placing them in real-life, three-dimensional environments. Accessibility through multimedia is also enhanced through the use of adaptive interfaces, audio descriptions, and captioning, which ensure that all students receive inclusive education. In all respects, multimedia tools and systems revolutionize the process of imparting knowledge, enhancing the effectiveness and personalization of learning and making it more interactive. Table 2.2 summarizes the various uses of multimedia systems in education.

2.4 Applications in healthcare

Multimedia systems have transformed the healthcare sector through innovation in terms of the collection, visualization, and distribution of medical information. Medical imaging is one of the primary uses of advanced multimedia technologies to assist in capturing, storing, and interpreting complex images such as MRI, CT, and ultrasound scans. This visual data is required for planned treatment and accurate diagnosis. Through video conferencing, interactive graphics, and real-time data sharing, telemedicine has assisted patients and health practitioners who are separated by long distances by facilitating remote consultations, diagnosis, and subsequent care. Virtual reality (VR) and augmented reality (AR) technologies are some of the technologies that can be used in surgical simulation to give surgeons

Table 2.3 Multimedia applications in healthcare

Healthcare application	Description
Medical imaging	Visualizes complex scans like MRI, CT, and ultrasound, aiding in diagnosis and treatment planning.
Telemedicine	Enables remote consultations, diagnosis, and monitoring via video conferencing and interactive tools.
Surgical simulation	Uses VR/AR for immersive surgical training and rehearsal.
Patient education	Provides interactive videos and animations to explain medical conditions and treatments.
Electronic Health Records (EHRs)	Enhances patient records with images, charts, and multimedia content.
Rehabilitation	Offers interactive games and apps for physical and cognitive therapy.
Health awareness campaigns	Delivers multimedia presentations and mobile apps for public health education.
Virtual reality therapy	Uses VR to treat psychological conditions like phobias and PTSD through controlled exposure.

the opportunity to safely train on complex procedures by giving them an immersive setting. It is the other significant application. Patient education is useful through interactive movies and cartoons that can make people understand medical conditions and possible ways of treatment. Electronic Health Records (EHRs) include multimedia elements such as charts, pictures, and videos, making the record of patients more comprehensive and accessible [11,12].

Multimedia systems also facilitate the process of rehabilitation with interactive games and programs involving patients in both mental and physical therapy. Health awareness campaigns use mobile apps and multimedia presentations to effectively deliver the message about the health of the population. Lastly, through exposing patients to a virtual environment where they can manage their conditions, virtual reality therapy provides new psychological disorder treatments such as PTSD and phobias. The different healthcare uses of the multimedia systems are listed in Table 2.3.

2.5 Applications in business and industry

The multimedia systems are significant to the present-day business and industry, as they have fundamentally transformed the way businesses promote, train, and communicate their goods and services. Among the key applications is corporate training, where multimedia technologies such as e-learning modules, movies, and simulations provide dynamic, interactive, and engaging learning experiences. These platforms improve the productivity and the level of skills of the employees, especially in aspects such as safety measures, handling of equipment, and use of software.

Table 2.4 Multimedia applications in business and industry

Application	Description
Corporate training	E-learning modules, videos, and simulations to train employees in skills, safety, and operations.
Marketing and advertising	Multimedia content (videos, graphics, animations) for brand promotion and customer engagement.
Product demonstrations and virtual tours	Virtual experiences of products or facilities for customers and partners.
Video conferencing	Real-time meetings and collaborations across locations, reducing travel costs.
Collaborative platforms	Tools for teamwork, sharing ideas, and managing projects effectively.
Data visualization	Interactive charts, graphs, and dashboards to support data-driven decision-making.
Customer support	Multimedia tutorials, chatbots, and interactive FAQs for efficient, personalized service.

The multimedia systems in marketing and advertising allow the creation of catchy promotional pieces that appeal to the audience through integration of text, images, animations, and videos. Multimedia is used in mobile applications, social media, and websites to create more brand awareness and consumer engagement. Virtual tours and product demos are also necessary applications, which save time and money as they allow potential customers to have a virtual tour of the facilities and items. Dispersed geographically, teams can interact and make decisions in real time through the assistance of video conferencing and collaboration tools, which enhance production and reduce the expenditure on travel. Moreover, the data visualization technologies will allow more informed decision-making and insights because complex corporate data are transformed into interactive charts, graphs, and dashboards. Finally, chatbots, interactive FAQs, and multimedia lessons allow customer care to offer effective and personalized support. Altogether, multimedia systems provide companies with the possibility to be innovative, more productive, and maintain a competitive advantage in the rapidly evolving digital market [13,14]. Table 2.4 summarizes various uses of multimedia systems in business and industry.

2.6 Applications in entertainment and media

Multimedia technology has become an essential part of the entertainment and media sectors and has transformed the manner in which material is produced, distributed, and consumed. In movies and TV series, multimedia technologies enable high-definition pictures, computer-generated images (CGI), and computer effects, which enhance the visual appeal and storyline. Postproduction processes such as video editing, sound mixing, and animation highly depend on advanced multimedia technologies to create

Table 2.5 Multimedia applications in entertainment and media

Application area	Description
Digital film and animation	Creation of movies, cartoons, and visual effects using multimedia tools like 3D modeling, CGI, and postproduction software.
Video games and interactive media	Development of immersive gaming experiences with multimedia systems that blend audio, video, and interactive interfaces.
Music production and distribution	Multimedia tools for recording, editing, mixing, and distributing music through platforms like streaming services.
Broadcasting and streaming	Use of multimedia systems for live TV, video streaming, and radio, including interactive features and on-demand content.
Virtual and Augmented Reality (VR/AR)	Immersive environments for gaming, simulations, and interactive storytelling using headsets and real-time rendering.
Digital art and graphic design	Multimedia applications for creating and editing digital illustrations, advertisements, and web content.
Social media content creation	Tools for producing, editing, and sharing multimedia posts, videos, and live streams on platforms like Instagram and YouTube.
Advertising and marketing	Multimedia systems used for designing eye-catching advertisements, animations, and interactive promotional content.
Interactive storytelling	Multimedia-based platforms for creating interactive movies, web series, and choose-your-own-adventure experiences.

high-quality final products. The music business uses multimedia systems to support the processes of recording and mixing music as well as creation of interactive albums and music videos. The producers and artists add effects, work with sound, and produce great music using sophisticated software. The other significant use is gaming, where multimedia systems integrate sound, animation, graphics, and interactive storytelling to produce immersive experiences on PCs, consoles, and mobile devices [15]. Live events and performances utilize multimedia systems to generate dynamic live performances and captivating shows with the help of lighting, sound design, visual projections, and stage effects. Also, through the creation of movies, television shows, and music, online streaming services such as Netflix, YouTube, and Spotify are transforming the media consumption process as they are used to distribute multimedia content worldwide. Finally, multimedia storytelling assists digital journalism through the use of interactive information, infographics, and films that can capture people in new and interesting ways. Table 2.5 summarizes a variety of applications of multimedia systems in entertainment and the media.

2.7 Applications in cultural heritage and tourism

Multimedia systems and technologies are needed in order to maintain and enhance tourism experiences and promote the cultural assets. The 3D modeling, virtual

Table 2.6 Multimedia applications in cultural heritage and tourism

Application area	Description
Virtual tours and reconstructions	Using 3D modeling, VR, and AR to recreate historical sites and artifacts for immersive exploration.
Digital archives and preservation	Multimedia systems digitize artifacts, artworks, and documents for long-term preservation and accessibility.
Interactive kiosks and apps	On-site multimedia kiosks and mobile apps provide interactive maps, guides, and audiovisual content to enhance visitor experiences.
Storytelling and educational content	Multimedia storytelling – videos, animations, and interactive narratives – brings cultural history to life for diverse audiences.
Marketing and promotion	Videos, social media, and websites leverage multimedia to promote destinations and attract tourists.
Augmented Reality (AR) experiences	AR overlays digital information onto physical sites, enriching on-site tours with contextual information and historical insights.
Intangible heritage preservation	Multimedia recordings of music, dance, and oral traditions safeguard cultural expressions for future generations.

reality (VR), and augmented reality (AR) allow the digital reproduction of historical locations, artifacts, and monuments, offering the audiences all over the world the chance to take a virtual tour of the place and feel as part of it. Mobile applications that are multimedia-enabled and interactive kiosks provide visitors with audio tours, real-time information, and engaging stories to increase accessibility and education. The cultural background and the historical narratives are also brought to life through multimedia storytelling, and in this way, the various audiences are in a position to appreciate and understand such cultural traditions and historical events. The capability to retain the intangible cultural heritage, such as dance, music, and oral traditions, by means of multimedia databases and digital archives can ensure future generations' access to such information. Tourism promotion uses multimedia presentations, films, and dynamic websites to show the diversity of places in terms of culture and attract tourists. Everything said and done, multimedia technologies transform the way people access and enjoy cultural and historical resources by closing the gap between technology and history [16,17]. Table 2.6 summarizes various uses of multimedia systems in cultural heritage and tourism.

2.8 Applications in scientific research and engineering

Multimedia systems and technologies enhance the visualization, analysis, and communication of data, and this is transforming scientific research and engineering into a revolution. The intuitive and interactive visualization of complex phenomena, such as fluid dynamics and molecular structures, can be achieved by scientists and engineers through sophisticated visualization methods such as 3D modeling,

Table 2.7 Multimedia applications in scientific research and engineering

Application area	Description
Data visualization and analysis	Multimedia tools enable 3D modeling, interactive graphs, and simulations to interpret complex scientific data.
Simulation and animation	Multimedia-based simulations model dynamic processes in physics, chemistry, and engineering for better understanding and prediction.
Computer-Aided Design (CAD) and CAM	Multimedia systems enhance product design, prototyping, and manufacturing through interactive modeling and visualization.
Remote sensing and GIS	Multimedia technologies process satellite imagery, visualize environmental data, and support geographical analyses.
Virtual Reality (VR) and Augmented Reality (AR)	Immersive environments enable interactive exploration of scientific and engineering phenomena, improving comprehension and engagement.
Scientific presentations and dashboards	Multimedia-enhanced presentations and interactive dashboards facilitate research communication and collaboration.
Training and education platforms	Multimedia learning systems provide interactive tutorials, virtual labs, and demonstrations to train researchers and engineers.

virtual reality, and augmented reality. Simulations and animations can help researchers to test theories, understand dynamic processes, and make correct predictions. The interactive dashboards and presentations where the multimedia is added will facilitate dissemination of findings, information, and insights, thereby encouraging collaborative research. The Computer-Aided Design (CAD) and CAM technologies are integrated with multimedia features and help in engineering design, prototyping, and production. Multimedia finds application in remote sensing, GIS, and image processing systems in the modeling and analysis of the environment. Besides, through the integration of theory and practice, multimedia learning systems facilitate learning and training. Everything said and done, multimedia systems are very conducive to creativity and efficiency as well as teamwork in scientific and engineering activities [6]. Table 2.7 summarizes various uses of multimedia systems in scientific research and engineering [18].

2.9 Challenges and opportunities

Some of the challenges (shown in Figure 2.2) that multimedia systems encounter include high storage requirements, data integration, and platform interoperability. Bandwidth, security, and copyright protection are also problems that inhibit adoption. Conversely, advancements in VR, AR, and AI-based content development offer a number of opportunities for immersive experiences and interactive learning. Scalable systems, cloud storage, and enhanced data compression are

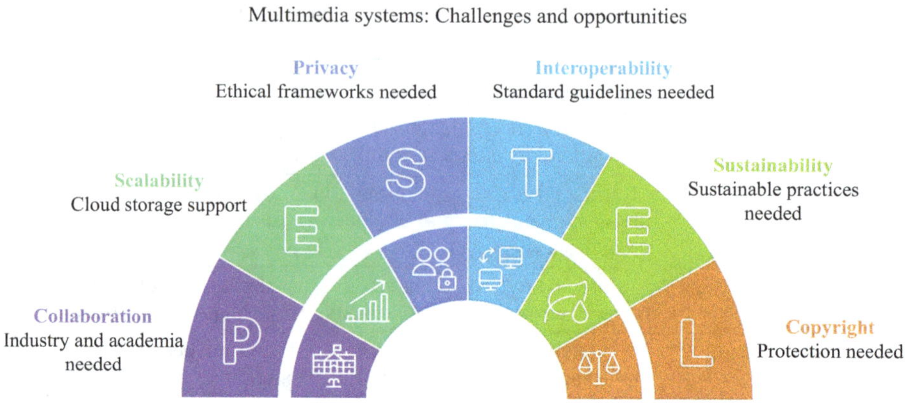

Figure 2.2 Challenges and opportunities in deploying multimedia systems

supporting real-time multimedia applications. In order to achieve the full potential of multimedia, collaboration between industry and academic institutions is needed.

2.9.1 Technical challenges and interoperability

Some of the technical challenges in multimedia system and tools include handling vast, complex information, the need to compress and transmit data effectively, and the need to store data and transfer it at high bandwidth. Real-time multimedia content processing and rendering require powerful hardware and advanced algorithms. The other significant challenge is to ensure the quality of service (QoS) in numerous networks. Interoperability is presented by different data formats, proprietary standards, and different hardware and software platforms. There is a lack of standardization between devices and applications that impedes multimedia content integration and sharing. There should be standard guidelines, flexible design, and powerful frameworks to face these challenges and ensure efficiency and compatibility [19].

2.9.2 Ethical and privacy considerations

Ethics and privacy should also be put into serious consideration by multimedia systems and tools, especially with the increased use of sensitive and personal information. To prevent abuse and ensure openness, issues such as data ownership, permission, and user rights must be addressed in a proper way. The problem of privacy also emerges due to the potential of multimedia systems to collect, store, and transmit individual information accidentally through pictures, sounds, and videos. Facial recognition and other multimedia systems that are enhanced by AI have the potential to lead to a higher probability of discrimination and spying. To reconcile innovation and respect for human privacy and fundamental rights, there is a need to have ethical frameworks to guide the proper design and use of multimedia technologies.

2.9.3 Emerging trends and future directions

One of the new trends in multimedia systems and tools is the use of AI, which has made it possible to create automated content, do automated compression, and render with adaptations. Immersive technologies such as mixed reality, augmented reality, and virtual reality are transforming training, education, and entertainment since they offer realistic and engaging experiences. Cloud-based multimedia platforms support scalable streaming services and real-time collaboration. The two low-latency multimedia applications that are enhanced by the advent of 5G networks are telemedicine and remote diagnostics. The future directions focus on sustainable multimedia practices, privacy-sensitive architectures, and cross-platform interoperability. Multimodal data integration and explainable AI will further influence the environment and ensure effective, ethical, and transparent multimedia experiences.

2.10 Conclusions

The powerful role played by multimedia tools and systems in a broad spectrum of areas is illustrated in this chapter. The integration of text, graphics, audio, and video into coherent, interactive experiences has transformed these technologies completely and changed the way we work, communicate, learn, and entertain ourselves. Multimedia enhances understanding, interaction, and access in various sectors such as engineering, tourism, cultural heritage, healthcare, and education. Nevertheless, challenges still persist, including the complexity of managing massive information, ensuring seamless interoperability, and managing privacy and ethical challenges. Emerging technologies such as AI, VR, AR, and 5G are enhancing the potential of multimedia by making it possible to engage in an immersive and real-time experience and encourage international collaboration. These benefits should be achieved appropriately through standardization, good structures, and interdisciplinary collaboration. Ultimately, multimedia tools and systems are not only technical advances but also social change agents and innovators; they fill in the gaps and provide access to more inclusive, interactive, and meaningful solutions in the digital age.

References

[1] F. Zhang, "Significances of multimedia technologies training," *Physics Procedia*, vol. 33, pp. 2005–2010, 2012.

[2] N. Das, N. Padhy, N. Dey, H. Paul, and S. Chowdhury, "Exploring explainable AI methods for bird sound-based species recognition systems," *Multimedia Tools and Applications*, vol. 83, no. 24, pp. 64223–64253, 2024.

[3] B. Furht, *Multimedia Tools and Applications*. Springer Science & Business Media, 2012.

[4] A. Salkintzis and N. Passas, *Emerging Wireless Multimedia: Services and Technologies*. John Wiley & Sons, 2005.
[5] B. Çeken and N. Taşkın, "Multimedia learning principles in different learning environments: a systematic review," *Smart Learning Environments*, vol. 9, no. 1, p. 19, 2022.
[6] R. Parekh, *Principles of Multimedia*. CRC Press, 2025.
[7] J. Ohm, *Multimedia Communication Technology: Representation, Transmission and Identification of Multimedia Signals*. Springer Science & Business Media, 2012.
[8] R. García, C. Tsinaraki, O. Celma, and S. Christodoulakis, "Multimedia content description using semantic web languages," in *Semantic Multimedia and Ontologies: Theory and Applications*. Springer, 2008, pp. 17–54.
[9] B. Furht, S. W. Smoliar, and H. Zhang, *Video and Image Processing in Multimedia Systems*. Springer Science & Business Media, 2012.
[10] S. A. Savov, R. Antonova, and K. Spassov, "Multimedia applications in education," in *Smart Technologies and Innovation for a Sustainable Future: Proceedings of the 1st American University in the Emirates International Research Conference—Dubai, UAE 2017*. Springer, 2019, pp. 263–271.
[11] A. Briassouli, J. Benois-Pineau, and A. Hauptmann, "Overview of multimedia in healthcare," in *Health Monitoring and Personalized Feedback Using Multimedia Data*. Springer, 2015, pp. 1–6.
[12] A. Alamri, "Monitoring system for patients using multimedia for smart healthcare," *IEEE Access*, vol. 6, pp. 23271–23276, 2018.
[13] V. Kumar, A. R. Saboo, A. Agarwal, and B. Kumar, "Generating competitive intelligence with limited information: a case of the multimedia industry," *Production and Operations Management*, vol. 29, no. 1, pp. 192–213, 2020.
[14] S. M. Rahman, R. Sarker, and B. Bignall, "Application of multimedia technology in manufacturing: a review," *Computers in Industry*, vol. 38, no. 1, pp. 43–52, 1999.
[15] B. Furht, *Handbook of Multimedia for Digital Entertainment and Arts*. Springer, 2009.
[16] L. S. Yin and S. A. Mubin, "Interactive multimedia for promoting cultural heritage tourism in Penang," in *2022 International Visualization, Informatics and Technology Conference (IVIT)*. IEEE, 2022, pp. 17–23.
[17] Ilaria Bartolini, Vincenzo Moscato, Ruggero G. Pensa, *et al.*, "Recommending multimedia visiting paths in cultural heritage applications," *Multimedia Tools and Applications*, vol. 75, no. 7, pp. 3813–3842, 2016.
[18] G. Höhne and V. Henkel, "Application of multimedia in engineering design education," *European Journal of Engineering Education*, vol. 29, no. 1, pp. 87–96, 2004.
[19] G. Yang, M. A. Jan, A. U. Rehman, M. Babar, M. M. Aimal, and S. Verma, "Interoperability and data storage in internet of multimedia things: investigating current trends, research challenges and future directions," *IEEE Access*, vol. 8, pp. 124382–124401, 2020.

Chapter 3

Internet of Multimedia Things: key role, framework, and security issues

Abstract

Internet of Multimedia Things (IoMT) is the innovative advancement of the Internet of Things, which allows multimedia-rich data (audio, video, and photos) to be easily incorporated and interacted with between intelligent devices and platforms. This chapter considers the important contribution of IoMT to various industries, including healthcare, security, entertainment, and smart environments. It provides a comprehensive architectural base with the focus on such key aspects as sensing, networking, data processing, and cloud integration. In the chapter, key security concerns that are imperative in ensuring trust and reliability in the installations of IoMT are discussed and they include data privacy, secure communication, access control, and intrusion detection. The discussion of the emerging themes, including edge computing and AI-powered processing, gives us an insight into the possible future developments and the efficient, scalable, and safe management of multimedia data in smart ecosystems.

Keywords: data privacy; Internet of Multimedia Things (IoMT); IoMT architecture; multimedia data integration; secure communication; smart applications

3.1 Introduction

The Internet of Multimedia Things (IoMT) is the complex paradigm that involves integrating multimedia devices, such as cameras, sensors, microphones, and displays, into the giant network called the Internet of Things (IoT). The manner in which multimedia data is recorded, processed, transported, and consumed is transformed by the fact that it makes it easy to establish smooth connectivity and real-time communication among various multimedia-enabled devices. The IoMT has a significant positive impact on user experiences in such sectors as smart homes, healthcare, surveillance, entertainment, and business. The primary role, conceptual framework, and immediate security issues surrounding IoMT are explored in this chapter. To begin with, we explain how IoMT can be utilized to facilitate rich multimedia interactions that cannot be achieved using the standard

IoT systems [1]. This creates possibilities of real-time analytics, remote monitoring, and customized services. Then we explain a typical design of an IoMT system, with a focus on the integration of the application, networking, storage, and multimedia processing layers. Finally, we address such crucial security concerns as trust in the user, authentication of devices, privacy of the data, and safe transmission of the data. To achieve the widespread adoption of IoMT systems and make them resilient, these issues have to be addressed. The revolutionary nature of the IoMT, the technical basis of its operation, and the need to have high-level security to ensure safe and efficient operation are all well-explained to the readers in this chapter.

3.1.1 Background and motivation

Internet of Multimedia Things (IoMT) is a new era that has come up due to the convergence of multimedia technologies and the Internet of Things (IoT). The classical IoT systems were aimed at linking sensors and devices with few or no multimedia features. Nevertheless, the spread of devices with a high level of multimedia (cameras, microphones, and sophisticated sensors) has extended the notion of IoT to facilitate real-time processing and transmission of audio, video, and images. This convergence has enormous potential in aspects such as smart cities, health care, entertainment, and industry, where multimedia data is used to improve decision-making and user experiences. Though these have benefits, IoMT also comes with its own set of challenges, especially when it comes to dealing with high-bandwidth multimedia traffic, interoperability among heterogeneous devices, and critical security and privacy concerns. The rationale behind this chapter is to explore these opportunities and challenges, providing a full-scale framework and discussion of security provisions that are necessary to ensure the successful deployment of the IoMT systems.

3.1.2 Scope and objectives of the chapter

This chapter aims to provide a comprehensive introduction to the Internet of Multimedia Things (IoMT) and its key aspects, including the overall architecture of the system, its transformational potential, and the key security concerns. The scope indicates the unique characteristics and needs of multimedia data, such as audio, video, and images in dispersed environments, and the intersection of multimedia technologies and the Internet of Things ecosystem. To make sure that the readers capture the entire lifecycle of multimedia data in the IoMT settings, the chapter examines the architecture of IoMT systems, such as device heterogeneity, data acquisition, processing pipelines, networking protocols, and application domains. One of the primary objectives is the clarification of the critical role that IoMT is playing in the provision of rich, interactive, and context-aware services in industries of various domains such as healthcare, smart cities, entertainment, surveillance, and industry. The chapter also seeks to offer a systematic structure that brings into the limelight the major components of the IoMT designs with special emphasis on the real-time analytics, multimedia data management, and interconnection of devices. Another important objective is analyzing the pressing security and privacy concerns that emerge during the implementation of IoMT, including the safe authentication of the devices, the integrity of the data, its confidentiality, and the trustworthiness of the users. To make IoMT systems safe and reliable in practice, these problems should be addressed. Through accomplishing these objectives, the chapter is expected to provide the reader with an in-depth understanding of the technological background of IoMT, its potential, and the importance of good security practices. This comprehensive perspective is essential to researchers, developers, and practitioners interested in relying on the use of IoMT to develop innovative and secure multimedia-based applications in the fast-evolving digital ecosystem.

3.2 Overview of the Internet of Multimedia Things (IoMT)

The Internet of Multimedia Things (IoMT) is an extension of the general Internet of Things (IoT) that integrates devices that can record, process, and transmit multimedia information, such as audio, video, and photos. Unlike other traditional IoT systems that typically handle structured information that is collected by simple sensors, IoMT allows real-time, immersive, and interactive experiences in various sectors such as smart cities, entertainment, healthcare, and surveillance. This paradigm incorporates the use of high-bandwidth connections, advanced analytics, and multimedia processing techniques to offer context-aware services. The IoMT infrastructure typically includes cloud platforms, communication networks, multimedia devices, and cognitive analytics in order to introduce a smooth flow of multimedia data and decision-making. But it also comes with security, interoperability, and bandwidth issues, which require comprehensive frameworks to address.

3.2.1 Definition and concepts

The Internet of Multimedia Things (IoMT) is a specialized branch of the Internet of Things (IoT) concerned with connecting, controlling, and sharing rich multimedia content, including audio, video, and images, across dispersed and heterogeneous devices. Unlike traditional IoT, IoMT operates with multimedia data streams that are characterized by high bandwidth and latency and are often unstructured, unlike traditional IoT, which typically operates with structured numerical or textual data.

Key concepts in IoMT include [1–3]:

- Multimedia devices: Cameras, microphones, sensors, and displays, among other devices that produce and consume multimedia data.
- Networking and connectivity: High-speed and low-latency communication technologies (e.g., 5G, Wi-Fi, Bluetooth) that enable real-time data transmission of multimedia data.
- Data processing and analytics: Data compression, streaming, computer vision, and real-time analytics techniques to process multimedia data.
- Integration frameworks: These are architectures that integrate devices, networks, and applications to provide end-to-end multimedia services.

- Security and privacy: Safety measures to provide safe transmission and storage as well as access control of sensitive multimedia information.

IoMT is designed to bring a flawless and interactive multimedia experience to a wide range of applications, which provides unprecedented possibilities in healthcare, surveillance, entertainment, smart cities, and so forth.

3.2.2 Evolution of IoMT

The Internet of Multimedia Things (IoMT) was formed by combining multimedia processing and the Internet of Things (IoT). Initially, IoT systems focused on the connection of simple sensors and devices that transmitted small amounts of structured data to be automated and monitored. Nonetheless, multimedia devices, such as cameras, microphones, and displays, became more connected with the development of networking technology (e.g., 4G, 5G, Wi-Fi 6), and more sophisticated applications became possible. The emergence of cloud and edge computing allowed processing large multimedia datasets in real time and contributed to the resolution of the problem of latency and bandwidth. Meanwhile, the development of artificial intelligence, machine learning, and computer vision has made it possible to have IoMT systems able to interpret and understand complex multimedia content and thus allow smart applications in smart cities, healthcare, and entertainment. Such trends as real-time multimedia streaming, AI-based video analytics, and integrated cybersecurity frameworks are examples of how IoMT continues to evolve today. This growth characterizes the fact that the disparate multimedia technologies have yielded to a fully integrated, intelligent, and secure multimedia environment that has enabled the opening up of revolutionary opportunities regarding the digital services [4,5].

3.2.3 Comparison with the Internet of Things (IoT)

The Internet of Multimedia Things (IoMT), an extension of the traditional Internet of Things (IoT), uses devices that create, process, and transfer multimedia data, such as audio, video, and images. IoMT focuses on unstructured, bandwidth-intensive multimedia content and requires advanced communication and processing functions, and IoT primarily connects devices that produce structured data, e.g., temperature sensors, actuators, and RFID tags. IoT systems are usually designed to support low-latency, low-bandwidth uses such as asset monitoring, industrial control, environmental surveillance, and the periodical gathering of information. Instead, IoMT needs real-time data processing, data transmission, and analytics to enable interactive multimedia experiences in applications like entertainment, smart cities, remote surveillance, and health monitoring. Moreover, the IoMT systems, despite the fact that simpler connectivity technologies such as Zigbee or Bluetooth are often employed in IoT, rely on edge computing and high-speed networks (5G, Wi-Fi 6) to meet the requirements of latency and bandwidth. Security is another vital distinction: IoMT requires managing complex copyright, privacy, and streaming security issues on top of the basic IoT authentication and encryption systems [4]. IoMT also brings new challenges in the area of data management,

Table 3.1 Comparison of IoT and IoMT

Aspect	**IoT**	**IoMT**
Data type	Primarily structured data (e.g., temperature, pressure)	Unstructured multimedia data (audio, video, images)
Data volume	Low to moderate	High-volume, bandwidth-intensive multimedia streams
Latency needs	Often tolerant of delays	Requires low latency for real-time multimedia applications
Devices	Sensors, actuators, and simple edge devices	Cameras, microphones, augmented reality (AR)/virtual reality (VR) devices, multimedia sensors
Processing	Primarily numeric data analysis	Requires multimedia processing (compression, streaming, AI)
Network	Standard connectivity (e.g., Wi-Fi, Zigbee)	High-speed networks (e.g., 5G, Wi-Fi 6) for real-time data
Applications	Industrial automation, smart metering, logistics	Healthcare monitoring, surveillance, entertainment, smart cities
Security	Encryption, authentication, and device management	Advanced security (privacy, digital rights management (DRM), watermarking, secure streaming)
Challenges	Device heterogeneity, scalability	Bandwidth, latency, device heterogeneity, and multimedia privacy

quality of service, and security, even though it enables the creation of rich multimedia applications that provide better user experiences [6]. Table 3.1 shows a detailed comparison of the IoT and IoMT with the focus on different aspects.

3.3 Key roles and applications of IoMT

IoMT also improves the real-time multimedia communications in such areas as healthcare (remote monitoring, diagnostics), smart cities (traffic surveillance, safety), entertainment (AR/VR, live streaming), and industry (process monitoring, training). It has major functions in the form of data collection, multimedia analytics, decision-making, and personalized services, which change user experiences [7,8].

3.3.1 Smart cities and surveillance

IoMT is based on multimedia data (cameras, sensors, and drones) to deliver real-time monitoring and control of urban infrastructure in smart cities. It enables the management of trash, energy efficiency, monitoring the environment, and optimization of traffic flow. IoMT is a surveillance system that integrates behavioral analysis, facial recognition, and video analytics and enhances response to emergencies, safety, and prevention of crimes. These multimedia-driven systems make it possible to involve proactive decision-making, improved situational awareness, and seamless coordination between the city services. The IoMT systems are based on edge computing and artificial intelligence (AI) to offer scalable and smart solutions that help in transforming urban landscapes into safer, more efficient, and livable places for citizens [9–11].

3.3.2 Healthcare and telemedicine

IoMT is revolutionizing the healthcare system with remote diagnosis and real-time monitoring with the use of multimedia devices such as wearable sensors, cameras, and imaging equipment. It fosters telemedicine by facilitating remote monitoring of patients, virtual rehabilitation, and quality video calls. Multimedia data may include vital signs, patient video recordings, and medical imaging to enhance the accuracy of diagnosis and personalized care. Second, cognitive health analytics can be achieved through IoMT to handle chronic illnesses and early disease detection. IoMT plays a crucial role in modern telemedicine and smart healthcare systems since it improves access to healthcare, reduces expenditures, and encourages long-term care due to the integration of AI and cloud computing [12].

3.3.3 Industrial automation and monitoring

IoMT enhances the automation of industries by using multimedia equipment such as cameras, microphones, and sensors to observe machines and processes in real-time. It enables visual inspection, quality control, and identification of the problem by utilizing video analytics and audio analysis. Remote monitoring by use of multimedia streams reduces downtimes and maintenance costs due to the issuance of early notifications and predictive information. IoMT promotes training and safety by offering immersive simulations and the use of augmented reality (AR) advice. Its ability to process rich multimedia data in the manufacturing, energy, and logistics industries ensures that they control the operations accurately, become more effective in their operations, and work in safer conditions [13].

3.3.4 Entertainment and media streaming

IoMT transforms media streaming and leisure through the easy, real-time sharing of high-quality multimedia content between connected devices. It enables interactive gaming, live video streaming, and immersive, augmented reality (AR) and virtual reality (VR) experiences through the use of cameras, microphones, and sensors. Advanced multimedia analytics enhance adaptive streaming, audience interaction, and content personalization. IoMT also facilitates remote production and creation of collaborative content through live multimedia sharing and synchronization. IoMT can also change the way the audience views and consumes media and entertainment content through the application of edge computing and high-speed networks to ensure scalable distribution, lower latency, and better user experiences [9].

3.3.5 Education and remote learning

IoMT improves distance learning and education by supporting the sharing of interactive multimedia content through smart cameras, microphones, and AR/VR tools. It facilitates student interaction and cooperation irrespective of the location in real time by facilitating immersive simulation, virtual classes, and live lectures. Multimedia content can be interactive tests, virtual laboratories, and video lessons, which enhance understanding and personalized learning. IoMT can also be used to continuously assess student performance and participation through audiovisual analytics. IoMT is turning traditional learning into dynamic, engaging, and technology-driven learning experiences, integrating AI and cloud computing to assist in creating inclusive, accessible, and adaptive learning environments [10].

3.4 Architectural framework of IoMT

The IoMT architectural framework consists of several interdependent layers that allow the flow of multimedia data to proceed easily. Rich data is recorded at the bottom using multimedia equipments such as cameras, microphones, and sensors. The communication layer ensures that the networks, such as 5G and Wi-Fi 6, are fast with low latency. Edge computing nodes are used to reduce the latency and bandwidth used by processing data on the edges. Cloud systems provide massive storage, advanced analytics, and AI-based insights. Application layer offers various services in the industry, entertainment, smart cities, and healthcare sectors. To maintain system integrity and user confidence, the security practices are carried out at all levels, ensuring privacy of data, authentication, and secure transmission [14].

3.4.1 IoMT architecture layers

The Internet of Multimedia Things (IoMT) Layered Architecture is a collection of interrelated layers that combine to process and handle multimedia data. The Sensor and Device Layer, which is at the bottom, acquires real-life data by using multimedia sensors such as cameras and microphones. Network Layer uses wireless networks to transmit this data, and thus, low latency and reliable communication are guaranteed. The Edge/Fog Layer offers local processing, filtering, and real-time analytics to minimize cloud reliance. On top, there is the Application Layer that provides the domain-specific services such as remote patient monitoring, video conferencing, and smart surveillance. The Management and Security Layer manages the work of systems, user authentication, data protection, and implementation of the policy to ensure the safe and effective deployment of IoMT [15,16]. Figure 3.1 indicates IoMT layered architecture.

3.4.2 Sensor and device layer

The Sensor and Device Layer is the heart of the IoMT architecture and it collects multimedia data about the environment. It entails various multimedia-capable

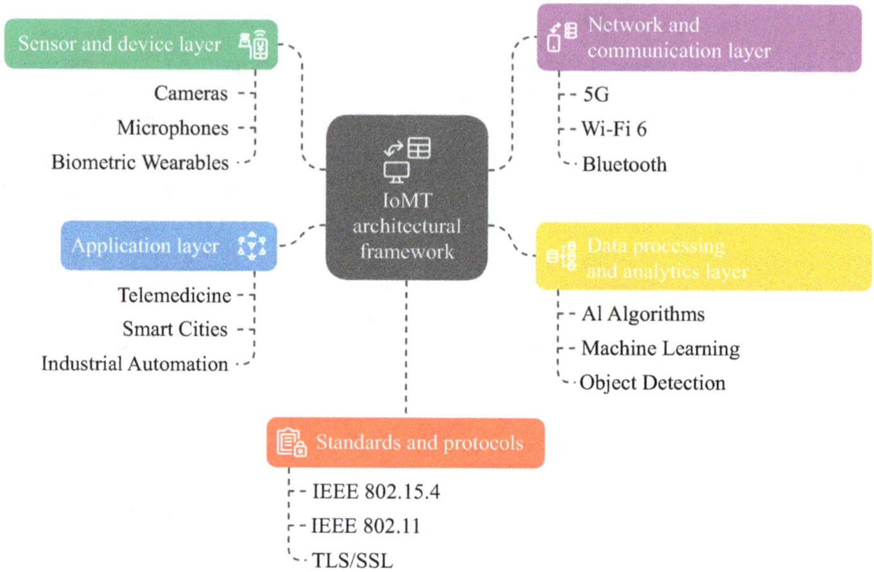

Figure 3.1 IoMT layered architecture

devices and gadgets like RFID tags, cameras, microphones, biometric wearables, and medical devices. These devices detect and collect images, audio, video, physiological signals, and other sensory data required in real-time monitoring and analysis. To optimize the bandwidth and enhance the quality of data, they also perform initial processing of data such as noise filtering and compression. This layer enables the applications in smart cities, industrial automation, and healthcare monitoring through an easy interface with the physical world. Ultimately, it assists multimedia IoT ecosystems to close the divide between the physical and digital worlds.

3.4.3 Network and communication layer

The Network and Communication Layer of the IoMT architecture provides the basis for reliable multimedia data transfer between devices and cloud or edge services. It ensures that there is easy connectivity through a diverse range of wired and wireless technologies, including Ethernet, Bluetooth, Zigbee, 4G/5G, and Wi-Fi. To facilitate high-bandwidth multimedia applications, this layer is involved in data forwarding, routing, and real-time streaming. In the case of real-time multimedia transmission like video conferencing and telemedicine, it uses protocols that provide Quality of Service (QoS), low latency, and jitter control. Moreover, it provides valuable security functions such as secure routing and encryption as a means of protecting confidential multimedia information during its transmission. Eventually, it connects the upper processing layers and the application layer to the physical sensor layer.

3.4.4 Data processing and analytics layer

The Data Processing and Analytics Layer of IoMT architecture transforms raw multimedia data into valuable information. It is located between the network and application layers and performs preprocessing, filtering, and data aggregation to prepare big multimedia datasets (audio, video, and biometric signals) to be analyzed. It utilizes AI and machine learning algorithms to detect anomalies, derive useful information, and also support decision-making in the present moment. This layer also applies advanced data analytics techniques such as object detection, pattern recognition, and image segmentation to enhance the interpretation of data. It also increases the efficiency and performance of the network and systems by reducing the amount and complexity of data before transmission to the application layer to enable timely responses in key fields such as smart cities, health, and security.

3.4.5 Application layer

Application Layer in the IoMT architecture is the interface between end users and processed multimedia data, and it provides domain-specific services. It supports applications such as real-time video conferencing, telemedicine, industrial automation, multimedia streaming, remote patient monitoring, and so on. This layer helps to make informed decisions because it displays information in easily navigable dashboards and visualization tools based on the insights generated by the Data Processing and Analytics Layer. Also, it supports such AI-driven functionalities as anomaly detection, personalized suggestions, and predictive diagnostics. The critical elements of security, privacy, and regulatory compliance in this layer ensure that sensitive data is handled in an appropriate way. All said and done, the Application Layer helps to enable real-time, seamless multimedia services by connecting the IoMT data processing and user interactions.

3.4.6 Standards and protocols

In IoMT architecture, standards and protocols are essential for ensuring interoperability, security, and reliable communication across diverse multimedia devices and systems. Common communication standards include:

- IEEE 802.15.4 (for low-rate wireless personal area networks like Zigbee)
- IEEE 802.11 (Wi-Fi) for high-bandwidth wireless data transfer
- Bluetooth/Bluetooth Low Energy (BLE) for short-range connectivity
- 5G/6G for high-speed multimedia streaming

Application-layer protocols such as MQTT, CoAP, and HTTP/RESTful APIs facilitate efficient multimedia data exchange and device communication. Multimedia streaming often uses protocols like RTSP (Real-Time Streaming Protocol) and RTP (Real-Time Transport Protocol). For security, TLS/SSL, IPSec, and encryption standards (Advanced Encryption Standard (AES), RSA) ensure data confidentiality and integrity.

Additionally, IoMT systems often adopt interoperability frameworks like HL7 and FHIR for medical data exchange, ensuring compliance with healthcare standards. These standards and protocols collectively support seamless, secure, and scalable IoMT deployments.

3.5 Security issues in IoMT

Security concerns in the IoMT are caused by the sensitive nature of multimedia data and the devices that are connected. Breach of data, privacy invasion, and unauthorized access are significant problems. Poor encryption, weak authentication, and unsafe network protocols make the systems susceptible to attacks. Malicious attacks like ransomware and DDoS can compromise trust and availability. The security of the IoMT systems against the dynamic cyber threats depends on robust security models, including access control, secure protocols, and end-to-end encryption [17–20].

3.5.1 Threat landscape

The threat landscape for IoMT is complex due to its interconnected and multimedia-rich environment. Key threats include:

- **Unauthorized access:** Hackers exploit weak authentication to gain control over devices and data.
- **Data breaches:** Sensitive multimedia data (e.g., medical videos, images) intercepted during transmission or stored insecurely.
- **Privacy violations:** Personal information exposed through eavesdropping or inadequate data protection.
- **Malware/Ransomware:** Infecting devices to disrupt services or demand ransom.
- **Denial-of-Service (DoS/DDoS):** Overloading networks to degrade multimedia service availability.
- **Man-in-the-Middle (MitM) attacks:** Intercepting and altering data streams between devices and servers.
- **Physical attacks:** Tampering with or stealing IoMT devices.
- Various types of IoMT threats are shown in Figure 3.2.

Effective defense requires layered security: strong encryption, robust authentication, secure protocols, and real-time monitoring.

3.5.2 Data privacy and confidentiality

Since the IoMT deals with sensitive and rich multimedia information, including movies, photos, and audio streams that often include personal or medical evidence, data privacy and confidentiality are highly important. To prevent unlawful access or interception, this information should be strongly encrypted to protect it during storage and transmission. Access control systems allow only authorized people and devices to manipulate the data. Tough data governance, such as anonymization, user consent control, and safe data lifecycle management, is needed to meet privacy

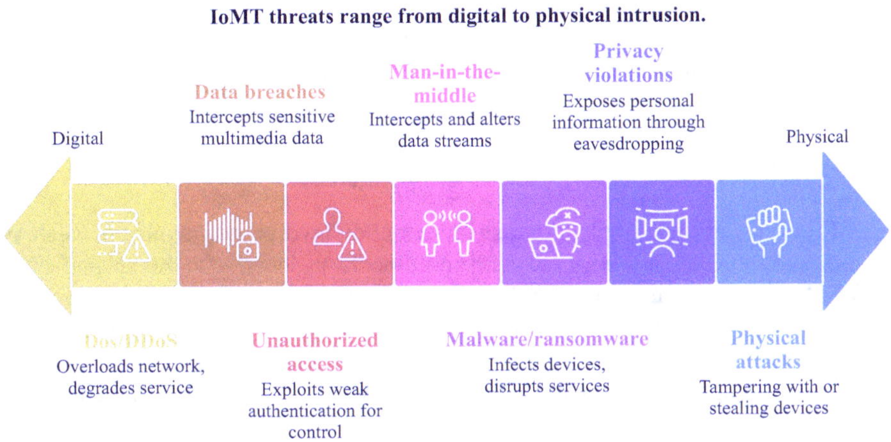

Figure 3.2 IoMT threat landscape

regulations such as GDPR and HIPAA. Privacy and confidentiality in the IoMT are very vital in ensuring safe implementation in the surveillance, healthcare, and smart environments where the multimedia data is omnipresent. It also adds security and confidence to the user and prevents identity theft and exploitation.

3.5.3 Authentication and access control

Access control and authentication play an important role in the protection of private multimedia information and devices in the IoMT. Authentication is used to identify people and machines before they are granted access. This is typically carried out through digital certification, passwords, biometrics, or multifactor authentication. Strong authentication prevents the entry of unwanted users into the system. Then, with role-based or attribute-based access control, access control methods restrict the permissions depending on roles or contexts and implement policies to define what authenticated individuals or devices are allowed to do. These safeguards only allow authorized entities to view, modify, or transmit multimedia content. Strong authentication and fine-grained access control prevent data breaches and misuse, enhancing the general system security in the IoMT, where privacy and real-time data integrity are highly essential, especially in healthcare and surveillance.

3.5.4 Secure communication and encryption

In the Internet of Medical Things, to avoid interception, alteration, or access of critical multimedia data by unauthorized individuals, secure communication and encryption are essential. Data transport and protection are ensured using data encryption algorithms such as RSA and AES (Advanced Encryption Standard) that ensure data integrity and secrecy. To avoid eavesdropping and man-in-the-middle attacks, secure communication protocols such as TLS/SSL, IPSec, and DTLS provide encrypted channels of multimedia streaming and device interactions.

Given the volume and real-time nature of the multimedia data, lightweight encryption methods are often used to provide a tradeoff between security and performance. Together, these security measures can maintain privacy, enhance user trust, and secure IoMT systems deployed in smart cities, health, and industry.

3.5.5 Intrusion detection and prevention

In IoMT, intrusion detection and intrusion prevention involve maintaining a watch on IoT networks and devices enabled with multimedia to identify and stop malicious traffic. Due to the large volume of data and real-time nature of multimedia streams, specialized intrusion detection systems (IDS) use machine learning and anomaly detection methods to detect anomalous behaviors, including unauthorized access, data tampering, or network attacks. To prevent harm or loss of data, intrusion prevention systems (IPS) actively prevent or mitigate threats that are identified. In order to provide continuous multimedia services, efficient IDS/IPS solutions in IoMT have to balance security and low latency. These are the solutions that would protect the private multimedia information and ensure reliability and security of the IoMT applications in smart environments, surveillance, and healthcare. Table 3.2 summarizes various security concerns and corresponding mitigation strategies of IoMT.

Table 3.2 Summarization of various security issues in IoMT

Security issue	**Description**	**Impact**	**Mitigation techniques**
Unauthorized access	Unauthorized users or devices gaining system access	Data theft, device control loss	Strong authentication, access control
Data breaches	Leakage or interception of sensitive multimedia data	Privacy violations, data misuse	Encryption, secure communication
Privacy violations	Exposure of personal or medical multimedia information	Loss of user trust, legal issues	Data anonymization, user consent
Weak authentication	Use of weak or single-factor authentication	Easy exploitation by attackers	Multifactor authentication
Insecure communication	Data transmitted over unprotected or vulnerable networks	Eavesdropping, man-in-the-middle attacks	TLS/SSL, secure protocols
Malware and ransomware	Malicious software disrupting IoMT devices and services	Service downtime, data loss	Intrusion detection/ prevention, regular updates
Denial-of-Service (DoS)	Attacks overwhelming the network or devices	Service unavailability	Network monitoring, traffic filtering
Physical attacks	Tampering with or stealing IoMT devices	Data compromise, device damage	Device hardening, tamper detection

3.6 Challenges and future directions

Some of the issues that the Internet of Multimedia Things (IoMT) is grappling with include managing large volumes of data, ensuring privacy of data, addressing interoperability among numerous devices, and even providing real-time protection against cyberattacks. To ensure smooth connectivity, real-time analytics, and adaptive security, the future directions will focus on the standardized frameworks, AI-based security, and energy-efficient protocols. User privacy, data integrity, and scalability should be considered the priority of IoMT to be implemented successfully and sustainably.

3.6.1 Scalability and interoperability

Internet of Multimedia Things (IoMT) has serious challenges in scalability and interoperability due to the proliferation of devices, protocols, and platforms. The larger the number of interconnected devices, the harder it is to ensure a smooth communication process and efficient resource management. Some of the future directions are the development of lightweight protocols, dynamic resource allocation methods, and standard communication frameworks. AI-based solutions can adaptively process network traffic, and distributed ledger and blockchain technologies can ensure the safety and transparency of interoperability as well as scaling. In order to address these challenges and make the integration of IoMT systems in different settings a seamless process, collaborative research and inter-industry standardization efforts are vital.

3.6.2 Resource constraints and energy efficiency

Since many IoMT devices run on a limited amount of power and computing capacity, resource restrictions and energy efficiency are significant challenges. Performance and device longevity may be impacted by high multimedia processing demands that quickly deplete resources. The development of energy-harvesting technologies, hardware accelerators to offload demanding workloads, and low-power multimedia processing techniques are some future directions. Energy conservation and performance can be achieved by dynamic resource management, edge computing, and adaptive duty cycling. Reliable, scalable, and sustainable IoMT deployment depends on cooperative efforts in resource-aware architecture and energy-efficient protocol design. Resource constraints and energy efficiency are also problems because most IoMT devices operate with a small amount of power and computing capacity. High multimedia processing needs, which rapidly use up resources, may affect performance and device life. Some of the future directions are the advancement of energy-harvesting technologies, hardware accelerators to offload workloads that are demanding, and the development of low-power multimedia processing methods. Such techniques as dynamic resource management, edge computing, and adaptive duty cycling can be used to achieve energy conservation and performance. Cooperative resource-aware architecture and energy-efficient protocol design are the keys to reliable, scalable, and sustainable IoMT deployment.

3.6.3 Real-time processing and Quality of Service (QoS)

One of the challenges of the Internet of Multimedia Things (IoMT) is real-time processing and Quality of Service (QoS) because multimedia applications have a high rate of data and low latency. Delivery, synchronization, and smooth user experiences are not easy to ensure and are particularly challenging when there are dynamic network conditions. The way forward will be the combination of edge computing to do local data processing, use of adaptive QoS frameworks that are AI-driven, and advanced traffic prioritization network slicing. Real-time performance may also be improved by standardized QoS protocols, predictive analytics, and machine learning to manage the resources. These developments will promote scalable, efficient, and reliable IoMT solutions.

3.6.4 Emerging trends: AI, blockchain, and quantum-safe security

Some of the new technologies in the Internet of Multimedia Things (IoMT) that are transforming the scene are blockchain, artificial intelligence (AI), and quantum-safe security. The AI-driven frameworks are changing multimedia analytics, resource management, and real-time decision-making and enabling adaptive streaming, intelligent compression, and predictive maintenance. The AI models also enhance user experiences by overseeing networks, providing personalized information, and addressing such challenges as latency and congestion. The blockchain technology has made decentralized architectures that facilitate the sharing of data between different IoMT devices safely, openly, and with trust. Its ability to guarantee data integrity and immutability makes it possible to decentralize identity management, provide secure device authentication, and tamper-proof multimedia transactions. Smart contracts enhance interoperability and scalability as they provide the opportunity to have automated trustless interactions between IoMT nodes. To conquer the limitations that quantum computing presents to conventional cryptographic tools, quantum-safe security seems to be an important frontier. Future quantum attacks will be mitigated by multimedia data and IoMT infrastructures due to strategies such as post-quantum algorithms, quantum key distribution (QKD), and lattice-based cryptography. The combination of these, the trends intelligence of AI, trust of blockchain, and the resilience of quantum-safe cryptography builds safe, scalable, and intelligent IoMT ecosystems, transforming multimedia-rich applications in smart cities, healthcare, and entertainment and addressing significant privacy, security, and performance concerns.

Various challenges and possible future research directions in IoMT are summarized in Table 3.3.

Table 3.3 Key challenges and future direction in IoMT

Aspect	Key challenges	Future directions/ solutions	Expected outcomes
General IoMT issues	Large data volumes, privacy risks, interoperability issues, cyber threats	Standardized frameworks, AI-based security, energy-efficient protocols	Secure, scalable, and sustainable IoMT deployment
Scalability and interoperability	Increasing number of devices, heterogeneous protocols, complex communication, and resource management	Lightweight protocols, dynamic resource allocation, standard communication frameworks, AI-based traffic management, blockchain for secure interoperability	Seamless integration, secure communication, transparent and scalable systems
Resource constraints and energy efficiency	Limited power and computing capacity, high multimedia processing demands, reduced device lifespan	Energy-harvesting technologies, hardware accelerators, low-power processing, edge computing, adaptive duty cycling, energy-efficient protocols	Improved energy efficiency, longer device life, reliable and sustainable operation
Real-time processing and QoS	High data rates, latency sensitivity, synchronization issues, fluctuating network conditions	Edge computing, AI-driven QoS frameworks, network slicing, predictive analytics, standardized QoS protocols	Low latency, efficient resource use, improved multimedia quality, and user experience
Emerging trends: AI, blockchain, quantum-safe security	Security vulnerabilities, trust issues, future quantum threats, network congestion	AI for analytics and resource optimization, blockchain for secure data sharing and authentication, smart contracts, post-quantum cryptography, quantum key distribution	Intelligent, secure, tamper-proof, and future-ready IoMT ecosystems

3.7 Case studies and practical implementations

IoMT applications in practice can be industrial automation (e.g., real-time process monitoring), smart cities (e.g., traffic management, surveillance), and healthcare (e.g., remote surgery, patient monitoring). Examples of such benefits as improved effective operations and service delivery are explained with case examples. There are, however, issues of interoperability, security, and scalability. Real-time analytics, trust, and resource management can all be enhanced by using edge computing, blockchain, and artificial intelligence, which should result in the wide and sustainable implementation of IoMT.

3.7.1 Smart home surveillance

Smart home surveillance is an ideal example of the Internet of Multimedia Things (IoMT) in practice, as it is implemented using a range of multimedia gadgets and sensors to enhance the security of the home. To offer real-time tracking, event identification, and remote control using mobile applications, case studies accentuate installation of networked cameras, microphones, motion sensors, and smart doorbells. Through video analytics, including behavior analysis and object recognition, using AI, the homeowner is able to get notified of suspicious activity, reducing false alarms and enhancing situational awareness. An example of practical applications can be systems such as Ring and Nest, which can be easily integrated with the IoMT ecosystems to offer cloud storage, intelligent notifications, and voice support with virtual assistants such as Alexa or Google Assistant. Cloud-based services are scalable in data storage and advanced in analytics, whereas edge computing can perform on-device processing in order to detect dangerous situations instantly. There has been an exploration of blockchain techniques to enhance security of device-to-device communications and integrity of data to ensure that the video captured is true. Some of the concerns that still persist in spite of the significant benefits are energy efficiency, privacy concerns, and the interoperability of the devices across vendors. To deliver dependable, scalable, and reliable smart home monitoring systems in the IoMT context, the upcoming developments will be dedicated to the development of lightweight AI models, standardized communication protocols, and quantum-safe security systems [21,22–25].

3.7.2 Healthcare monitoring systems

Healthcare monitoring systems are a significant field of practical implementation of the Internet of Multimedia Things (IoMT). To support continuous monitoring of patients and early detection of diseases, as well as personalized treatment, real-world applications integrate wearable devices, medical imaging devices, and multimedia solutions. To illustrate, smartwatches and ECG patches with IoMT features can constantly monitor heart rate, transmit information to cloud-based servers, and alert medical specialists about an abnormal tendency immediately. The case studies, such as GE Mural Virtual Care Solution and Philips HealthSuite, demonstrate successful implementation of IoMT in healthcare. HealthSuite supports remote consultations and full-scale patient care, combining multimedia data from imaging devices, wearables, and electronic health records (EHRs). Mural Virtual Care Solution by GE helps in remote monitoring cases and critical care units with the help of multimedia dashboards, which visualize real-time patient data on a large number of devices. Through the analysis of multimodal data, such as voice data, physiological data, and medical imaging, AI-based analytics are vital in identifying health risks and recommending solutions. Issues that still require solutions include ensuring privacy of data, making sure that the energy is well used so that the medical device can be used continuously, and ensuring that the different medical devices can work with each other. To deliver reliable and scalable IoMT healthcare solutions, the future directions will focus on energy-efficient multimedia processing, secure data exchange models, and quantum-safe security protocols.

3.7.3 Multimedia streaming platforms

One of the most successful fields of IoMT application is multimedia streaming platforms, which are transforming the way individuals watch and listen to audio-visual content. Useful implementations are those that use networked devices, e.g., edge servers, VR headsets, smart TVs, and mobile devices, to deliver high-quality, lag-free streaming experiences. The case studies of Netflix, Disney+, and YouTube are the best examples of large-scale IoMT streaming ecosystems that use AI-driven adaptive bitrate streaming, content recommendation systems, and edge caching to enhance their performance. As an illustration, Netflix uses AI-based encoding methods and multimedia-aware edge servers to adapt video quality dynamically to ensure smooth play in a variety of network conditions. To understand the preferences of users and optimize the distribution of content on a wide range of devices, including smart home hubs and IoMT-enabled TVs, Disney+ uses multimedia analytics. Adaptive streaming protocols and real-time analytics are the two strategies that YouTube employs to deliver a uniform watching experience regardless of the different capabilities of devices and bandwidth. Some of the challenges include the management of heavy traffic on the network, ensuring compatibility with other devices, and protecting user privacy. To ensure safe and uninterrupted streaming, the future directions will be the development of lightweight streaming protocols, AI-based content personalization, and blockchain-based digital rights management (DRM). Also, quantum-safe cryptography is being developed to safeguard content delivery in the future against the threats of quantum computing to ensure integrity and trust in IoMT systems streaming multimedia [26].

3.8 Conclusion

The Internet of Multimedia Things (IoMT) enables real-time data processing and smart applications in many industries, like healthcare, smart homes, and entertainment, and is entirely transforming the way multimedia devices communicate and connect. Its success depends on strong structures that offer easy interoperability, standardized communication protocols, and good management of the vast amount and diversity of multimedia data. Due to the increased cases of cyber-attacks on sensitive multimedia information, security remains a critical issue. These issues should be addressed by using advanced encryption techniques, blockchain to enhance data integrity and trust, and quantum-safe cryptographic solutions to future-proof the ecosystem. Examples of new technologies that are vital in performance optimization, adaptive analytics, and low-latency responses are AI and edge computing. These technologies should be combined with scalable architectures and privacy-saving solutions in order to realize resilient, efficient, and secure IoMT deployments in the future. Researchers, industry stakeholders, and standardization organizations should not stop collaborating to stimulate innovation and wide adoption and ensure that IoMT has the capacity to meet the growing demands of a connected, multimedia-rich world.

References

[1] A. Nauman, Y. A. Qadri, M. Amjad, Y. B. Zikria, M. K. Afzal, and S. W. Kim, "Multimedia Internet of Things: a comprehensive survey," *IEEE Access*, vol. 8, pp. 8202–8250, 2020.

[2] V. Kumar, S. Kushwaha, I. Singh, R. K. Barik, G. Singh, and M. Sabraj, "Internet of Multimedia Things (IoMT): communication techniques perspective," *5G and Beyond Wireless Networks*, pp. 147–162, 2024.

[3] S. Rani, S. H. Ahmed, R. Talwar, J. Malhotra, and H. Song, "IoMT: a reliable cross layer protocol for internet of multimedia things," *IEEE Internet of Things Journal*, vol. 4, no. 3, pp. 832–839, 2017.

[4] G. Yang, M. A. Jan, A. U. Rehman, M. Babar, M. M. Aimal, and S. Verma, "Interoperability and data storage in internet of multimedia things: investigating current trends, research challenges and future directions," *IEEE Access*, vol. 8, pp. 124382–124401, 2020.

[5] H. Sahu, N. Joshi, and S. V. Chande, "Security and privacy preservation of multimedia objects over the Internet of Multimedia of Things (IoMT)," in *International Conference on Emerging Trends in Expert Applications & Security*. Springer, 2024, pp. 1–21.

[6] J. Areia, I. A. Bispo, L. Santos, and R. L. d. C. Costa, "IoMT-TrafficData: dataset and tools for benchmarking intrusion detection in internet of medical things," *IEEE Access*, vol. 12, pp. 115370–115385, 2024.

[7] S. A. Alvi, B. Afzal, G. A. Shah, L. Atzori, and W. Mahmood, "Internet of multimedia things: vision and challenges," *Ad Hoc Networks*, vol. 33, pp. 87–111, 2015.

[8] Y. B. Zikria, M. K. Afzal, and S. W. Kim, "Internet of multimedia things (IoMT): opportunities, challenges and solutions," *Sensors*, vol. 20, no. 8, p. 2334, 2020.

[9] R. Sharma, D. Gavalas, and S.-L. Peng, "Smart and future applications of Internet of Multimedia Things (IoMT) using big data analytics," ed: MDPI, vol. 22. 2022, p. 4146.

[10] J. Yan, A. Chen, and J. Chao, "Application of Internet of Things and multimedia technology in English online teaching," *Journal of Computational Methods in Science and Engineering*, vol. 23, no. 6, pp. 3147–3162, 2023.

[11] M. P. Nath, S. B. B. Priyadarshini, M. Ray, and D. S. Das, "An overview of multimedia technologies in current era of Internet of Things (IoT),"

Multimedia Technologies in the Internet of Things Environment, vol. 2, pp. 1–23, 2021.

[12] T. K. Vashishth, V. Sharma, K. K. Sharma, B. Kumar, S. Chaudhary, and S. Agarwal, "IoT-enabled multimedia applications in healthcare, telemedicine, and imaging," in *Multimedia Technologies in the Internet of Things Environment*, vol. 4. Springer, 2025, pp. 135–160.

[13] Y. Kondratenko, O. Kozlov, O. Korobko, and A. Topalov, "Complex industrial systems automation based on the Internet of Things implementation," in *International Conference on Information and Communication Technologies in Education, Research, and Industrial Applications*. Springer, 2017, pp. 164–187.

[14] J. Campbell, P. B. Gibbons, S. Nath, P. Pillai, S. Seshan, and R. Sukthankar, "Irisnet: an internet-scale architecture for multimedia sensors," *in Proceedings of the 13th Annual ACM International Conference on Multimedia*, 2005, pp. 81–88.

[15] N. Sharma and P. G. Shambharkar, "Multi-layered security architecture for IoMT systems: integrating dynamic key management, decentralized storage, and dependable intrusion detection framework," *International Journal of Machine Learning and Cybernetics*, pp. 1–48, 2025.

[16] D. C. Nguyen, P. N. Pathirana, M. Ding, and A. Seneviratne, "BEdgeHealth: a decentralized architecture for edge-based IoMT networks using blockchain," *IEEE Internet of Things Journal*, vol. 8, no. 14, pp. 11743–11757, 2021.

[17] Maria Papaioannou, Marina Karageorgou, Georgios Mantas, *et al.*, "A survey on security threats and countermeasures in internet of medical things (IoMT)," *Transactions on Emerging Telecommunications Technologies*, vol. 33, no. 6, p. e4049, 2022.

[18] S. Rani, A. Kataria, P. Bhambri, P. K. Pareek, and V. Puri, "Artificial intelligence in personalized health services for better patient care," in *Revolutionizing Healthcare: AI Integration with IoT for Enhanced Patient Outcomes*. Springer, 2024, pp. 89–108.

[19] S. N. Hegde, D. Srinivas, M. Rajan, S. Rani, A. Kataria, and H. Min, "Multi-objective and multi constrained task scheduling framework for computational grids," *Scientific Reports*, vol. 14, no. 1, p. 6521, 2024.

[20] S. Kumar, S. Rani, S. Sharma, and H. Min, "Multimodality fusion aspects of medical diagnosis: a comprehensive review," *Bioengineering*, vol. 11, no. 12, p. 1233, 2024.

[21] G. Kokkonis, K. E. Psannis, M. Roumeliotis, and D. Schonfeld, "Real-time wireless multisensory smart surveillance with 3D-HEVC streams for internet-of-things (IoT)," *The Journal of Supercomputing*, vol. 73, no. 3, pp. 1044–1062, 2017.

[22] C. Su, and W. Chen, "Design of remote real-time monitoring and control management system for smart home equipment based on wireless multihop sensor network," *Journal of Sensors*, vol. 2022, no. 1, p. 6228440, 2022.

[23] S. Rani, A. Kataria, S. Kumar, and V. Karar, "A new generation cyber-physical system: a comprehensive review from security perspective," *Computers & Security*, vol. 148, p. 104095, 2025.

[24] S. Rani, P. Bhambri, and M. Chauhan, "A machine learning model for kids' behavior analysis from facial emotions using principal component analysis," in *2021 5th Asian Conference on Artificial Intelligence Technology (ACAIT)*. IEEE, 2021, pp. 522–525.

[25] D. Mittal, H. Singh, and S. Rani, "Exploring explainable artificial intelligence techniques for hate speech detection," in *International Conference on Innovative Computing and Communication*. Springer, 2024, pp. 545–554.

[26] Alcardo Alex Barakabitze, Nabajeet Barman, Arslan Ahmad, Saman Zadtootaghaj, Lingfen Sun, and Maria G. Martini, "QoE management of multimedia streaming services in future networks: a tutorial and survey," *IEEE Communications Surveys & Tutorials*, vol. 22, no. 1, pp. 526–565, 2019.

Chapter 4

Challenges in the adoption of ML and DL techniques for securing multimodal data

Abstract

Due to the increasing application of multimodal data in an ever-expanding range of applications, such as autonomous systems, healthcare, and surveillance, strong security measures are now more important than ever. Deep Learning (DL) and Machine Learning (ML) techniques offer a promising solution to safeguard such a complex data environment. However, there are numerous challenges in embracing them. These are computational constraints, interpretability of models, heterogeneity of data, absence of labeled data, and vulnerability to malicious attacks. Moreover, the multimodal data is sensitive, and therefore, privacy and ethical concerns are raised. This chapter discusses the technical and practical barriers that do not allow the successful implementation of ML/DL-based security structures. It also discusses the current research trends along with the description of potential strategies to encourage the use of reliable and secure multimodal data processing with the help of clever techniques.

Keywords: adversarial attacks; data privacy; deep learning; machine learning; multimodal data; security challenges

4.1 Introduction

Due to the rapid evolution of digital technologies, the creation and use of multimodal data have grown exponentially in diverse disciplines, such as healthcare, finance, autonomous systems, and smart cities [1]. Multimodal data can be textual, visual, auditory, or sensor-based and this opens up possibilities of enhancing situational awareness and decision-making that have never been considered before. However, there is also a dark side to privacy and security in this richness. The availability, security, and integrity of such extensive data, especially at the point where sensitive information is involved, must be ensured. Machine learning (ML) and deep learning (DL) are now considered useful tools in the context of detecting and mitigating security threats in multimodal data. These methods are attractive for installing powerful security measures due to their capability to detect trends, spot abnormalities, and provide predictive insight. Nonetheless, some of the problems that make them difficult to apply in real-life situations include model interpretability, heterogeneity of data, adversarial vulnerabilities, and resource-consuming training requirements. This chapter aims to discuss the several challenges to the widespread application of ML and DL techniques to multimodal data security. The chapter takes a close examination of these issues in an attempt to assist academics, practitioners, and policymakers in developing multimodal data security solutions that are more reliable, efficient, and deployable.

4.1.1 Overview of multimodal data

Multimodal data is information that brings together multiple types of data such as text, images, audio, video, and sensor measurements, among others. This mixture of different modalities captures free characteristics of a system or phenomenon, which is beneficial in analysis and decision-making. The healthcare industry can combine wearable sensor data with medical imaging and electronic health records to improve patient monitoring and diagnosis, e.g., through multimodal data. Autonomous cars have better safety and situational awareness due to LiDAR, video, and radar sensor fusion. The special challenges of multimodal data are despite its advantages. To begin with, it is often nonhomogeneous and has varying formats, structures, and sampling rates, which complicates preprocessing and data integration. Second, complicated procedures are required to maintain both temporal and semantic consistency in the process of aligning information across modalities, including synchronizing textual annotations with video. Third, multimodal data tends to be high-dimensional, which means that dimensionality reduction and successful feature extraction are required to ensure that computing complexity is limited. Multimodal data is capable of demonstrating hidden trends that indicate threats or anomalies in security situations, yet due to its complexity, it also increases the attack surface. Thus, developing effective ML and DL systems that safeguard multimodal data is a challenging but required task. To realize the full use of multimodal systems in practice, a number of issues should be addressed [2–4].

4.1.2 Role of Machine Learning (ML) and Deep Learning (DL) in security

Deep learning (DL) and machine learning (ML) are emerging as essential approaches to addressing security problems in modern data systems, in particular, multimodal data. These scalable, automated, and flexible strategies enable effective threat identification and mitigation. Classification, clustering, and anomaly detection are machine learning methods that are quite useful in determining trends in historical data, which allows detecting suspicious activity, illegal access, and data breaches at an early stage. Examples of the use of ML models include text, log, or user behavior analysis to identify malware or phishing activity. Deep Learning (DL) has a tremendous advantage in the analysis of high-dimensional and heterogeneous multimodal data, as it can model nonlinear relationships. Whereas transformers can be used to combine a wide range of input types to perform a thorough threat analysis, Convolutional Neural Networks (CNNs) and Recurrent Neural Networks (RNNs) can handle pictures, audio, and time series. DL models can identify the smallest anomalies that a rule-based system might overlook, such as identifying deepfake movies or scanning sensor data to identify violations in Internet of Things networks. All said and done, ML and DL provide data-driven proactive security systems. However, their use has disadvantages such as explainability, resistance to malicious attacks, and the need to have large, labeled datasets, which are also significant and discussed in the following sections [5,6].

4.2 Characteristics and complexity of multimodal data

The multiple types of multimodal data include text, images, music, and sensor signals, and only a few of them are listed. Its heterogeneity, high dimensionality, and different sample rates make it more difficult to integrate and analyze. It is hard to synchronize and integrate different modalities and preserve the temporal and semantic consistency. Moreover, multimodal data is often incomplete and noisy, which requires powerful modeling and preprocessing techniques to be used in effective machine learning and security [7]. The various challenges experienced in multimodal data are shown in Figure 4.1.

4.2.1 Data heterogeneity and integration challenges

Multimodal data is inherently diverse, with each modality having its own format, structure, and sample rates. Audio is continuous waves, images are high-dimensional pixel arrays, sensor data may be time-series or event-driven, and text is often unstructured or semi-structured. All these modalities are very hard to unite. There is also the need to manage various temporal and spatial resolutions, different noise properties, and uneven labeling standards to match modalities. As an example,

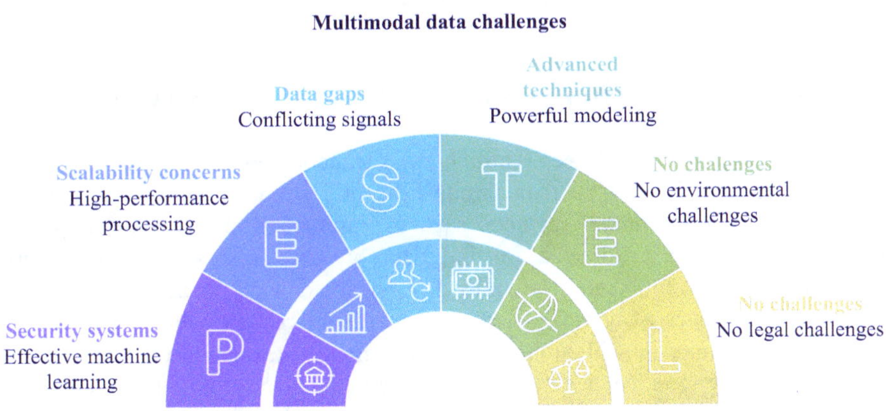

Figure 4.1 Complexities and challenges in multimodal data

sophisticated preprocessing and time-warping algorithms would be required to match physiological data with medical images or match video frames with textual annotations. To retain the information of modality specificity and enable thorough analysis, the data fusion strategies, such as early fusion (raw data integration) and late fusion (model-level integration), must be planned appropriately. Semantic consistency across modalities is required in order to make accurate decisions. Moreover, the heterogeneity may exacerbate such issues as conflicting signals, data gaps, and imbalance in modalities and complicate the training and inference processes. These issues need to be solved to develop effective and reliable machine learning and deep learning solutions for multimodal security systems.

4.2.2 High dimensionality and scalability concerns

As a result of the interrelation of numerous modalities, each of which adds its own distinct features, the dimensionality of multimodal data is often extremely high. As an example, high-frequency time series can be generated by sensor data, intricate embeddings can be generated by text, and photos can contain thousands of pixel values per frame. The combination of these modalities generates massive feature spaces that are computationally and storage-intensive. This high dimensionality may lead to the so-called curse of dimensionality, where the volume of the feature space grows exponentially and makes it difficult to generalize models. The training of deep learning models on such data may be computationally challenging and require specialized equipment, large memory requirements, and efficient distributed training algorithms. The problem of scalability is also aggravated by the reality that real-time security systems often require prompt processing of multimodal streams of data. Scalable architectures are essential in managing high-dimensional and large-scale data with high performance in terms of security, particularly as the number of data sources increases in areas such as healthcare, the Internet of Things, and autonomous systems. These issues necessitate advanced dimensionality reduction techniques, parallel computing systems, and optimized model structures to ensure that they can be used in real-world problems and that they are viable and perform well.

4.3 ML and DL techniques for multimodal data security

Machine learning (ML) and deep learning (DL) technologies are increasingly being used to safeguard multimodal data through the utilization of patterns in multiple modalities. Machine learning methods such as ensemble learning, clustering, and anomaly detection can be used to find data breaches and suspicious activity. Transformers, Recurrent Neural Networks (RNNs), and convolutional neural networks (CNNs) are examples of complex and cross-modal interaction patterns that can be effectively represented in a DL architecture. By combining textual, visual, and auditory data, they are able to detect advanced threats, including adversarial attacks and deepfakes. Security is an ongoing research focus since, even though it is effective, model interpretability, robustness, and computation requirements remain an issue [8,9].

4.3.1 Overview of ML approaches (e.g., classification, clustering)

Machine learning (ML) methods are necessary to secure multimodal data by identifying trends and detecting abnormalities. Supervised learning algorithms, such as decision trees, random forests, and support vector machines, are very useful in classifying known threats using labeled data. Examples of unsupervised learning methods that are useful in uncovering hidden patterns and previously unknown attacks in unlabeled data are clustering and anomaly detection. In practice, semi-supervised methods are more accurate in detection since they use both labeled and unlabeled data. Combining multiple models, ensemble methods enhance resilience and flexibility and address the challenges posed by the large dimensionality and heterogeneity of multimodal data.

4.3.2 Overview of DL approaches (e.g., autoencoders, GANs)

Deep Learning (DL) methods have revolutionized multimodal data security by modeling high-dimensional, complex patterns. Although Recurrent Neural Networks (RNNs) and Long Short-Term Memory (LSTM) networks excel at temporal correlations in sequential data, which are the audio and sensor streams, Convolutional Neural Networks (CNNs) are the most effective in analyzing picture and spatial data. Transformers make it possible to combine data and understand across modalities by learning effectively through attention. Generative Adversarial Networks (GANs) and variational autoencoders (VAEs) enhance the stability of models by generating synthetic training samples and aiding in the detection of anomalies. Despite their efficiency, DL models are disadvantaged with respect to explainability, adversarial robustness, data privacy, and high computational cost.

4.3.3 Advantages of ML/DL techniques in security

Machine learning (ML) and deep learning (DL) methods have significant advantages in the security of multimodal data by leveraging their ability to automatically find complex patterns in large and heterogeneous datasets. This is because the ML/DL models can dynamically identify new threats and small anomalies that cut across multiple data types, such as text, pictures, audio, sensor data, etc., which distinguishes them against traditional rule-based security systems and signature-based security systems. This flexibility is vital in light of the way cyberattacks and data breaches are changing. At least, DL architectures are remarkably good at integrating dissimilar data sources to derive holistic information, which enhances the ability to detect coordinating and multifaceted attacks that would otherwise not be detected when data of a specific modality is considered individually. As an example, sensor signals can be used in conjunction with video surveillance data to enhance the precision of intruder detection in smart settings. Moreover, with the ability to process high-dimensional and large volumes of multimodal data, ML/DL models can be scaled, which is essential in real-time security surveillance in large systems, such as IoT networks and healthcare systems [10–15]. Their ability to

Table 4.1 *ML and DL techniques for multimodal data security*

Aspect	Machine Learning (ML) techniques	Deep Learning (DL) techniques
Feature extraction	Requires manual/handcrafted features	Automatically learns features from raw multimodal data
Data handling	Effective for structured and low-dimensional data	Well-suited for high-dimensional, complex multimodal data
Common models	SVM, Decision Tree, Random Forest, KNN, Clustering	CNN, RNN, LSTM, Autoencoders, Transformers
Computational cost	Low to moderate	High (requires GPUs/accelerators)
Interpretability	Higher and more transparent	Lower, often considered black-box
Scalability	Limited for very large datasets	Highly scalable with big data
Accuracy	Good for known attack patterns	Superior for complex and unknown threats
Real-time suitability	Suitable for resource-constrained IoMT devices	More suitable for edge–fog–cloud architectures
Multimodal fusion	Limited fusion capability	Strong cross-modal and attention-based fusion
Robustness	Less robust to complex/ adversarial attacks	More robust with advanced training strategies
Typical applications	Intrusion detection, access control, anomaly detection	Biometric security, surveillance analytics, content integrity
Deployment complexity	Easier to deploy and maintain	Complex deployment and training pipeline

learn using unstructured and unlabeled data also increases their applicability to dynamic environments with limited labeled data. Nevertheless, in spite of the challenges such as interpretability and resource demands, ML and DL strategies remain essential in enhancing multimodal data security, such as better accuracy, robustness, and proactive threat mitigation. An overview of both ML and DL methods of securing multimodal data is illustrated in Table 4.1.

4.4 Key challenges in adoption

The implementation of the ML and DL algorithms for multimodal data security has several challenges. The time and cost of data labeling are constraints of supervised learning. The variety of modalities complicates model design and data integration. Models are often not interpretable, which hinders trust and regulatory compliance. Adversarial attacks pose a threat to robustness and exploit the vulnerabilities of ML/DL systems. The high requirements in terms of computation and storage impede deployment in situations where the available resources are limited. The privacy concerns the usage of sensitive multimodal data. There is also the issue of ethical and legal concerns with regard to data control, which makes adoption difficult. To ensure that multimodal security solutions are reliable and successful, these challenges have to be resolved [16–18].

4.4.1 Data labeling and annotation challenges

In the case of security applications, multimodal data labeling is a challenging and costly task. To be annotated properly, every modality – text, photos, audio, and sensors – requires specialized knowledge, which often incorporates different formats and standards. Multimodal datasets are large and high-dimensional, which makes manual labeling expensive and time-consuming. Moreover, attacks and abnormalities relating to security are either rare or evolving, resulting in unbalanced or poorly labeled samples. This scarcity limits the effectiveness of supervised learning and model generalization. Although they are partial solutions, automated labeling and weak supervision methods can produce noise. These problems should be addressed in order to train a reliable ML and DL model in multimodal security [19].

4.4.2 Model interpretability and explainability

Multimodal data security ML and DL models are often black boxes, and thus, their judgments are difficult to comprehend. This is a disadvantage to trust, especially in critical security fields where it is imperative to understand the logic behind the alerts. The multimodal models that involve heterogeneous data make explainability more challenging due to the complexity of interactions of features across modalities. Ethical and regulatory limitations demand explainable systems, but approaches to deciphering deep models are computationally expensive and scarce. Among the largest challenges of establishing reliable and responsible multimodal security solutions is improving interpretability without reducing performance [20,21].

4.4.3 Data privacy and confidentiality concerns

Multimodal data often contains sensitive information in various formats, posing a significant threat to privacy and confidentiality of security applications. There is a threat of misuse, data breaches, and unlawful access to such data collection, storage, and processing. ML and DL models require large datasets, which increases the chances of a privacy breach, especially when the data is shared among organizations. It is made complicated by ensuring adherence to laws such as GDPR and HIPAA. Although techniques such as federated learning, encryption, and data anonymization minimize risks, they can also influence the quality of the model or increase the cost of computing. The balancing between the high levels of privacy and effective security is a significant challenge in multimodal data settings.

4.4.4 Adversarial attacks and robustness issues

Multimodal security can be adversarially attacked by attackers who secretly modify input data in one or more modalities to evade detection or cause a false result. These attacks are threatening the reliability and integrity of critical security systems by exploiting vulnerabilities in the models. The complexity of multimodal fusion is increased, and defense is complicated. Development of adversarial training and resilient designs is required to offer robustness, yet they often increase the cost of computing. A balance between model correctness and resilience remains one of the largest obstacles to the implementation of safe and reliable multimodal learning systems.

4.4.5 Resource and infrastructure requirements

Multimodal data security based on ML and DL needs a lot of computational power, including large memory, rapid storage, and powerful GPUs, to process the volume and complexity of many data types. Deep models require much time and effort to be trained using high-dimensional multimodal datasets, and distributed computing environments are often required. Real-time security applications impose further burden on those systems that demand low processing latency. Besides, model maintenance and updates need scalable and reliable technologies. The adoption is limited by the resource constraints, especially in edge or IoT applications. Hybrid architecture based on the clouds and efficient algorithms is required to find a balance between infrastructure limitations and performance.

4.4.6 Legal, ethical, and regulatory considerations

The process of adopting ML and DL to ensure the security of multimodal data involves operating in complex regulatory, ethical, and legal landscapes. Data privacy laws such as GDPR and HIPAA have strict rules of data collection, processing, and sharing, especially of sensitive multimodal data. Ethical considerations include fairness, the removal of bias, and maintaining openness in automated security judgments. Noncompliance may be followed by legal consequences and loss of user confidence. Besides, ML/DL models need to be audited and responsible for meeting regulatory demands. These factors should be considered to have multimodal security solutions implemented in a responsible manner.

Summarization of all the above challenges is presented in Table 4.2.

4.5 Case studies and real-world examples

More and more machine learning and deep learning are being applied in various areas to safeguard multimodal data. Anomaly detection systems identify inconsistencies in different types of data using these techniques to enhance data confidentiality and integrity. Visual, aural, and sensor multimodal analyses are useful in the identification of potential threats in security and surveillance systems.

Table 4.2 Summarization of the key challenges in the adoption of ML and DL techniques for multimodal security

Challenge	Key issues	Impact on multimodal security	Possible solutions/ directions
General ML/DL implementation challenges	High data labeling cost, modality diversity, lack of interpretability, adversarial threats, high computational needs, privacy risks, legal and ethical issues	Limits trust, scalability, deployment, and adoption of multimodal security systems	Efficient algorithms, privacy-preserving techniques, explainable AI, and regulatory-compliant frameworks
Data labeling and annotation	Expensive and time-consuming labeling, need for domain expertise, large and high-dimensional datasets, rare and evolving attack patterns, imbalanced data	Reduces model accuracy, generalization, and effectiveness of supervised learning	Automated labeling, weak supervision, semi-supervised learning, improved annotation tools
Model interpretability and explainability	Black-box nature of ML/DL models, complex multimodal feature interactions, limited explainability tools	Reduces trust, transparency, and regulatory compliance	Explainable AI (XAI), interpretable models, visualization tools
Data privacy and confidentiality	Sensitive multimodal data, risk of data breaches, unauthorized access, compliance with regulations (GDPR, HIPAA)	Privacy violations, legal risks, reduced adoption	Federated learning, encryption, anonymization, privacy-preserving ML
Adversarial attacks and robustness	Manipulation of input data, multimodal fusion vulnerabilities, evasion attacks	Reduced system reliability, incorrect predictions, security failures	Adversarial training, robust model design, defensive architectures
Resource and infrastructure requirements	High computational power, large storage, GPU dependency, real-time processing demands, infrastructure cost	Limits deployment in edge, IoT, and resource-constrained environments	Efficient models, cloud-edge hybrid systems, model optimization
Legal, ethical, and regulatory issues	Compliance with privacy laws, bias, fairness, lack of transparency, accountability requirements	Legal penalties, ethical concerns, reduced user trust	Ethical AI frameworks, bias mitigation, regulatory compli-ance, audit mechanisms

Besides enhancing resistance to malicious assaults, smart data combination of diverse sources reveals the importance of AI-based approaches to defending complex data environments [22–26].

4.5.1 Healthcare data security

Machine learning (ML) and deep learning (DL) strategies are playing a major role in ensuring that multimodal data are secure in the healthcare sector by addressing challenges such as data heterogeneity, privacy, and adversarial threats. One of such applications is anomaly detection of diagnostic imaging and electronic health records (EHRs). Anomalous patterns or unauthorized access to both organized (lab findings) and unstructured (clinical notes, medical photos) data can be identified by machine learning models like isolation forests and DL-based autoencoders. Organizations can also collaborate in developing models on private patient data without transferring information between systems by applying privacy-preserving techniques such as federated learning. This approach has been applied by Google Health to safely detect diabetic retinopathy by examining retinal scans. Multi-mode biometric identification systems employ the use of fingerprint, voice, and facial information to verify users in telehealth systems safely. Also, DL models can be used to detect hostile attacks on medical imaging equipment that could alter the outcomes of diagnostic tests. Besides, although patient confidentiality is preserved, safe data fusion methods can be used to integrate information using imaging instruments, wearable sensors, and the medical history. These examples demonstrate how the solutions based on ML/DL can be essential in enhancing the resilience of healthcare systems or enhancing trust in digital health solutions by ensuring data integrity, access management, and defense against evolving cyberthreats [27].

4.5.2 Financial and banking data

Multimodal data, such as voice commands, digital documents, transaction records, and biometric information, require machine learning (ML) and deep learning (DL) to safeguard such data in the banking and finance sector. Machine learning algorithms can also be applied to detect fraud and identify suspicious activities by analyzing trends in a great number of data sources, such as voice recordings, metadata of transactions, and wording in email messages. DL models, especially transformers and Recurrent Neural Networks (RNNs), make it possible to perform real-time anomaly detection on high-volume, multimodal streams, including ATM footage, transaction history, and user behavior data. Multimodal biometric systems IDV Multimodal biometric systems incorporate voice prints, facial recognition, and keystroke dynamics to verify users with accuracy using DL models. Financial institutions can also apply machine learning (ML) to detect insider risks and phishing by comparing data on chat logs, emails, and access records. Regulatory compliance makes use of natural language processing (NLP) models, which process legal papers and communications with consumers to ensure that financial requirements are adhered to. Federated learning is also being explored in order to enhance privacy through collaborative model training between universities without sharing raw sensitive information. Such innovative ML/DL solutions significantly decrease the number of financial frauds, enhance multimodal data security, and enhance trust in online banking services [28].

4.5.3 Smart city and IoT systems

ML and DL play a vital role in securing multimodal data of diverse origins, such as connected devices, traffic cameras, surveillance cameras, and environmental scanners in smart cities and Internet of Things systems. To detect abnormalities, potential attacks, or system malfunctions in real-time, machine learning models process multimodal data, such as text messages, voice messages, video streams, and sensor data. An example of such systems is smart traffic, whereby it uses GPS, accelerometers, and traffic lights to correlate data in order to detect events accurately and applies the DL-based video analytics to detect an accident or illegitimate vehicle movement. Machine learning algorithms in smart grids defend against the data on energy consumption by cross-examining user behaviors and grid performance metrics to identify anomalies in consumption or cyberattacks. DL models are also intelligent and can be used to power intelligent surveillance, such as combining motion data, audio data, and video data and determining questionable activity without compromising user privacy. In the context of public safety, multimodal integration of postings in social media, street camera videos, and emergency call logs enables fast threat detection and response. Moreover, approaches such as homomorphic encryption and federated learning are being implemented to protect confidential urban information and enable cross-departmental model training. These ML/DL-based methods ensure sound and shrewd city management by enhancing the resilience and integrity of smart city environments [29].

4.6 Emerging trends and research directions

Some of the emerging trends in multimodal data security based on machine learning (ML) and deep learning (DL) are adversarial learning to enhance data integrity, multimodal fusion models used in anomaly detection, and federated learning as data privacy-preserving analytics. Self-supervised learning can support the process of working with unlabeled data, and studies progress to explainable AI to achieve transparency and trust. To ensure high levels of multimodal security, the implementation of edge AI, safe data-sharing procedures, and cross-domain generalization are the priorities of future efforts [30,31].

4.6.1 Federated and distributed learning approaches

Distributed and federated learning is an emerging trend as an approach to protection of multimodal data. Such techniques preserve privacy and reduce the chances of information leakage through collaborative training of models on dispersed devices or organizations without sharing raw data. In the case of sensitive multimodal data, such as surveillance or healthcare, federated learning is ideal as local models are trained on-device, and only model updates are communicated to the center. Distributed learning also increases scalability and robustness through the application of parallel computing between nodes. These strategies can be combined to make sure that the laws of data protection, such as GDPR, are upheld. Present studies are focused on making sure that multimodal intelligence, which is security-friendly and privacy-conscious, can be provided in various fields by improving the efficiency of communication, handling non-IID information, and securing model updates through homomorphic encryption and differential privacy.

4.6.2 Explainable AI (XAI) in security

Explainable AI (XAI) is necessary to enhance transparency and trustworthiness of multimodal data security systems. XAI methods help to understand the decision-making mechanisms in complex ML and DL models that accept different types of inputs, such as text, images, and sensor data, revealing possible biases or weaknesses. This is important in sectors such as healthcare, banking, and defense, where compliance and risk analysis require an understanding of the logic underlying models. XAI can ensure that stakeholders can confirm the security measures, detect abnormalities, and ensure that data is used ethically. Examples of emerging XAI methods are saliency mapping, attention visualization, and counterfactual explanations tailored to multimodal inputs. Further research will be done to integrate XAI into real-time systems seamlessly to improve interpretability without compromising on accuracy and speed of processing.

4.6.3 Integration with blockchain and other technologies

One of the possible solutions to enhance multimodal data security is to combine blockchain with machine learning and deep learning. Blockchain provides decentralized, impenetrable, and traceable data integrity, transparency, and traceability across distributed systems. It makes data exchange and auditing safe in combination with ML/DL models, particularly in sensitive domains such as healthcare, smart cities, and financial services. Consensus mechanisms prevent unwanted changes, whereas smart contracts can be used to verify data and control access. Moreover, it can also be enhanced with real-time processing and privacy, combining it with such technologies as secure multiparty computation, homomorphic encryption, and edge computing. The primary areas of contemporary research are interoperability, energy efficiency, and lightweight blockchain frameworks. This convergence enables a stable, scalable infrastructure to monitor and safeguard multimodal data environments of a complex nature.

4.7 Recommendations and best practices

Applied to the use of ML and DL to preserve the privacy of multimodal data, use privacy-preserving techniques such as federated learning and differential privacy.

Apply powerful data fusion and anomaly detection models, and apply XAI techniques to ensure explainability. To ensure safe access control and traceability, include blockchain. Test the models on diverse and changing datasets and refresh them regularly to counter malicious attacks. To achieve ethical and efficient multimodal data protection, promote transparency, cross-domain generalization, and data protection laws.

4.7.1 Data governance and policy considerations

Data policy and governance are necessary when applying ML and DL algorithms to secure multimodal data. Effective governance ensures that data quality, integrity, and regulatory compliance, such as GDPR, HIPAA, and the DPDP Act in India, are met. Important components include data classification, access controls, permission management, and accountability in data utilization. Policies should outline roles, duties, and protocols of data exchange, retention, and auditability of all modalities. The ethical standards should be part of the governance systems to prevent prejudice and abuse, and the decisions related to AI models should be made transparent. Security and uniformity are also enhanced by adopting lifecycle management and data interchange standards. To ensure safe, legal, and reliable AI-driven multimodal systems, the future directions suggest the coordination of governance and the latest technology such as blockchain and federated learning.

4.7.2 Designing robust ML/DL models

To develop powerful ML/DL models to secure multimodal data, strategies to ensure accuracy, robustness, and adaptability to diverse sources of data are required. In managing the heterogeneity, such significant methods are feature alignment, noise reduction, and multimodal data normalization. Adversarial training is applied to help models identify bad inputs and resist manipulation. The powerful models ought to be capable of processing missing or distorted modalities and be applicable to different domains. Regularization, dropout methods, and ensemble learning enhance the stability of the model and prevent overfitting. The inclusion of explainability tools enhances interpretability and trust. Applicability with respect to the changing situations is achieved through real-time retraining and continuous model validation. Moreover, privacy-preserving algorithms such as secure computing and differential privacy are applied to enhance data protection and make the models suitable for sensitive tasks such as surveillance and medical care.

4.7.3 Collaborative approaches and open datasets

Cooperative approaches and the use of publicly available datasets are the key factors in the development of ML and DL algorithms in the field of multimodal data security. By sharing information, benchmarking of models, and data collection of different types through cross-institutional collaborations, innovation becomes faster and transparency and reproducibility are promoted. Open datasets make models more robust and generalized by enabling them to be trained on diverse multimodal real-world inputs such as text, audio, pictures, and sensor data. Programs such as federated learning enable institutions to collaborate without sharing any private information. Examples of best practices include standardization of dataset formats, ensuring that the process of anonymization is properly performed, and removing bias by incorporating diverse data in the data curation process. More secure, open, and ethical paradigms are being developed as well due to open challenges and community-based platforms. Ultimately, these collaborative efforts assist in developing multimodal security systems, which are dependable and scalable.

4.8 Conclusion

The application of machine learning (ML) and deep learning (DL) methods to guarantee the security of multimodal data has a number of challenges and enormous opportunities. Powerful models that can process heterogeneous inputs are needed since multimodal data, a combination of text, images, audio, and sensor signals, makes integration, preprocessing, and feature alignment complex. Security concerns, such as privacy of data, attacks by enemies, and unauthorized access, complicate the deployment. Even though recent methods such as explainable AI, federated learning, and blockchain integration can offer a solution to the issue, their practical application is limited by regulatory barriers, computing constraints, and the absence of standardized frameworks. Moreover, the quality of high-quality and annotated multimodal data and the necessity of domain-specific adjustment limit the model's generalization and scalability. Ethical considerations, such as prejudice, fairness, and responsibility, also play an important role in high-stakes environments, such as healthcare, banking, and surveillance. Thus, to achieve good governance, promote ethical AI uses, and ensure interoperability, further development will depend on a collaborative ecosystem of academics, industry, and politicians. Thus, both ML and DL methods are powerful tools for securing multimodal data, yet their effective application requires the elimination of operational, ethical, and technical challenges. A multidisciplinary approach involving the development of policy, involvement of stakeholders, and technical development is necessary to realize the potential of safe multimodal intelligence fully.

References

[1] D. Lahat, T. Adali, and C. Jutten, "Multimodal data fusion: an overview of methods, challenges, and prospects," *Proceedings of the IEEE*, vol. 103, no. 9, pp. 1449–1477, 2015.

[2] K. Sharma and M. Giannakos, "Multimodal data capabilities for learning: what can multimodal data tell us about learning?," *British Journal of Educational Technology*, vol. 51, no. 5, pp. 1450–1484, 2020.

[3] S. R. Stahlschmidt, B. Ulfenborg, and J. Synnergren, "Multimodal deep learning for biomedical data fusion: a review," *Briefings in Bioinformatics*, vol. 23, no. 2, p. bbab569, 2022.

[4] F. Zhao, C. Zhang, and B. Geng, "Deep multimodal data fusion," *ACM Computing Surveys*, vol. 56, no. 9, pp. 1–36, 2024.

[5] Muhammad Imran Tariq, Nisar Ahmed Memon, Shakeel Ahmed *et al.*, "A review of deep learning security and privacy defensive techniques," *Mobile Information Systems*, vol. 2020, no. 1, p. 6535834, 2020.

[6] H. Attar, "Joint IoT/ML platforms for smart societies and environments: a review on multimodal information-based learning for safety and security," *ACM Journal of Data and Information Quality*, vol. 15, no. 3, pp. 1–26, 2023.

[7] Q. Zhang, Y. Wei, Z. Han *et al.*, "Multimodal fusion on low-quality data: a comprehensive survey," *Information Fusion*, vol. 135, p. 104437, 2026.

[8] M. Moshawrab, M. Adda, A. Bouzouane, H. Ibrahim, and A. Raad, "Reviewing multimodal machine learning and its use in cardiovascular diseases detection," *Electronics*, vol. 12, no. 7, p. 1558, 2023.

[9] W. Lin, "Design of a multimodal network data security detection model based on self-supervised learning," *Security and Privacy*, vol. 8, no. 5, p. e70062, 2025.

[10] F. Hu and X. Hei, *AI, Machine Learning and Deep Learning: A Security Perspective*. CRC Press, 2023.

[11] Aboubakr Bajenaid, Maher Khemakhem, Fathy E. Eassa *et al.*, "Towards robust SDN security: a comparative analysis of oversampling techniques with ML and DL classifiers," *Electronics*, vol. 14, no. 5, p. 995, 2025.

[12] Z. Mustafa, R. Amin, H. Aldabbas, and N. Ahmed, "Intrusion detection systems for software-defined networks: a comprehensive study on machine learning-based techniques," *Cluster Computing*, vol. 27, no. 7, pp. 9635–9661, 2024.

[13] S. Rani, A. Kataria, P. Bhambri, P. K. Pareek, and V. Puri, "Artificial intelligence in personalized health services for better patient care," in *Revolutionizing Healthcare: AI Integration with IoT for Enhanced Patient Outcomes*. Springer, 2024, pp. 89–108.

[14] S. Rani, P. Bhambri, and M. Chauhan, "A machine learning model for kids' behavior analysis from facial emotions using principal component analysis," in *2021 5th Asian Conference on Artificial Intelligence Technology (ACAIT)*. IEEE, 2021, pp. 522–525.

[15] S. N. Hegde, D. Srinivas, M. Rajan, S. Rani, A. Kataria, and H. Min, "Multi-objective and multi constrained task scheduling framework for computational grids," *Scientific Reports*, vol. 14, no. 1, p. 6521, 2024.

[16] K. Bayoudh, R. Knani, F. Hamdaoui, and A. Mtibaa, "A survey on deep multimodal learning for computer vision: advances, trends, applications, and datasets," *The Visual Computer*, vol. 38, no. 8, pp. 2939–2970, 2022.

[17] Qingzhi Liu, Yuchen Huang, Chenglu Jin *et al.*, "Privacy and integrity protection for IoT multimodal data using machine learning and blockchain,"

ACM Transactions on Multimedia Computing, Communications and Applications, vol. 20, no. 6, pp. 1–18, 2024.

[18] S. W. Shende, J. V. Tembhurne, and N. A. Ansari, "Deep learning based authentication schemes for smart devices in different modalities: progress, challenges, performance, datasets and future directions," *Multimedia Tools and Applications*, vol. 83, no. 28, pp. 71451–71493, 2024.

[19] P. Nanjundan, L. Thomas, P. Indu, and S. Eslamian, "Challenges and opportunities in multimodal learning research," *Multimodal Learning Using Heterogeneous Data*, pp. 239–246, 2026.

[20] Z. Tolba, "Cryptanalysis and improvement of multimodal data encryption by machine-learning-based system," *arXiv preprint arXiv:2402.15779*, 2024.

[21] M. Amirian, "Deep learning for robust and explainable models in computer vision," *arXiv preprint arXiv:2403.18674*, 2024.

[22] T. Sadiq and C. W. Omlin, "Sensing in smart cities: a multimodal machine learning perspective," *Smart Cities*, vol. 9, no. 1, p. 3, 2025.

[23] A. Kumar, R. Gupta, S. Kumar, K. Dutta, and M. Rani, "Securing IoMT-based healthcare system: issues, challenges, and solutions," *Artificial Intelligence and Cybersecurity in Healthcare*, pp. 17–56, 2025.

[24] S. Kumar, S. Rani, S. Sharma, and H. Min, "Multimodality fusion aspects of medical diagnosis: a comprehensive review," *Bioengineering*, vol. 11, no. 12, p. 1233, 2024.

[25] D. Mittal, H. Singh, and S. Rani, "Exploring explainable artificial intelligence techniques for hate speech detection," in *International Conference on Innovative Computing and Communication*. Springer, 2024, pp. 545–554.

[26] V. Puri, A. Kataria, S. Rani, and P. K. Pareek, "DLT based smart medical ecosystem," in *2023 International Conference on Network, Multimedia and Information Technology (NMITCON)*. IEEE, 2023, pp. 1–6.

[27] H. Singh, M. Deshmukh, and L. K. Awasthi, "Secure healthcare data management using multimodal image fusion and dual watermarking," *Scientific Reports*, vol. 15, no. 1, p. 9047, 2025.

[28] S. Paleti, *Smart Finance: Artificial Intelligence, Regulatory Compliance, and Data Engineering in the Transformation of Global Banking*. Deep Science Publishing, 2025.

[29] S. Mehta and A. Bhalla, "Smart cities reimagined: enhancing traffic management through federated multimodal learning," in *2024 3rd International Conference for Advancement in Technology (ICONAT)*. IEEE, 2024, pp. 1–6.

[30] M. Shamim, A. R. Faridi, and F. Masood, "Analysis of emerging trends and challenges in multimodal data," in *2025 12th International Conference on Computing for Sustainable Global Development (INDIACom)*. IEEE, 2025, pp. 1–7.

[31] V. Dankan Gowda, D. Palanikkumar, K. Prasad, M. Kaur, and S. Singh, "Future directions and emerging trends in multimodal data fusion for bioinformatics," *Multimodal Data Fusion for Bioinformatics Artificial Intelligence*, pp. 247–282, 2025.

Chapter 5

Analysis and management of multimodal data: big data approach

Abstract

The rapid growth of different digital content necessitates the urgency to find effective ways of managing and assessing multimodal data. Heterogeneous sources such as text, photos, audio, video, sensors, and social media generate massive datasets of large volume, velocity, and variety, which makes them hard to integrate and process. Examples of scalable big data systems that allow it to store complex data efficiently, analyze it in real time, and retrieve it fast include Hadoop, Spark, and distributed NoSQL systems. The presence of meaningful patterns in multiple modalities is easier to find with advanced methods such as data fusion, feature engineering, and representation learning using deep learning. These techniques are used in autonomous systems, smart cities, healthcare, and personalized services to demonstrate how the techniques can deliver game-changing insights. In order to ensure trustworthiness and ethical outcomes, equal focus is directed to data quality, privacy, and governance. The article provides researchers and practitioners with a systematic way of applying big data technologies to extract valuable information from multimodal data.

Keywords: big data analytics; data fusion; deep learning; distributed computing; multimodal data

5.1 Introduction

The multimodal datasets are complicated by the fact that the digital information has become exponentially large (text, images, audio, video, sensors, and social media platforms). The analysis and handling of such a wide variety of data require scalable big data methods capable of operating with large volume, high velocity, and heterogeneous data. This chapter describes the fundamental concepts and challenges of multimodal data processing, including integration, storage, and real-time analytics. It also highlights the role played by distributed computing systems such as Hadoop and Spark, in addition to state-of-the-art techniques such as data fusion and deep learning. The discussion forms the basis of gaining practical insights without compromising data governance, privacy, and quality [1].

5.1.1 Overview of multimodal data

Multimodal data denotes information collected through different sources or modalities like text, photos, audio, video, sensor data, and social media feeds. Multimodal data is capable of making deeper insights and decision-making more accurate as the multimodal data represents richer and more detailed representations of real-world phenomena than traditional single-mode datasets do. Nevertheless, it has a number of challenges due to its complexity. The information is generated fast and in bulk and the formats of data can be unstructured text and images to semi-structured and fully structured numerical data. To match the modalities, both in terms of time, space, and meaning, the synchronization and integration of these different formats require sophisticated preprocessing, synchronization, and feature extraction methods. Typical components of an effective multimodal data pipeline are data acquisition, cleaning, fusion, and advanced analytics based on machine learning and deep learning models with cross-modal understanding. The large data models, such as Hadoop and Spark, are used to provide distributed processing and scalable storage. The applications can be real-time surveillance, smart cities, autonomous cars, healthcare diagnostics, and personalized recommendations. The complementary data of multiple sources can be integrated to reveal relationships and patterns that may not be identified by single-modality methods using multimodal analytics. The data governance, privacy, and quality are also important in order to maintain dependability and trust. It is all said and done that multimodal data provides a powerful foundation of perceptive, data-driven innovations across a wide range of disciplines [2].

5.1.2 Role of big data in multimodal analytics

The use of big data technologies is necessary to ensure the successful analytics of multimodal data that is characterized by its high volume, rapid creation, and numerous formats. Text, image, audio, video, and sensor streams are too large and varied to be managed using the traditional methods of data management. The big data frameworks, such as Hadoop, Spark, and distributed NoSQL databases, make high-performance computing and scalable storage possible as they allow real-time processing and integration of these various sources. They also ensure the seamless integration and coordination of multimodal inputs through fault tolerance, parallel processing, and scalable data management. Big data ecosystems have the advantage of being computationally powerful and providing feature extraction and pattern recognition across modalities for advanced analytics, including machine learning and deep learning. These capabilities can be used in such applications as healthcare, autonomous systems, and smart cities to find the relationships that were not observed before, enhance predictive accuracy, and deliver actionable insights. Efficient multimodal analytics and decision-making are thus based on big data [3–5].

5.1.3 Motivation and scope of the chapter

The analysis and management have become a critical necessity because of the growing volume of heterogeneous information from different sources such as text, photos, audio, video, and sensors. The amount, variety, and speed of such data are often too large to be processed using conventional methods. This chapter is driven by the challenge of using big data technologies to combine and extract meaningful insights from complex multimodal information. It includes scalable storage, real-time processing, data fusion, and advanced analytics through deep learning and machine learning. The chapter is applicable and useful as evidenced by the applications in autonomous systems, smart cities, healthcare, and personalized services.

5.2 Foundations of multimodal data

Multimodal data is a type of data that represents complementary information about real-world phenomena by integrating information found in multiple sources, such as text, images, audio, video, sensors, etc. Its base of effective data integration, synchronization, and representation enables its meaningful analysis. Proper preprocessing, feature extraction, and modality alignment are required in the interpretation and provision of useful insights.

5.2.1 Definition and types

The multimodal data refers to the data sets that describe the complementary perspectives on real-world phenomena through the integration of information from multiple sources. Contrary to single-modality data, multimodal datasets combine different types of inputs, which can be more effectively analyzed and can be presented in a richer form. Each of the modalities is unique in its characteristics and applications. Text data provides semantic and context information and consists of both structured and unstructured data in the form of documents, reports, and posts to social media. The tasks, such as visual interpretation, classification, and recognition, can be assisted with the help of images where visual content, textures, and spatial patterns are captured. Video data is needed to combine image sequences with temporal dynamics, which makes analysis of motion, events, and behavioral patterns possible. Audio data has temporal signals that are often exploited to detect emotions, analyze the environment, and recognize speech. Sensor data on wearables, Internet of Things (IoT) devices, and environmental monitors can be used to provide real-time numerical or categorical measurements needed to monitor and control applications. The additional modalities include social media feeds, geospatial information, and physiological information such as ECG/EEG recordings. The process of heterogeneity that requires preprocessing, feature extraction, and alignment is needed to ensure meaningful integration when making use of multimodal data. The combination of these different types in such areas as healthcare, autonomous systems, smart cities, and personalized services will enable deeper insights and higher prediction accuracy and decision-making. The concept of multimodal data definition and types is the prerequisite for big data methods and advanced analytics.

5.2.2 Characteristics and challenges

Multimodal data is heterogeneous, high-volume, and high-velocity data that can be obtained by text, images, audio, video, and sensors. Each modality has unique formats, structures, and semantics and offers additional data enhancing the overall understanding. The multicultural representation, temporal and spatial relations, and complex intermodal connections are useful features that contribute to further understanding and increase the complexity of analysis. These traits pose grave challenges. The modalities are difficult to integrate and align due to the different scales, resolutions, and formats. Preprocessing and data cleaning are challenging process that deal with inconsistent, noisy, or missing data. The feature extraction and fusion require sophisticated techniques that will not only be able to retain information but will also capture meaningful correlations. Moreover, the multimodal datasets are enormous, and therefore, they need scalable processing and storage structures. The requirement to guarantee data governance, data privacy, and quality makes the analysis more challenging. These issues should be addressed to make full use of multimodal data in order to accurately predict, recognize patterns, and make informed decisions in such fields as healthcare, smart cities, and autonomous systems. Table 5.1 presents several features and issues of multimodal data.

5.2.3 Sources and acquisition of multimodal data

The diversity of real-world phenomena is mirrored in the multimodal data, which is generated with a great variety of sources. Textual data can be used as a source of semantic and contextual data and may be located in documents, reports, emails, blogs, social media posts, and online forums. Some of the sources of images that

Table 5.1 Summarization of characteristics and challenges of multimodal data

Characteristics	Challenges
Heterogeneous data from multiple modalities (text, image, audio, video, sensors)	Integration and alignment across different modalities
High volume and high velocity	Scalable storage and real-time processing requirements
Diverse data formats and structures	Preprocessing and cleaning of noisy, missing, or inconsistent data
Temporal and spatial dependencies	Capturing intermodal relationships without information loss
Complex intermodal correlations	Feature extraction and effective data fusion
Complementary information across modalities	Ensuring data quality, privacy, and governance
Rich representations enabling deeper insights	Computational and analytical complexity for large datasets

capture visual content and spatial patterns include cameras, satellites, medical imaging equipment, and internet repositories. Video data or a combination of visual and temporal information is collected using wearable devices, traffic monitoring, entertainment media, and surveillance devices. Audio data created by speech recordings, ambient noise, sensors, and multimedia applications is what makes speech recognition, emotion recognition, and sound analysis possible. Industrial monitors, wearable devices, environmental stations, and Internet of Things devices are the sources of sensor data, which is available in the form of real-time numeric or categorical measurements. Others also cover social media feeds, which use text, photos, and interactions; physiological data like ECG, EEG, or EMG; and geospatial data of GPS and GIS systems. Acquisition of multimodal data has challenges related to keeping track of the synchronization between modalities, handling large quantities of data, and ensuring the quality of data. Techniques to store data in a structured format, in a real-time stream, and to collect data automatically are necessary. Big data platforms and distributed frameworks enable the efficient use of multimodal datasets for analytics, pattern recognition, and actionable insights across applications, including healthcare, smart cities, and autonomous systems, since it is easier to acquire, combine, and run preprocessing data in a scalable fashion. Various data modalities, their sources, and key characteristics are summarized in Table 5.2.

Table 5.2 Data modalities, sources, and key characteristics

Modality	Sources	Type of information	Key applications	Acquisition challenges
Text	Documents, reports, emails, blogs, social media, forums	Semantic and contextual information	NLP, sentiment analysis, information retrieval	Unstructured format, noise, language ambiguity
Image	Cameras, satellites, medical imaging, internet repositories	Visual content and spatial patterns	Medical diagnosis, object detection, remote sensing	Image quality, storage size, annotation effort
Video	Wearables, traffic systems, entertainment media, surveillance	Visual and temporal information	Activity recognition, surveillance, behavior analysis	Large data volume, synchronization, processing complexity
Audio	Speech recordings, ambient sound sensors, multimedia	Speech and acoustic patterns	Speech recognition, emotion detection, sound classification	Noise interference, sampling quality
Sensor data	IoT devices, industrial monitors, environmental stations, wearables	Real-time numeric and categorical measurements	Smart cities, industrial monitoring, healthcare	Real-time processing, calibration, missing data
Physiological data	ECG, EEG, EMG devices	Biological and health signals	Healthcare monitoring, diagnosis, brain-computer interfaces	Signal noise, synchronization, privacy concerns

(Continues)

Table 5.2 (Continued)

Modality	Sources	Type of information	Key applications	Acquisition challenges
Geospatial data	GPS, GIS systems	Location and spatial information	Navigation, urban planning, tracking systems	Accuracy, integration with other modalities
Social media data	Social platforms (text, images, interactions)	Combined multimodal user-generated content	Trend analysis, recommendation systems	Data heterogeneity, privacy, reliability
Acquisition infrastructure	Big data platforms, distributed systems, automated pipelines	Data storage, integration, preprocessing	Scalable analytics, AI model training	Synchronization, scalability, data quality management

5.3 Big data technologies and architectures

Big data technologies make scalable storage, processing, and analysis of multiple multimodal data, such as text, images, video, and sensor streams, possible. The architecture of distributed computing, such as Hadoop, Spark, and Flink, and the flexibility of storage are provided by the NoSQL databases, data lakes, and cloud platforms. Among the stream-processing frameworks; Extract, Transform, Load (ETL) pipelines; and microservices, the high availability, fault tolerance, and real-time insights are the foundation of effective analysis and management in multi-modal big data settings [6].

5.3.1 Hadoop ecosystem and MapReduce

The open-source Hadoop ecosystem aims at massive processing and distributed storage of data. Basically, Hadoop Distributed File System (HDFS) is a storage system that is scaled and fault-tolerant through the provision of large datasets on a cluster of commodity computing hardware. Critical components of the ecosystem are Sqoop/Flume to ingest data, Hive and Pig to query it at a high level, HBase to store data in NoSQL format, and YARN to manage resources. The fundamental processing model of Hadoop is MapReduce, which divides the work into two parts: Map sorts data into pairs with keys and values, and Reduce combines the output to form the final output. This parallel processing approach enables batch analytics to be done on petabytes of data, which is quite efficient in handling structured and unstructured data. Hadoop and MapReduce are associated with helping businesses undertake high-performance, affordable analytics and thus are fundamental to big data applications such as recommendation systems, log analysis, and comprehensive machine learning procedures in multimodal data management [7].

5.3.2 Spark, Flink, and streaming frameworks

The most used big data engines are Apache Spark and Apache Flink, which are designed to support real-time analytics and fast and distributed computations. The in-memory processing of Apache Spark is much faster than traditional MapReduce in terms of batch and streaming processing. Some of its key components include MLlib, which is scalable machine learning; GraphX, which is graph analytics; Spark SQL, which is structured data queries; and Structured Streaming, which is near real-time data pipelines. Spark can be used in multimodal data processing of text, image, and sensor streams; ETL processing; and iterative algorithms due to its robustness, integration with Hadoop, and compatibility with Python, Scala, and Java. Apache Flink is an expert in low latency, high-throughput stream processing with support for both event-time and processing-time semantics. Unlike Spark, Flink does real-time streaming with exactly-once state consistency and advanced windowing, which is micro-batched. It excels in continuous data streams where fast insights are needed such as IoT telemetry, financial transactions, and social media analytics. More elaborate streaming systems, including Apache Kafka, Apache Storm, and Pulsar, as well as Spark and Flink, are needed to provide scalable ingestion and message queuing. Storm is a framework that supports distributed, real-time computing with minimal overhead, whereas Kafka is a fault-tolerant publish-subscribe model of event streaming. These frameworks are often used together with Spark or Flink when it comes to the development of end-to-end streaming architecture. In its present form, the basis of modern big data analytics consists of Spark, Flink, and similar frameworks. Their capacity to process numerous multimodal inputs, such as video feeds, sensor signals, and logs, makes real-time decision-making, anomaly detection, and predictive modeling possible. They are essential in managing and analyzing high-velocity and dynamic data, both in cloud and on-premise environments, due to their flexibility, scalability, and ecosystems [8–10].

5.3.3 NoSQL databases for multimodal storage

The ability of NoSQL databases to store heterogeneous multimodal data such as text, photos, videos, and sensor streams is due to the flexibility and the absence of any schema. They are also horizontally scaled and dispersed across clusters, unlike traditional relational systems, to provide high availability and performance as well as dynamic data models. Key types include document stores (such as Couchbase or MongoDB) of semi-structured data in JSON or BSON, key–value stores (such as Redis or Amazon DynamoDB) of quick lookups, wide-column stores (such as Apache Cassandra or HBase) of time-series and large-scale analytics, and relationship-driven queries (such as a graph database like Neo4j or JanusGraph). Image and video repositories, social media analytics, and IoT sensor management are some of the applications that are perfectly suited to these databases since they can process unstructured and real-time data. Scalability and fault tolerance are achieved through such features as sharding, replication, and eventual consistency. The ability of NoSQL to adapt enables easy integration with big data systems in multimodal settings, which ensures that data in the form of various formats can be stored, accessed, and analyzed without strict adherence to a schema [11].

5.4 Preprocessing and fusion techniques

Preprocessing of multimodal data, such as text, images, video, and sensor signals, is done to remove noise, handle missing values, normalize formats, and extract significant features. PCA (t-SNE) and data augmentation enhance quality. Fusion techniques can be used to make richer correlations and enable more accurate, complex big data analytics and decision-making by combining heterogeneous sources into a single data set. Early fusion integrates raw features, late fusion integrates individual model outputs, and hybrid fusion integrates both [12].

5.4.1 Data cleaning and transformation

In the multimodal datasets, comprising text, images, video, and sensor signals, data processing and purification are critical steps to make the analytics of multimodal data reliable. Data cleaning helps to enhance quality by removing errors such as duplicates, outliers, inconsistent formats, and missing values. Some of the methods include imputation of missing data, noise removal of sensor values, text spelling correction, and image or video metadata normalization. The use of anomaly detection and validation rules will help to guarantee the accuracy and consistency of different sources. Diverse data is converted into standardized forms, which can be processed and combined. It consists of encoding categorical attributes, normalization or scaling numerical values, and feature extraction, such as text embedding or converting images to pixel matrices or feature vectors. In the case of time-series or streaming data, events get synchronized across modalities with the aid of temporal alignment. Advanced workflows often automate these processes at scale using ETL (Extract, Transform, Load) pipelines and big data technologies such as Apache Spark and Hadoop. Dimensionality reduction (PCA, autoencoders) can further be used to transform high-dimensional datasets in order to be handled. Together with cleaning, transformation ensures that structured, consistent, and analytically ready datasets are produced to ensure that big data analytics and downstream machine learning models can provide consistent and reliable insights based on complex multimodal settings [13].

5.4.2 Feature extraction from heterogeneous modalities

Raw multimodal inputs can be text, images, audio, video, and sensor streams, to name but a few, but they all include extracting and transforming inputs into useful numerical forms to be analyzed. Each modality requires specific methods: Tokenization, TF-IDF, and word embeddings (Word2Vec, BERT) are used in text; convolutional neural networks (CNNs), edge detection, or optical flow are used in images and video; spectrograms, MFCCs, and pitch analysis are used in audio; statistical descriptors, frequency-domain transforms, and temporal pattern mining are used in sensor data. Cross-modal methods such as autoencoders, contrastive learning, and multimodal transformers facilitate correlation between different types of data and are trained to know shared latent spaces. The features are then optimized in order to use them in further machine learning activities, i.e., feature selection and dimensionality reduction (PCA, t-SNE). The aim is to take noise-robust, discriminative representations that minimize complexity without any semantic relationships. Efficient feature extraction allows creating a crucial connection between raw non-homogeneous data and accurate big data analytics or multimodal decision-making, thereby enhancing classification, clustering, and predictive modeling [14].

5.4.3 Data alignment, synchronization, and fusion strategies

Heterogeneous multimodal inputs include text logs, sensor streams, images, and video that need to be temporally as well as semantically matched to be meaningfully analyzed. This is guaranteed through data alignment and synchronization. Alignment of data in different sources to a shared reference is done (e.g., timestamps, spatial coordinates, or contextual events). To maintain uniform sequences in modalities, signals are synchronized to remove time drifts and adjust variable sampling rates; synchronization resamples signals. Fusion strategies are used to combine these complementary datasets in order to exploit the complementary information. Before modeling, early fusion transforms intermodal correlations by fusing low-level features or raw features into one. Late fusion is flexible when the data is received asynchronously and it is necessary to combine predictions or decisions of other models. The fusion of features at multiple levels brings about a compromise between strength and fineness in hybrid or intermediate fusion. Graph-based fusion, multimodal transformers, and attention mechanisms are some of the methods that enhance cross-modal reasoning and feature interaction. Alignment, synchronization, and fusion combine in a complex big data environment to generate coherent, analytically ready datasets that enable accurate pattern recognition and real-time decision-making.

5.5 Multimodal data analytics using big data tools

Big data tools such as Apache Spark, Flink, and Hadoop are capable of allowing scalable analytics on text, image, video, and sensor data. The combination of multimodal datasets with NoSQL databases, Kafka streams, and machine learning libraries is what makes it possible to make accurate predictions and make decisions based on the obtained data. They also enable distributed processing and real-time insights as well as advanced modeling [15,16].

5.5.1 Descriptive and exploratory analytics

To provide the answer to the question of what happened, descriptive analytics applies statistics aggregation, dashboards, and time-series analysis to reduce the historical multimodal data, such as text, photos, and sensor logs, to the pertinent measures, trends, and visualizations. Exploratory analytics will identify the concealed patterns, relationships, and anomalies without predefined hypotheses. The use of techniques such as clustering, correlation analysis, dimensionality reduction, and interactive visualization in big data environments supports the formulation of hypotheses and is used to guide more detailed prediction or prescriptive modeling.

5.5.2 Predictive modeling and machine learning approaches

Predictive modeling is the extrapolation of future actions or behavior using multimodal and past data. Machine learning (ML) techniques (supervised, unsupervised, and reinforcement learning) are used to extract patterns in text, images, video, and sensor streams. Although the unsupervised methods, such as clustering and anomaly detection, reveal underlying structures, the supervised approaches, such as regression, decision trees, and neural networks, predict. Sequential decision-making is maximized in reinforcement learning in dynamic environments. In the case of heterogeneous data, feature engineering, dimensionality reduction, and cross-modal embeddings enhance the accuracy of the model. Powerful representation learning is enabled by advanced deep learning models, including CNNs, RNNs, and transformers. It can be brought to big data training and deployment, with big data tools including PyTorch, TensorFlow, and Spark MLlib. Predictive modeling and machine learning can be applied collaboratively in complex multimodal and high-velocity data landscapes to make data-driven, real-time forecasts and intelligent decisions.

5.5.3 Deep learning for cross-modal representations

Deep learning facilitates the effective practice of shared representations of heterogeneous modalities, such as text, images, video, and audio, and encourages integrated decision-making and analysis. To learn semantic correlations, transformer-based architectures, contrastive learning, multimodal autoencoders, and others map data of different types into a shared latent space. Intermodal dependencies are represented by attention mechanisms; sequential text and audio are processed by recurrent neural networks (RNNs) or transformers; and spatial features of images and video are extracted by convolutional neural networks (CNNs). Some of the tasks that cross-modal embeddings can be used in include multimodal recommendation systems, audiovisual speech recognition, video summarization, and image captioning. Deep learning addresses the heterogeneity problem and feature fusion as well as enhances classification, retrieval, and predictive modeling accuracy by learning shared representations. These techniques are necessary for multimodal big data analytics and enable strong interpretation, retrieval, and reasoning of a range of data sources [17–21].

A broader view of multimodal data analytics using big data tools is shown in Figure 5.1.

5.6 Scalability and real-time processing

Multimodal big data needs architectures that can scale efficiently with volume, velocity, and variability. Distributed systems such as Apache Spark, Flink, and Kafka enable parallel ingestion and streaming analytics, whereas the dynamic workload

Multimodal data analytics

Characteristic	Descriptive & exploratory analytics	Predictive modeling & machine learning	Deep learning for cross-modal representations
Goal	Understand past events, identify patterns	Extrapolate future actions, predict behavior	Create shared representations, integrated analysis
Techniques	Statistics aggregation, dashboards, time-series analysis, clustering, correlation analysis, dimensionality reduction, interactive visualization	Supervised, unsupervised, reinforcement learning, feature engineering, dimensionality reduction, cross-modal embeddings, deep learning models (CNNs, RNNs, transformers)	Transformer-based architectures, contrastive learning, multimodal autoencoders, attention mechanisms, RNNs, CNNs
Applications	Reduce historical data, formulate hypotheses	Real-time forecasts, intelligent decisions	Multimodal recommendation systems, audio-visual speech recognition, video summarization, image captioning

Figure 5.1 Multimodal data analytics - big data perspective

surges are facilitated by scalable cloud resources. In-memory computation, low-latency messaging, and rapid storage are combined in real-time pipelines to support decision-making and sustained data fusion across multiple modalities in real-time, without any loss of accuracy or performance when data complexity increases.

5.6.1 Handling high-volume and high-velocity data

Sensors, social media, IoT devices, and transactional systems often contribute to the receipt of massive, rapidly changing streams of multimodal big data. Distributed storage systems such as cloud object storage, Hadoop Distributed File System (HDFS), and NoSQL databases are required to manage this scale and be able to scale to petabyte levels. Continuous streams with low latency are buffered and directed through message brokers, like Apache Kafka or RabbitMQ, which support high-velocity ingestion. Real-time analytics, filtering, and enrichment of stored data can occur before storing it in persistent storage by using real-time processing engines such as Apache Spark streaming, Flink, and Storm. On the one hand, constrained resource utilization is ensured by such strategies as event-driven architectures, windowed computations, and micro-batching to ensure timely insights. Adaptive load balancing, data compression, and partitioning are further features that enhance throughput and fault tolerance. A combination of these tactics allows businesses to consistently gather, process, and model various high-speed data, making real-time decisions and predictive modeling a possibility without any loss of accuracy or system stability, even during unpredictable spikes.

5.6.2 Real-time analytics architectures

Real-time analytics require an end-to-end pipeline that is efficient in terms of ingesting, processing, and visualizing streaming data. Traditional designs use stream-processing engines (Apache Flink, Spark streaming, Storm) to compute low-latency data ingestion layers (Apache Kafka, Pulsar, or MQTT) to capture high-throughput events, and fast data stores (Redis, Cassandra, Elasticsearch) to query and retrieve data. A lambda or kappa design often integrates batch and streaming paths to achieve fault tolerance and exactly-once semantics. In-memory computing and micro-batching enable continuous aggregation, anomaly detection, and predictive modeling of multimodal streams. Scalable cloud deployments comprising autoscaling and container orchestration (Kubernetes) maintain performance even on traffic spikes, delivering real-time actionable insights to applications such as real-time recommendation systems, financial trading, and IoT monitoring.

5.6.3 Edge and fog computing for multimodal big data

Edge and fog computing in multimodal big data environments can minimize latency and network congestion through the expansion of processing to data sources. Edge nodes, sensors, gateways, or embedded devices perform preparatory operations such as light analytics, feature extraction, and filtering before sending important data. Fog layers (which consist of micro-data centers or intermediate servers) provide additional computation, caching, and aggregation in order to offload cloud loads. This hierarchical nature of data protection ensures privacy by retaining sensitive data locally and real-time decision-making in cases of poor connectivity. Frameworks like EdgeX Foundry and OpenFog enable scalable deployment, orchestration of containers, and inference of AI models at the edge. By distributing computation at edge, fog, and cloud layers, organizations can realize strong management of diverse and high-throughput multimodal streams of data, reduce bandwidth expenditure, and accelerate response times.

5.7 Applications and case studies

Multimodal big data analytics supports diverse and practical solutions (shown in Figure 5.2). Combined sensor, video, and social information can be used to optimize energy consumption and control adaptive traffic in intelligent cities. Wearable, genomic, and imaging data are used together in applications in healthcare to facilitate early diagnosis and individualized care. Industrial IoT combines vibration, thermal, and operational logs to predict equipment failures and improve

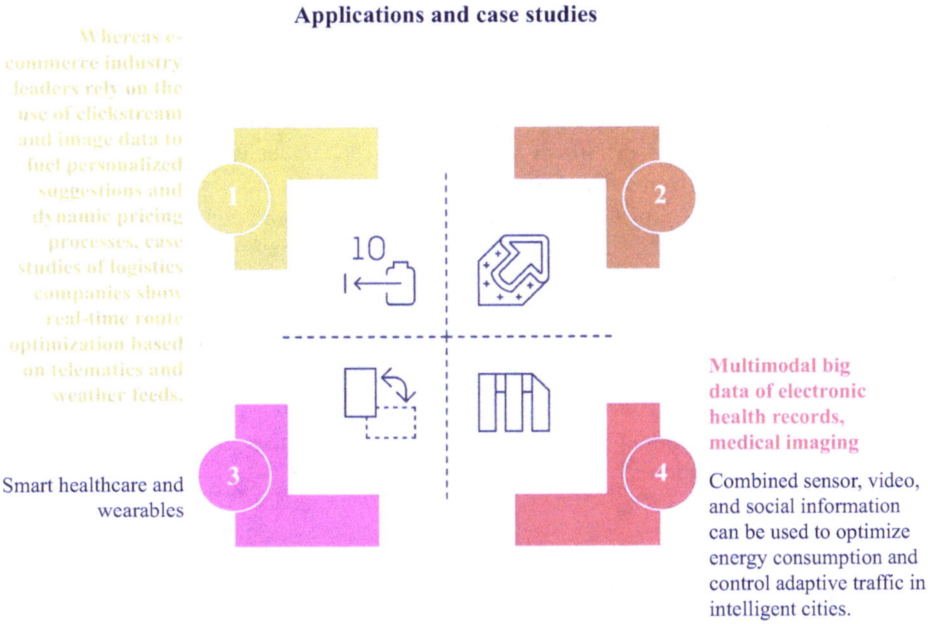

Figure 5.2 Applications and case studies of multimodal big data analytics

maintenance strategies. Finance applies sentiment analysis and multimodal transaction streams to detect fraud and direct algorithmic trading. Whereas e-commerce industry leaders rely on the use of clickstream and image data to fuel personalized suggestions and dynamic pricing processes, case studies of logistics companies show real-time route optimization based on telematics and weather feeds.

5.7.1 Smart healthcare and wearables

Multimodal big data of electronic health records, medical imaging, and wearable technology enables personalized and continuous healthcare. Wearable technology, including fitness trackers, smartwatches, biosensors, and others, can monitor heart rate, blood pressure, oxygen saturation, sleep patterns, and activity levels in real time. Cloud and edge analytics are used to integrate these streams with clinical data and predict hypoglycemic events, arrhythmias, and chronic conditions. Smart healthcare systems integrate imaging, genomic, and lifestyle data with machine learning in order to provide accurate diagnoses and a personalized treatment plan. Remote patient monitoring platforms alert physicians to abnormalities, reduce hospitalization, and improve outcomes. These applications/case studies illustrate how safe and privacy-sensitive pipelines ensure timely insights, can support pandemic surveillance, tracking the progress of rehabilitation, and early sepsis detection without risking the privacy of patient information [22].

5.7.2 Multimedia content analysis and recommendation

Multimodal big data methods allow intelligent text, audio, image, and video stream analysis and recommendations. With the help of advanced feature extraction and deep learning methods such as convolutional networks and transformer networks, automatic tagging, object detection, sentiment analysis, and scene understanding are all feasible. Examples of the platforms that utilize user interaction logs, contextual metadata, and visual and audio cues to provide users with personalized recommendations in real-time include YouTube, Netflix, and Spotify. Cross-modal retrieval links the similarities between various forms. As an example, it can synchronize video highlights with music or captions that accompany them. Adaptive recommendation engines are based on the principles of reinforcement learning and collaborative filtering, which are used to improve suggestions as tastes of users evolve. Scalable architectures ensure that large volumes of various forms of media can be handled in a short time, which enhances the engagement, advertisement performance, and the general user experience within the entertainment, education, and social media ecosystems [23].

5.7.3 Autonomous systems and IoT

Multimodal big data is used to assist autonomous systems and the Internet of Things (IoT) in combining multiple forms of sensory information (LiDAR, radar, cameras, GPS, and environmental sensors) to provide real-time perception, decision-making, and control. Data fusion will allow self-driving vehicles to identify roadblocks, remain on course, and divert when the environment changes. Industrial IoT makes use of vibration, temperature, and operating variables to ensure things are running fine and that they will require repair at some point. Smart infrastructure makes use of sensor networks to monitor traffic, energy consumption, and building conditions. Edge and fog computing ensure that analytics occur promptly, and the machine learning algorithms identify peculiar behavior patterns and self-learn. The examples of cases in robots, smart manufacturing, and connected transportation demonstrate how the use of multimodal data can turn systems into smarter, more autonomous, and more aware of the surrounding environment in a large variety of areas [24].

5.7.4 Surveillance and security systems

Multimodal big data enhances modern security and surveillance by integrating video feeds, audio signals, sensor readings, and social media streams to have a comprehensive understanding of the situation. Intelligent video analytics based on deep learning make it possible to detect objects in real-time, recognize faces, monitor crowds, and detect behavior anomalies. Sensor networks are used to detect motion, intrusion, or environmental threats; audio processing is used to identify strange sounds, such as gunshots or glass breaking. Heterogeneous data fusion improves emergency response coordination, access control, and prediction of threats. Edge and fog computing help to receive timely notices and make decisions by reducing latency. Case studies of markets Multimodal analytics is essential in security systems, which are demonstrated by the smart cities, airports, and critical infrastructure case studies, faster response times, proactive mitigation of threats, and improved citizen safety [25].

5.8 Future trends and research directions

Multimodal big models, edge–cloud collaboration, and privacy-preserving analytics will all be advanced by future research. Real-time multimodal interaction made possible by 5G/6G, energy-efficient computing for sustainable processing, and graph and causal learning for interpretable insights are important directions. Reliable, scalable big data applications will continue to depend on explainable AI and ethical governance.

- **Multimodal large models and foundation models**
  Uniform multimodal understanding will be made possible by next-generation foundation models that have been trained on text, image, video, and sensor streams. Efficient fine-tuning, domain adaptation, and privacy-preserving training for sector-specific tasks will be the main areas of research.
- **Collaborative intelligence between edge and cloud**
  Hybrid systems that integrate cloud, fog, and edge computing will lower latency without sacrificing scalability. Future research will focus on adaptive resource allocation, dynamic workload balancing, and lightweight inference models for real-time multimodal analytics.
- **Responsible AI, security, and privacy**
  Strong privacy features – federated learning, differential privacy, and secure multiparty computation – will continue to be essential when handling sensitive data from wearables, healthcare, and surveillance. Explainable decision pipelines and ethical data governance will be the focus of the research.
- **Causal and graph learning**
  In order to improve predictive accuracy and enable interpretable reasoning, relationships between modalities will be found using graph neural networks and causal inference.
- **Sustainable and energy-efficient computing**
  In order to manage ever-increasing multimodal datasets sustainably, green AI initiatives will propel the development of energy-aware algorithms, hardware accelerators, and data compression techniques.
- **Multimodal interaction in real time**

5G/6G and streaming framework developments will enable interactive, real-time analytics for applications like smart cities, immersive AR/VR, and autonomous systems.

5.9 Conclusion

The application of big data methods in the analysis and processing of multimodal data is a revolutionary paradigm to gain useful insights on a wide range of information sources. This chapter showed that heterogeneous modalities, such as text, images, audio, video, and sensor streams, can significantly enhance the process of decision-making in various areas of human endeavor, such as healthcare, smart cities, autonomous systems, and multimedia analytics. The convergence of distributed storage, scalable big data platforms, and advanced analytics allows handling such high-volume, high-velocity, and high-variety data with ease. Preprocessing, feature extraction, fusion tactics, and machine learning techniques were all highlighted as viable steps toward ensuring that the data is of good quality and that the representations are insightful. Another point made in the chapter was that effective multimodal analytics require robust architectures that are integrated with edge/fog computing, real-time streaming frameworks, and AI-driven models capable of adapting to varying conditions. Although the potential of greater automation, personalization and prediction is tremendous, numerous hurdles have yet to be surmounted, among them being standardization, synchronization, data privacy, and computational complexity. The interdisciplinary collaboration and the integration of the latest technologies, such as cross-modal representation learning and deep learning, will help to overcome these challenges. Multimodal analysis based on big data can provide more comprehensive, context-sensitive, and scalable solutions to the complexity of modern data ecosystems and has vast potential in creating future intelligent systems.

References

[1] K. Bayoudh, R. Knani, F. Hamdaoui, and A. Mtibaa, "A survey on deep multimodal learning for computer vision: advances, trends, applications, and datasets," *The Visual Computer*, vol. 38, no. 8, pp. 2939–2970, 2022.

[2] C. Zhang, Z. Yang, X. He, and L. Deng, "Multimodal intelligence: representation learning, information fusion, and applications," *IEEE Journal of Selected Topics in Signal Processing*, vol. 14, no. 3, pp. 478–493, 2020.

[3] F. Li and J. Xu, "Revolutionizing AI-enabled information systems using integrated big data analytics and multi-modal data fusion," *IEEE Access*, vol. 13, pp. 212316–212340, 2025.

[4] V. Bellandi, P. Ceravolo, S. Maghool, and S. Siccardi, "Toward a general framework for multimodal big data analysis," *Big Data*, vol. 10, no. 5, pp. 408–424, 2022.

[5] Y. Ning, "A study of interactive decision-making techniques in multimodal big data visual analytics," *International Journal of Educational Teaching and Research*, vol. 2, no. 12, 2025.

[6] P. Pääkkönen and D. Pakkala, "Reference architecture and classification of technologies, products and services for big data systems," *Big Data Research*, vol. 2, no. 4, pp. 166–186, 2015.

[7] Y. Demchenko, J. J. Cuadrado-Gallego, O. Chertov, and M. Aleksandrova, "Big data algorithms, MapReduce and Hadoop ecosystem," in *Big Data Infrastructure Technologies for Data Analytics: Scaling Data Science Applications for Continuous Growth*. Springer, 2024, pp. 145–198.

[8] S. Saxena and S. Gupta, *Practical Real-Time Data Processing and Analytics: Distributed Computing and Event Processing Using Apache Spark, Flink, Storm, and Kafka*. Packt Publishing Ltd, 2017.

[9] S. Kumar, S. Rani, S. Sharma, and H. Min, "Multimodality fusion aspects of medical diagnosis: a comprehensive review," *Bioengineering*, vol. 11, no. 12, p. 1233, 2024.

[10] S. Rani, P. Bhambri, and M. Chauhan, "A machine learning model for kids' behavior analysis from facial emotions using principal component analysis," in *2021 5th Asian Conference on Artificial Intelligence Technology (ACAIT)*. IEEE, 2021, pp. 522–525.

[11] C. Jiang, S. Liu, and P. Ma, "Innovative architecture and key technology of database for multiple scenarios," in *2024 International Conference on Ubiquitous Computing and Communications (IUCC)*. IEEE, 2024, pp. 286–291.

[12] I. Nazir, I. U. Haq, M. M. Khan, M. B. Qureshi, H. Ullah, and S. Butt, "Efficient pre-processing and segmentation for lung cancer detection using fused CT images," *Electronics*, vol. 11, no. 1, p. 34, 2021.

[13] P. Vassiliadis, Z. Vagena, S. Skiadopoulos, N. Karayannidis, and T. Sellis, "ARKTOS: a tool for data cleaning and transformation in data warehouse environments," *IEEE Data Engineering Bulletin*, vol. 23, no. 4, pp. 42–47, 2000.

[14] S. Iqbal, A. N. Qureshi, M. Alhussein, I. A. Choudhry, K. Aurangzeb, and T. M. Khan, "Fusion of textural and visual information for medical image modality retrieval using deep learning-based feature engineering," *IEEE Access*, vol. 11, pp. 93238–93253, 2023.

[15] K. L. O'Halloran, G. Pal, and M. Jin, "Multimodal approach to analysing big social and news media data," *Discourse, Context & Media*, vol. 40, p. 100467, 2021.

[16] C. Lemonde, E. Arsenio, and R. Henriques, "Integrative analysis of multimodal traffic data: addressing open challenges using big data analytics in the city of Lisbon," *European Transport Research Review*, vol. 13, no. 1, p. 64, 2021.

[17] L. Zhen, P. Hu, X. Wang, and D. Peng, "Deep supervised cross-modal retrieval," in *Proceedings of the IEEE/CVF Conference on Computer Vision and Pattern Recognition*, 2019, pp. 10394–10403.

[18] V. Puri, A. Kataria, S. Rani, and P. K. Pareek, "DLT based smart medical ecosystem," in *2023 International Conference on Network, Multimedia and Information Technology (NMITCON)*. IEEE, 2023, pp. 1–6.

[19] S. Rani, A. Kataria, P. Bhambri, P. K. Pareek, and V. Puri, "Artificial intelligence in personalized health services for better patient care," in *Revolutionizing Healthcare: AI Integration with IoT for Enhanced Patient Outcomes*. Springer, 2024, pp. 89–108.

[20] S. Rani, A. Kataria, S. Kumar, and V. Karar, "A new generation cyber-physical system: a comprehensive review from security perspective," *Computers & Security*, vol. 148, p. 104095, 2025.

[21] D. Mittal, H. Singh, and S. Rani, "Exploring explainable artificial intelligence techniques for hate speech detection," in *International Conference on Innovative Computing and Communication*. Springer, 2024, pp. 545–554.

[22] D. De, P. Bharti, S. K. Das, and S. Chellappan, "Multimodal wearable sensing for fine-grained activity recognition in healthcare," *IEEE Internet Computing*, vol. 19, no. 5, pp. 26–35, 2015.

[23] R. Di Massa, M. Montagnuolo, and A. Messina, "Implicit news recommendation based on user interest models and multimodal content analysis," in *Proceedings of the 3rd International Workshop on Automated Information Extraction in Media Production*, 2010, pp. 33–38.

[24] C. Anagnostopoulos, A. Gkillas, C. Mavrokefalidis, E.-V. Pikoulis, N. Piperigkos, and A. S. Lalos, "Multimodal federated learning in AIoT systems: existing solutions, applications, and challenges," *IEEE Access*, vol. 12, pp. 180864–180902, 2024.

[25] J.-h. Jeong, H.-h. Jung, Y.-h. Choi, S.-h. Park, and M.-s. Kim, "Intelligent complementary multi-modal fusion for anomaly surveillance and security system," *Sensors*, vol. 23, no. 22, p. 9214, 2023.

Chapter 6

Security issues and mechanisms in multimodal data

Abstract

There are several types of multimodal data such as text, image, audio, video, and sensor streams. It is evolving at a very high rate, which has resulted in not only complicated security issues but also enormous potential opportunities in advanced analytics and intelligent applications. The significant security issues in multimodal data management are analyzed in this chapter, such as data integrity, data confidentiality, authentication, access control, and privacy protection. Multimodal data is vulnerable to attacks such as adversarial attacks, data breaches, unauthorized access, and cross-modal inference, and due to its dispersed and heterogeneous nature, such attacks can compromise sensitive information. The chapter examines diverse security controls to address these challenges, such as safe multimodal fusion, blockchain architecture, cryptography, federated learning, differential privacy, and robust authentication processes. It is concentrated on scalable and real-time protection methods that are effective in edge-cloud designs and big data environments. This combination of approaches will enable businesses to ensure dependable multimodal data analytics that will safeguard user privacy and system reliability and allow making safe and efficient decisions in any field of application.

Keywords: authentication; blockchain; data privacy; multimodal security; secure data fusion

6.1 Introduction

The multimodal data, encompassing text, images, video, audio, and sensor streams, in industries such as healthcare, finance, surveillance, and smart cities, has changed analytics and decision-making due to the exponential growth. Nevertheless, the incorporation of different modalities has some grave security threats, including adversarial attacks, data breaches, unlawful access, and privacy violations. Traditional security methods do not always provide sufficient protection to heterogeneous and high-dimensional data. To achieve the availability, confidentiality, and integrity of data and support secure and reliable cross-modal information exchange, the chapter explores the essential security issues in multimodal data environments and presents the state-of-the-art solutions such as access control models, blockchain, federated learning, and encryption [1].

6.1.1 Overview of multimodal data

The combination of information obtained and input through different sources or modalities, such as text, images, audio, video, and sensor signals, is known as multimodal data. It gives more comprehensive information on complex phenomena and contains more contextual relationships compared to single-modality data. They can be examples of social media analytics, which combine text, images, and geolocation; autonomous cars, which combine cameras, LiDAR, and radar; and medical diagnostics, which combine imaging and clinical notes. The challenges of multimodal data management include heterogeneous formats, dissimilar sampling rates, synchronization, and combination of different features. The effective analysis requires advanced preprocessing, alignment, and machine learning tools to be able to extract valuable insights. Multimodal data enables good decision-making in areas such as healthcare, security, smart cities, and human–computer interaction by relying on complementary data provided by other modalities.

6.1.2 Importance of security in multimodal environments

Security is needed in multimodal environments where heterogeneous data, such as text, images, audio, video, and sensor streams, are being continuously collected, shared, and analyzed. These diverse sets of information are attractive targets of cyberattacks and unauthorized access because they often contain sensitive information, such as biometric identifiers, personal health records, and real-time surveillance feeds. Breaches may cause financial losses, impaired decision-making, and invasion of privacy. Also, the integration of various modalities increases the area of attack, and, therefore, adversarial manipulation or data poisoning may occur, leading to biased analytics and machine learning outcomes. Both securing the integrity and confidentiality of data and ensuring the safety of users, safeguarding their data availability is important. Multimodal systems should be secured with strong mechanisms such as access control, blockchain, federated learning, and encryption to be used in applications in healthcare, finance, the Internet of Things, and smart cities [1,2].

6.1.3 Objectives and scope of the chapter

The objectives of this chapter are to analyze the major security concerns that can occur in multimodal data environments and provide a description of effective solutions to the security of a range of data sources. However, when exploring the latest technologies, such as encryption, blockchain, secure fusion, and federated learning, the primary objectives will include finding possible threats, such as unauthorized access, data breaches, adversarial attacks, and privacy violations. The range encompasses theoretical foundations, practical systems, and emerging trends in multimodal data protection in such areas as surveillance, smart cities, healthcare, and the Internet of Things. The chapter provides researchers and practitioners with a comprehensive guide on how to develop robust and reliable multimodal systems, as it addresses both organizational and technical problems.

6.2 Multimodal data ecosystem and vulnerabilities

The sources that are included in the multimodal data ecosystem to be thoroughly analyzed are text, photos, audio, video, and sensors, to name a few. Attacks that are caused by this complexity are adversarial attacks, inconsistent fusion, unauthorized access, and data breaches. There should be robust protection systems in the data lifecycle since heterogeneous formats and high dimensionality cause even greater threats to security.

6.2.1 Types and sources of multimodal data

Multimodal data is defined as diverse types of information obtained using different modalities, and each has a different insight. Textual data that provides contextual and semantic information are documents, emails, social media posts, and medical records. Some examples of visual data include images, videos, and satellite imagery that capture the temporal and spatial trends. Audio data, including speech, background noise, and biometric indications, provides temporal and emotional context. Sensor data collected by wearables, industrial machines, and Internet of Things devices gives real-time information about motion, temperature, physiological signals, etc. Examples of physiological and biomedical data that are crucial in research and healthcare are EEG, ECG, and MRI scans. The source of multimodal data is varied. Text, photos, videos, and geolocation data are generated on social media sites at the same time. Healthcare systems are all combined with biosensor readings, imaging, and clinical notes. Autonomous systems employ GPS, LiDAR, radar, and cameras when it comes to navigation. Smart cities and industrial structures capture sensor streams to optimize and monitor them. In the case of recommendation systems, there is an online platform and multimedia repositories that integrate text, audio, and video. These different types have to be handled using heterogeneity, synchronization, and fusion techniques, which are to be handled with care. The richness of multimodal data makes comprehensive analytics possible; however, it also adds processing, storage, and security challenges, which highlights the importance of robust data management practices in all applications [3]. Table 6.1 presents various types and sources of multimodal data.

6.2.2 Data lifecycle and security exposure points

The lifecycle of multimodal data (shown in Figure 6.1) includes collection, transmission, storage, processing, and sharing, which are all essential steps of data

Table 6.1 Summary of types and sources of multimodal data

Data type/ modality	Examples	Key information provided	Typical sources/ applications
Textual data	Documents, emails, social media posts, medical records	Contextual and semantic information	Social media platforms, healthcare systems, enterprise databases
Visual data	Images, videos, satellite imagery	Spatial and temporal patterns, activities, environments	Surveillance, remote sensing, autonomous systems
Audio data	Speech, background sounds, biometric audio cues	Temporal, emotional, and identity-related context	Voice assistants, call centers, healthcare monitoring
Sensor data	Motion, temperature, environmental, and wearable data	Real-time physical and environmental states	IoT devices, wearables, industrial systems, smart cities
Physiological and biomedical data	EEG, ECG, MRI scans	Health, neurological, and physiological insights	Medical research, hospitals, clinical diagnostics
Social media data	Text, images, videos, geolocation	User behavior, interaction, and location patterns	Online social platforms, recommender systems
Autonomous system data	GPS, LiDAR, radar, cameras	Navigation and situational awareness	Self-driving vehicles, drones, robotics
Smart city and industrial data	Infrastructure and operational sensor streams	Monitoring, optimization, and control insights	Smart grids, factories, urban management systems
Multimedia repository data	Text, audio, video content	Preference and content relevance	Recommendation and content delivery systems
Cross-cutting challenges	Heterogeneity, synchronization, fusion	Data integration and consistency	All multimodal analytics applications

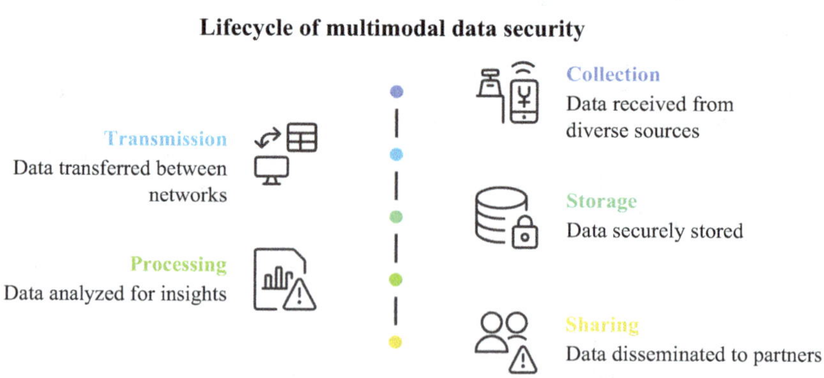

Figure 6.1 Lifecycle of multimodal data

lifecycle, and each of them is vulnerable to security issues. The collection phase is when data is received by a multiplicity of sources such as biomedical devices, cameras, microphones, sensors, and social media. One of the vulnerabilities at this stage that could compromise the integrity of the data, even before it gets into the system, is unauthorized access, tampering, data interception, and unprotected devices. During the transmission phase, multimodal data is transferred between networks, often between devices, cloud servers, or organizational systems. This step is highly susceptible to interception, eavesdropping, and man-in-the-middle attacks, especially in cases where the communication channels are not encrypted or authenticated. Storage risks involve poor encryption, information leakage, and unauthorized access. Multimodal datasets require a secure storage solution due to their size and diversity; poorly set up databases or cloud solutions may result in severe security violations. The processing and analysis of multimodal data involves the combination and analysis of data with the aim of extracting insights [4,5]. In this case, adversarial attacks, data poisoning, and model manipulation may compromise analytical results. Integrating various modalities into an algorithm will unintentionally propagate the flaws or vulnerabilities across the system. Finally, sensitive data faces the risk of privacy attacks, abuse, and violation of regulations in the sharing and dissemination phase when datasets are made available to other partners, platforms, or open repositories. Poor access control systems or auditing also adds to these risks. It is important to identify and safeguard exposure points at all stages of the entire life cycle. The integrity, confidentiality, and availability of the data are ensured through the practice of encryption, authentication, access control, secure data fusion, blockchain verification, and federated learning. This forms secure, dependable multimodal ecosystems.

6.2.3 Threat models in multimodal systems

Numerous security risks affect multimodal systems, which combine data from various sources like text, photos, audio, video, and sensors. Define threat models, which describe possible adversaries, their capabilities, and potential attack vectors, in order to comprehend these threats [6]. Typical threat models consist of:

- External attackers are unauthorized people who try to compromise the system, steal confidential data, or interfere with normal operations. Phishing attacks, eavesdropping, and network intrusions are a few examples.
- Insider threats are when authorized users take advantage of their access rights to purposefully or inadvertently leak or alter data. Because of authorized system access, these threats are frequently more difficult to identify.
- Adversarial attacks are malicious inputs intended to trick multimodal fusion algorithms or machine learning models, leading to inaccurate predictions or system failures.
- Data poisoning is the practice of introducing tainted or false data during training or collection, jeopardizing the accuracy of the model and the results of analytics.

- Privacy Attacks: Attempts to use reconstruction or inference techniques to extrapolate private information, such as identity, location, or behavioral patterns, from multimodal datasets.
- Systemic vulnerabilities are exploits of flaws in hardware, software, or networks, such as improperly configured storage, unpatched components, or unsecured APIs.

Establishing these threat models is crucial for creating strong security measures, setting defense priorities, and guaranteeing that multimodal systems continue to be secure, dependable, and resistant to known and unknown threats.

6.3 Security challenges in multimodal data

The security threats to multimodal data include heterogeneous data vulnerability, synchronization attacks, and sensor and IoT device exposure. These risks are data tampering, identity spoofing, privacy leakage, and adversarial manipulation. The assurance of secure fusion, transmission, and storage is still a challenge because of the existing variety of formats, real-time processing requirements, and distributed architecture [7].

6.3.1 Data fusion and integrity risks

Data fusion of multimodal systems involves combining data from various sources, including images, audio, text, and sensor streams, to produce rich and complete representations. Nevertheless, this integration creates serious integrity threats. Poor data quality, noise, or absence of modalities can yield erroneous results, whereas corrupted or adversarial inputs can propagate errors through fused layers and thus increase their effects. The unhomogenized data formats make the validation complicated and it is hard to prove authenticity and identify the existence of the manipulations. The fusion pipelines can be abused by malicious actors by either injecting fake sensor readings, manipulating metadata, or creating adversarial examples that can be used to fool machine learning models. The distributed IoT environment also creates additional vulnerability in the sense that a weak node or communication channel can modify the data before fusion. It is necessary to withstand preprocessing, ensure secure synchronization, detect anomalies, verify with the help of cryptography, and check cross-modality to ensure integrity. In the absence of effective protection, breached fusion processes may compromise the decision-making process, lower trust, and put safety-critical systems, including healthcare, surveillance, and autonomous systems, at risk [8].

6.3.2 Modality-specific and cross-modality attacks

Multimodal systems can be attacked by both modality-specific and cross-modality attacks that take advantage of the peculiarities of each type of data and the relations between them. Modality-specific attacks are attacks on the specific input, e.g., adversarial pertains to images, spoofed audio commands, manipulated sensor readings, or text that attempts to mislead machine learning models. The attacks are usually in a way that they go around the normal security measures because they seem natural and are not noticeable to humans. The attacks of cross-modality are more advanced, which take advantage of the fusion process to control or corrupt the system output overall. As an example, a change in visual perception without changing audio can cause misclassification, or falsified data from environmental sensors can cause distortion of cross-modal understanding. Another way in which attackers can use discrepancies across modalities is to mislead detection algorithms. Multimodal pipelines are so interconnected that it is not easy to isolate and determine the authenticity of each modality. Defense needs to be effectively addressed in terms of coordinated validation, multiple-layer anomaly detection, and strong fusion strategies in order to maintain system reliability [9,10].

6.3.3 Data annotation and labeling vulnerabilities

Annotating and labeling data are also crucial to the training of multimodal machine learning systems, but they also present serious security risks. Crowdsourcing, human labeling, or automated labeling systems can unintentionally cause biases, inconsistencies, or errors and undermine the model's accuracy. Labels can be intentionally attacked by malicious actors who can misclassify samples in other modalities, e.g., by matching wrong audio transcripts with images or manipulating sensor-event labels. Such small variations may pollute training data and models may learn incorrect relationships that harm their performance or produce backdoors. The complexity of multimodal data exacerbates these dangers, where there should be a strict correspondence between modalities; otherwise, misaligned timestamps, partial annotations, or invalidated metadata can disrupt the fusion mechanisms. Also, annotation pipelines usually do not have rigorous authentication or verification features and can be compromised by intruders and unauthorized access. To achieve secure labeling, it is necessary to perform stringent quality assurance and provenance tracking, access control, and cross-modal validation to ensure that the integrity of the data is upheld and the downstream applications are not affected by the compromised results of learning [11–17].

6.3.4 Model interpretability and privacy issues

The interpretability and privacy of models are serious issues in multimodal data systems, whereby the various inputs, including pictures, text, audio, and sensor inputs, make it hard to reason in a transparent manner. Deep learning models are usually black boxes, and it is not always easy to determine the contribution of particular modalities to the decision-making process or how biases might occur due to the integration of representations. Low interpretability prevents the identification of adversarial manipulations and decreases confidence in sensitive areas such as healthcare or surveillance. The threat to privacy is increased by the fact that models can accidentally disclose personal information during inference or by leaking feature embeddings. This weakness is magnified by multimodal data since the fusion of modalities raises the chances of recognizing individuals or recreating sensitive situations. Interpretability tools may also be used by attackers to learn training data or do model inversion. To assure privacy, there must be a trade-off between transparency and protection, and the methods of differential privacy, secure model auditing, federated learning, and controlled interpretability may be employed. These measures should be enhanced to maintain trust, equity, and confidentiality in multimodal systems [18,19]. Table 6.2 presents various security challenges in multimodal data.

Table 6.2 Multimodal data security challenges

Security aspect	Key challenges	Major threats	Implications
Overall multimodal security	Heterogeneity, synchronization, distributed architecture	Data tampering, identity spoofing, privacy leakage, adversarial manipulation	Difficult to secure fusion, transmission, and storage in real-time systems
Data fusion and integrity risks	Noisy, missing, or corrupted modalities; unstandardized formats	Fake sensor injection, metadata manipulation, adversarial inputs	Error propagation, compromised decisions, risks to healthcare, surveillance, and autonomous systems
Modality-specific attacks	Unique vulnerabilities per data type	Adversarial images, spoofed audio commands, falsified sensor readings, malicious text	Models misled while attacks remain human-imperceptible
Cross-modality attacks	Exploitation of inter-modality dependencies	Inconsistent modality manipulation, fusion-level corruption	System-wide misclassification and reduced reliability
Data annotation and labeling risks	Complex alignment across modalities	Label poisoning, misaligned timestamps, biased or incorrect labels	Polluted training data, backdoors, degraded model performance
Annotation pipeline weaknesses	Lack of authentication and verification	Unauthorized access, malicious relabeling	Loss of data provenance and trust in datasets
Model interpretability issues	Black-box nature of deep models	Hidden biases, undetected adversarial behavior	Reduced transparency and confidence in critical applications
Privacy leakage via models	Multimodal feature fusion	Model inversion, embedding leakage, re-identification	Exposure of sensitive personal information
Defense and mitigation needs	Secure validation and auditing	Differential privacy, federated learning, anomaly detection	Improved trust, confidentiality, and system robustness

6.4 Mechanisms for securing multimodal data

Multimodal data must be secured by the means of strong encryption, safe fusion of data, and authentic transmission across cross-heterogeneous sources (shown in Figure 6.2). Anomaly detection, cross-modal consistency checks, differential privacy, and federated learning are some of the techniques that can be used to increase protection. The use of access control, blockchain provenance, and even adversarial defense strategies also enhances the integrity of the data, their confidentiality, and resistance to complex attacks.

6.4.1 Cryptographic techniques for multimodal storage and transmission

The cryptographic methods are crucial in the protection of multimodal data in both storage and transmission in the distributed environment of IoT and multimedia. AES, RSA, and elliptic curve cryptography are used to provide confidentiality; secure hashing and digital signatures are used to provide integrity and authenticity. Homomorphic encryption allows privacy-preserving analytics on encrypted multimodal data by allowing computation of this encrypted data. Resource-constrained devices that have to deal with images, audio, text, and sensor streams require key management and lightweight cryptography. These methods can be used in

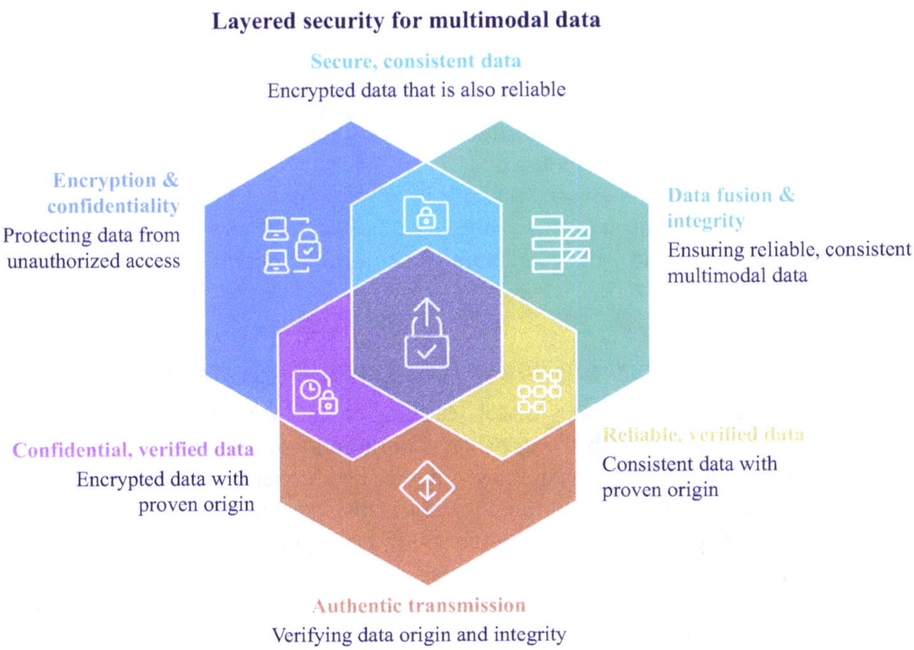

Figure 6.2 Security techniques for multimodal data

conjunction with secure communication systems such as TLS and blockchain provenance systems to safeguard against tampering, eavesdropping, and unauthorized access in multimodal systems [20,21].

6.4.2 Secure data fusion and aggregation

Secure data fusion and aggregation are used to ensure that multimodal sensor, image, audio, and text inputs are fused without causing vulnerability or integrity loss. Encrypted fusion pipelines, secure multiparty computation, and homomorphic encryption are some of the techniques that enable processing of data without making the raw information available. Cross-modal consistency checks and anomaly detection, as well as trust scoring, are used to detect corrupted or adversarial inputs prior to fusion. Provenance and blockchain-based logging are more resistant to unauthorized changes and increase the security of access control. Such mechanisms ensure confidentiality, reliability, and robustness of the fusion workflow, collection, synchronization, processing, and aggregation, making accurate decisions in distributed multimodal environments possible.

6.4.3 Access control and authentication schemes

Multimodal data in distributed IoT and multimedia systems requires access control and authentication schemes to protect multimodal data. The role-based, attribute-based, and context-aware access control models make sure that specific data modalities can be accessed or changed by authorized users or devices only. Multifactor authentication, biometric verification, and cryptographic credentials help boost identity assurance. Fine-grained policies are used in multimodal settings to control access to various types of data, and continuous authentication is used to identify anomalies during the interaction. Trust is further enhanced by secure token management, identity frameworks that are based on blockchain, and device attestation. Combining the mechanisms will avert unauthorized access, misuse of data, and identity spoofing and will secure safe and controlled operations of multimodal data [22].

6.4.4 Federated learning and privacy-preserving methods

Federated learning allows joint model learning on multimodal data without the transfer of raw data, thus improving privacy and minimizing the risks of exposure. All devices or nodes process local images, audio, text, or sensor data and only send model updates, which are combined safely. Other techniques like differential privacy, secure aggregation, and homomorphic encryption, as well as multiparty computation, also prevent inference attacks and reconstruction efforts. Privacy-sensitive techniques guarantee the decentralization of sensitive user information without adversely affecting the model performance. Such methods are especially useful in healthcare, smart cities, and IoT-based settings where multimodal data are highly personal, decentralized, and prone to unauthorized access or interference.

6.5 Adversarial attacks and robustness in multimodal AI

Adversarial attacks on multimodal AI systems attack the imagery, audio, text, or sensor data to deceive the fused models. Such attacks take advantage of modality interactions and mismatches. Adversarial training, cross-modal validation, anomaly detection, and resilient fusion strategies are needed to provide robustness in order to guarantee credible, secure, and tamper-resistant multimodal decision-making [23,24].

6.5.1 Attack vectors in multimodal learning systems

The multimodal learning systems are subjected to a variety of attack vectors against each individual modality and fusion mechanisms. Attackers can use distorted images, spoof audio cues, and change text input and/or sensor data to trick models. Training pipeline attacks like data poisoning, label manipulation, and metadata tampering, as well as inference attacks because of model vulnerabilities, compromise the training pipeline and evasion attacks. The cross-modality attacks use a single modality to corrupt fused results or introduce discrepancies that disorient the decision-making. Also, model inversion, membership inference, and feature extraction attacks are privacy threats that recreate sensitive multimodal information. All these vectors contribute to the lack of accuracy, integrity, and trust in multimodal AI applications.

6.5.2 Detection and mitigation strategies

Multimodal systems are detected and mitigated based on cross-modal consistency checks, anomaly detection, and robust feature validation in order to detect tampered or inconsistent inputs. Adversarial training, input sanitization, and ensemble defenses have increased protection against attacks. Data fusion is made secure, cryptographically verified, and provenance tracked to ensure intermodal manipulation. Further exposure capping is achieved by continuous monitoring and hardening of models, as well as fine-grained access control, which guarantees trustworthy and dependable multimodal AI behavior.

6.5.3 Case studies of adversarial scenarios

Multimodal systems in adversarial settings demonstrate the effect of coordinated manipulations in different types of data on the performance of AI. In autonomous driving, attackers can manipulate the roadside image in a subtle way or introduce the tiniest elements of audio feedback that can confuse vision-audio fusion models to perceive obstacles incorrectly or trigger false reactions to an emergency. The cross-modal discrepancies between person-tracking systems and adversarial patches on clothing, along with manipulated acoustic signals, can be used in smart surveillance. The threat to healthcare applications is also present: altered medical images and falsified sensor data or inaccurate text reports may confuse the diagnostic models and provide unsafe recommendations. The systems of social media moderation can be compromised when opponents control the video frames and use false captions or background audio to pass the content filters. In smart homes based on IoT, fed with fake sensor data and manipulated voice commands, it is possible to cause unauthorized actions. These case studies point to the importance of multimodal interactions that enhance the impact of attacks and the necessity of resilience to various fusion mechanisms, continuous monitoring, and adversarial robust design of models.

6.6 Regulatory, ethical, and legal considerations

Data security: Multimodal data demands compliance with privacy regulations, ethical data processing, and responsible AI. Policies such as GDPR and industry-related policies guarantee legal processing. The ethical issues include equity, openness, and avoiding abuse. Laws and regulations ensure responsibility, data security, and safety against attacks to ensure confidence in multimodal systems [25].

6.6.1 Compliance frameworks

The structured guidelines for the management and security of multimodal data exist in compliance frameworks including GDPR, HIPAA, and ISO/IEC standards. The GDPR requires consent of the user, minimization of data, and the right to access or delete personal data and guarantees privacy in various modalities. HIPAA regulates the safety of confidential healthcare information, the strict protection of confidentiality, safe storage, and controlled sharing of patient records. The ISO/IEC standards provide the information security management and risk mitigation best practices. The application of these frameworks will need strong access control, encryption, an audit trail, and anonymization of data. Compliance promotes legal responsibility, ethical management, and security of delicate multimodal data within the IoT and AI-driven settings.

6.6.2 Ethical use of sensitive multimodal data

The ethical use of sensitive multimodal data requires a responsible collection, processing, and analysis of the data based on privacy, consent, and fairness. Multimodal datasets are likely to include personal data in the form of images, audio, text, and sensors, which must remain anonymous and stored in a secure location to avoid abuse. The mitigation of bias is essential to prevent the discriminatory nature of AI models, particularly in the fields of healthcare, surveillance, and social use. Accountability is improved by transparent reporting of the source of data, limitations, and decision-making. Companies ought to use stringent access controls, surveillance, and ethical codes and regulations. The principles promote trust, safeguard the rights of people, and implement socially responsible multimodal AI systems.

6.6.3 Data ownership and consent

The management of multimodal datasets in terms of ethical and legal issues relies on data ownership and consent. The creators or producers of data have rights to the collection, storage, and use of their images, audio, text, or sensor information. Informed consent is required and should be explicit with the purpose of data use, time, and scope of data use, such as training AI models or across platforms. Transparency, accountability, and user autonomy are achieved through proper consent mechanisms. There are clear ownership policies, which eliminate unauthorized access, misuse, or commercial exploitation. Together with secure access controls and audit trails, the ownership of data and consent protection of privacy, the establishment of trust, and the alignment of multimodal data practices with regulatory and ethical standards are crucial.

6.7 Case studies and applications

In autonomous vehicles, smart cities, and surveillance systems, multimodal data security is essential in healthcare. Case studies indicate that it is difficult to defend against adversarial attacks, privacy violations, and manipulation of images, audio, text, and sensor data. Intense encryption, safe fusion, and adherence frameworks provide safe, trustworthy, and reliable multimodal AI applications.

6.7.1 Healthcare and biomedical systems

The examples of multimodal data applications in healthcare indicate the advantages and security issues of a combination of different data. In radiology, MRI, CT, and ultrasound images with patient electronic health records allow for making more accurate diagnoses of such complicated diseases as cancer and cardiovascular diseases. Adversarial examples have demonstrated that even minor manipulations of medical images, along with manipulated textual records, can be fooled by an AI model, and this is why it is necessary to have strong anomaly detection and safe fusion systems. Wearable sensors that record the heart rate, blood pressure, and activity levels are used with audio and video consultations in remote patient monitoring to monitor chronic conditions. The experience of case studies shows that lack of secure transmission of sensor information or hacked IoT devices may lead to privacy invasion or false alerts, which makes encryption, access control, and federated learning methods crucial. The other example is called genomics and personalized medicine, in which DNA sequences are studied and compared with medical histories and imaging data to determine the likelihood of a disease. Predictive accuracy can be impaired by data labeling errors or cross-modality inconsistencies, which highlights the importance of quality checks, provenance tracking, and privacy-preserving analytics. All these examples demonstrate a severe necessity for ethical, safe, and robust multimodal AI systems in healthcare.

6.7.2 Surveillance and smart cities

The multimodal data is central to the latest surveillance and smart city implementation, where video feeds, audio cues, sensor networks, and social media information can be incorporated to make cities safer, manage traffic, and respond to emergencies. Cameras, LiDAR, and vehicle sensors are combined in traffic monitoring to identify congestion, accidents, and violations in real-time. It has been demonstrated in case studies that the traffic AI systems may be misled with adverse effects on the camera feeds or GPS spoofing, and secure data fusion, anomaly detection, and strong sensor validation are necessary. Multimodal systems are used in the context of public safety and surveillance to analyze CCTV footage, acoustic sensors, and social media reports to identify suspicious activities, crowd behavior, or security threats. Studies have shown that audio cues or modified video frames can evade detection algorithms and this is a weakness in cross-modal interactions. Integrity and privacy are ensured by deploying cryptographic protection, access control, and real-time verification. Environmental monitoring is a smart city IoT application that incorporates air quality sensors, weather stations, and citizen reports. The case studies indicate that inconsistent or manipulated sensor measurements may affect analytics and policy-making decisions, which is why provenance tracking, secure transmission, and privacy-preserving aggregation are important. Together, these instances demonstrate the need for robust, beneficial as well as safe, multimodal information management within cities.

6.7.3 Industrial IoT and autonomous systems

Multimodal data, which integrates sensor measurements, images, audio, and logs of the operations, is becoming an important part of industrial IoT (IIoT) and autonomous systems to streamline manufacturing, robotics, and autonomous vehicles. Smart factories combine vibration sensors, thermal cameras, and machine logs in order to forecast equipment breakdowns and improve predictive maintenance. Case studies indicate that tampering with data, sensor spoofing, or incorrect labeling of operational logs may undermine model accuracy, which may lead to expensive downtimes or risk to lives and property. In self-driving cars, navigation, detection of obstacles, and decision-making are performed based on multimodal LiDAR, radar, cameras, and GPS information. Studies have shown that the fusion models, when perturbed by adversarial examples on visual or radar inputs, are vulnerable to making unsafe decisions in the driving process. Another risk to industrial robotics is seeing cross-modality inconsistencies, e.g., wrong sensor alignment or manipulated control signals, impacting task execution. Secure data fusion, anomaly detection, access control, and federated learning have been successfully implemented to overcome these threats. The cases highlight the importance of the existence of strong, privacy-friendly, and resilient multimodal AI in industrial and autonomous systems.

6.8 Research directions and future trends

Multimodal data security is an emerging field that is quickly developing because of the growing applications of AI and IoT in healthcare, smart cities, autonomous systems, and industry. Future work will be aimed at making it resistant to adversarial attacks, cross-modality manipulations, and data integrity threats. It will be important to build sophisticated adversarial defense systems, robust fusion systems, and real-time anomaly detection systems to ensure trust and reliability in multimodal AI. Privacy-sensitive methods, such as federated learning, secure multiparty computation, and differential privacy, will also keep gaining more and more influence, allowing jointly trained models without disclosing sensitive information. The IoT resource-constrained devices will require research on lightweight cryptography and energy-saving security protocols. Transparency issues will be dealt with through explainable AI and interpretable multimodal models that will enable accountability and ethical use, particularly in healthcare and critical infrastructure. Blockchain and distributed ledger technology integration can be a promising solution in the field of secure provenance tracking, auditability, and tamper-proof data sharing. Other new trends are quantum-safe cryptography, AI-based security automation, and cross-domain multimodal threat intelligence. Interdisciplinary solutions with cybersecurity, machine learning, and domain-specific knowledge will lead to resilient, ethical, and scalable solutions, which will become the future of secure multimodal data systems in a variety of applications.

6.9 Conclusion

Multimodal data provides the first-ever chances to improve decision-making, situational awareness, and predictive analytics in the fields of healthcare, intelligent cities, industrial IoT, and autonomous systems. Nonetheless, the combination of different modalities – images, audio, text, and sensor data – creates serious security, privacy, and integrity issues. All these can adversely affect model reliability, disclose sensitive data, and result in mistrust due to adversarial attacks, data tampering, labeling errors, and cross-modality inconsistencies. Strong mechanisms that may be deemed to deal with these risks include secure data fusion, cryptographic protection, access control, federated learning, and privacy-preserving analytics. Regulatory adherence, ethical treatment of sensitive information, and open model interpretability also enhance trust and accountability. The practical role of these challenges and the efficiency of mitigation strategies are illustrated in the case studies in healthcare, smart cities, and industrial applications. In the future, studies should be conducted on resilient architectures, explainable AI, real-time monitoring, and new technologies, such as the blockchain and quantum-safe cryptography. Multimodal systems can provide secure, dependable, and socially responsible deployment in a variety of fields by using technical, ethical, and regulatory protection.

References

[1] R. Na, Y. Jiao, and L. Yang, "Research on the privacy protection mechanism of multimodal fusion of data based on blockchain technology," in *2024 IEEE 7th International Conference on Information Systems and Computer Aided Education (ICISCAE)*. IEEE, 2024, pp. 1190–1194.

[2] D. Lahat, T. Adali, and C. Jutten, "Multimodal data fusion: an overview of methods, challenges, and prospects," *Proceedings of the IEEE*, vol. 103, no. 9, pp. 1449–1477, 2015.

[3] N. Algiriyage, R. Prasanna, K. Stock, E. E. Doyle, and D. Johnston, "Multi-source multimodal data and deep learning for disaster response: a systematic review," *SN Computer Science*, vol. 3, no. 1, p. 92, 2022.

[4] Vacius Jusas, Rita Butkiene, Algimantas Venĉkauskas *et al.*, "Sustainable and security focused multimodal models for distance learning," *Sustainability*, vol. 14, no. 6, p. 3414, 2022.

[5] S. Guo, Y. Liu, M. Dong, and Y. Tang, "A three-stage end-to-end security regulatory model for high-definition map data," in *CCF Intelligent Vehicles Symposium*. Springer, 2025, pp. 230–258.

[6] Y. Chai, Y. Zhou, W. Li, and Y. Jiang, "An explainable multi-modal hierarchical attention model for developing phishing threat intelligence," *IEEE Transactions on Dependable and Secure Computing*, vol. 19, no. 2, pp. 790–803, 2021.

[7] S. Kumar, M. K. Chaube, S. N. Nenavath, S. K. Gupta, and S. K. Tetarave, "Privacy preservation and security challenges: a new frontier multimodal machine learning research," *International Journal of Sensor Networks*, vol. 39, no. 4, pp. 227–245, 2022.

[8] P. Piyush, K. Singh, R. Kumar, S. Chhabra, A. Kashyap, and N. Goomer, "Enhancing the security of multimodal fused data with blockchain," in *2024 International Conference on Computational Intelligence and Computing Applications (ICCICA)*, vol. 1. IEEE, 2024, pp. 221–225.

[9] Ajian Liu, Zichang Tan, Jun Wan, Yanyan Liang, Zhen Lei, and Guodong Guo, "Face anti-spoofing via adversarial cross-modality translation," *IEEE Transactions on Information Forensics and Security*, vol. 16, pp. 2759–2772, 2021.

[10] Y. Gong, Q. Zeng, D. Xu, Z. Wang, and M. Jiang, "Cross-modality attack boosted by gradient-evolutionary multiform optimization," arXiv preprint arXiv:2409.17977, 2024.

[11] X. Zhou and R. M. Verma, "Vulnerability detection via multimodal learning: datasets and analysis," in *Proceedings of the 2022 ACM on Asia Conference on Computer and Communications Security*, 2022, pp. 1225–1227.

[12] T. H. M. Le and M. A. Babar, "Automatic data labeling for software vulnerability prediction models: how far are we?," in *Proceedings of the 18th ACM/IEEE International Symposium on Empirical Software Engineering and Measurement*, 2024, pp. 131–142.

[13] S. Kumar, S. Rani, S. Sharma, and H. Min, "Multimodality fusion aspects of medical diagnosis: a comprehensive review," *Bioengineering*, vol. 11, no. 12, p. 1233, 2024.

[14] V. Puri, A. Kataria, S. Rani, and P. K. Pareek, "DLT based smart medical ecosystem," in *2023 International Conference on Network, Multimedia and Information Technology (NMITCON)*. IEEE, 2023, pp. 1–6.

[15] S. Rani, A. Kataria, P. Bhambri, P. K. Pareek, and V. Puri, "Artificial intelligence in personalized health services for better patient care," in *Revolutionizing Healthcare: AI Integration with IoT for Enhanced Patient Outcomes*. Springer, 2024, pp. 89–108.

[16] S. Rani, P. Bhambri, and M. Chauhan, "A machine learning model for kids' behavior analysis from facial emotions using principal component analysis," in *2021 5th Asian Conference on Artificial Intelligence Technology (ACAIT)*. IEEE, 2021, pp. 522–525.

[17] A. Kumar, R. Gupta, S. Kumar, K. Dutta, and M. Rani, "Securing IoMT-based healthcare system: issues, challenges, and solutions," *Artificial Intelligence and Cybersecurity in Healthcare*, pp. 17–56, 2025.

[18] H. Montenegro, W. Silva, A. Gaudio, M. Fredrikson, A. Smailagic, and J. S. Cardoso, "Privacy-preserving case-based explanations: enabling visual interpretability by protecting privacy," *IEEE Access*, vol. 10, pp. 28333–28347, 2022.

[19] A. K. Roundtree, "AI explainability, interpretability, fairness, and privacy: an integrative review of reviews," *in International Conference on Human–Computer Interaction*. Springer, 2023, pp. 305–317.

[20] E. B. Tarif, S. Wibowo, S. Wasimi, and A. Tareef, "A hybrid encryption/hiding method for secure transmission of biometric data in multimodal authentication system," *Multimedia Tools and Applications*, vol. 77, no. 2, pp. 2485–2503, 2018.

[21] R. Shokri, M. Strobel, and Y. Zick, "On the privacy risks of model explanations," in *Proceedings of the 2021 AAAI/ACM Conference on AI, Ethics, and Society*, 2021, pp. 231–241.

[22] Y. Ding, Y. Zhang, B. Qin, Q. Wang, Z. Yang, and W. Shi, "A scalable cross-chain access control and identity authentication scheme," *Sensors*, vol. 23, no. 4, p. 2000, 2023.

[23] C. Jiang, Z. Wang, M. Dong, and J. Gui, "Survey of adversarial robustness in multimodal large language models," *arXiv preprint arXiv:2503.13962*, 2025.

[24] X. Cui, A. Aparcedo, Y. K. Jang, and S.-N. Lim, "On the robustness of large multimodal models against image adversarial attacks," in *Proceedings of the IEEE/CVF Conference on Computer Vision and Pattern Recognition*, 2024, pp. 24625–24634.

[25] D. Naik, I. Naik, and N. Naik, "Applications of AI chatbots based on generative AI, large language models and large multimodal models," in *The International Conference on Computing, Communication, Cybersecurity & AI*. Springer, 2024, pp. 668–690.

Chapter 7

ML and DL techniques to detect cyberattacks on multimodal databases

Abstract

The increasing trend in multimodal databases in the Internet of Multimedia Things (IoMT) poses distinct cybersecurity vulnerabilities as multimodal systems combine text, image, audio, video, and sensor information. Conventional security tools are not effective at identifying advanced attacks, such as deepfakes, data poisoning, and cross-modal manipulations. This chapter discusses the use of machine learning (ML) and deep learning (DL) to identify cyber threats within this type of environment. CNNs, RNNs, Transformers, autoencoders, and generative models are discussed as well as supervised, unsupervised, and semi-supervised models with attack detection in specific modalities and in cross-modality. Strategies of data fusion and cross-modality consistency checks contribute to a high level of robustness, whereas accuracy, precision, recall, and F1 score are used as evaluation measures to demonstrate the effectiveness. This chapter ends with a list of challenges, future research, and practical implementations in healthcare, smart cities, industrial IoT, and financial systems.

Keywords: adversarial attacks; cybersecurity; deep learning; multimodal databases; machine learning

7.1 Introduction

The fast growth of multimodal databases, such as a combination of text, images, audio, video, and sensor streams, has both given rise to intelligent services and provided systems with high vulnerability to complex cyberattacks. The conventional security approaches have difficulty identifying advanced and multimodal threats that take advantage of the relationships among different data types. Deep learning (DL) and machine learning (ML) methods currently have become of paramount importance in the protection of these environments due to their ability to operate in adaptive, context-sensitive, and real-time mode, detecting threats [1]. This chapter discusses sophisticated ML/DL models, intrusion detection systems, and multimodal fusion plans that would detect abnormalities, deter data breaches, and improve the resiliency of Internet of Multimedia Things systems.

7.1.1 Overview of cybersecurity challenges in multimodal databases

Multimodal databases are heterogeneous, including images, video, audio, text, and sensor streams, and are much more difficult to secure than more traditional datasets (shown in Figure 7.1). To take advantage of this variety, cyber enemies use sophisticated attacks to exploit cross-modal inconsistency, latent correlations, and vulnerabilities created during data combination. High volume of data, real-time requirements, and challenges in making unified modalities' security policies are some of the challenges. Also, multimodal systems are frequently based on distributed systems of IoT, which themselves expose them to spoofing, data modification, and man-in-the-middle attacks as well as to unauthorized access. It is challenging to offer integrity and authenticity when no two modalities share a common format, noise pattern, or attack surface. Furthermore, the traditional rule-based or one-mode detection systems do not detect complex and integrated attacks, which can simultaneously alter multiple data streams. Such complications highlight the necessity of ML- and DL-based systems that will be able to learn patterns of multimodal, identify anomalies, and offer adaptive protection to the Internet of Multimedia Things environments [2].

7.1.2 Importance of ML and DL for attack detection

Multimodal database security has been made easier through the use of machine learning (ML) and deep learning (DL) because the two can analyze multi-dimensional, complex, and heterogeneous data. Conventional security measures are

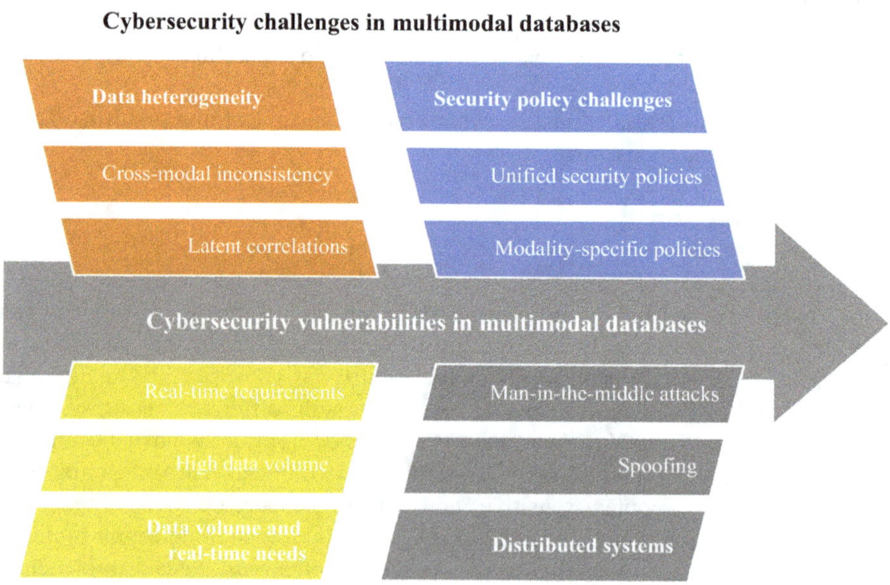

Figure 7.1 Cybersecurity issues and multimodal databases

based on predefined regulations or single-mode investigation, which cannot restrict evolving and cross-modal attacks. The ML and DL models are trained on various types of data, including images, audio, video, text, and sensor measurements and are capable of identifying subtle anomalies and correlations that a human or a rule-based system would not have easily noticed. Their ability to be more flexible to emerging threats, analyze in real-time, and extract features automatically enhances the intrusion detection, malware classification, deepfake detection, and data integrity verification. These smart approaches will make Internet of Multimedia Things ecosystems a lot more resilient [3–5].

7.2 Threats and attack vectors in multimodal systems

Multimodal systems are vulnerable to a variety of attacks (summarized in Table 7.1) against the combination of images, audio, text, video, and sensor information. Attackers take advantage of the vulnerabilities of a particular modality, including image tampering, audio spoofing, video deepfakes, and text injection, and cross-modal vulnerabilities introduced during data fusion. Some of the common attack vectors are data poisoning, adversarial examples, replay attacks, eavesdropping, model inversion, and unauthorized access to distributed IoT nodes. Any manipulation of one of the modalities may lead to misleading the entire system and generating

Table 7.1 Various types of attacks attempted on multimodal systems

Type of attack	Description	Impact on multimodal systems	Examples
Modality-specific attacks	Exploiting weaknesses in specific data types such as images, audio, text, video, or sensors.	Compromised system decisions if one modality is manipulated.	Image tampering, adversarial image perturbation, face spoofing, voice replay/cloning, phishing text, deepfake videos, sensor spoofing.
Cross-modality attacks	Manipulating correlations between different modalities to confuse fusion models.	Disrupted data fusion and incorrect decision-making.	Altered video with original audio, conflicting sensor inputs, fake metadata with manipulated video, multimodal misinformation.
Data poisoning and adversarial attacks	Injecting malicious samples into training data or adding subtle perturbations during inference.	Reduced model accuracy, biased predictions, hidden backdoors, loss of system trust.	Poisoned training datasets, coordinated multimodal adversarial inputs.

false predictions or corrupted analytics. Such threats negatively affect integrity, authenticity, and availability, and powerful ML- and DL-driven detection systems are necessary to secure Internet of Multimedia Things environments.

7.2.1 Modality-specific attacks

The attacks that are multimodal are those that focus on individual data types and take advantage of the specific vulnerabilities and qualities of individual data into account. Attacks based on images are tampering, adversarial perturbation, and face spoofing. Audio attacks use voice cloning, voice replay, or audio noise to corrupt recognition models. Phishing content, unauthentic metadata, and controlled natural language inputs are some of the threats to text modalities. Deepfakes, frame injection, and compression-based distortion can be used to compromise video streams. Sensor measurements are vulnerable to spoofing, signal jamming, and compromised measurements. A single modality can be compromised by attackers and, thus, system decisions will be corrupted, which is why the effective ML/DL strategies for each data type are essential [6–8].

7.2.2 Cross-modality attacks

Cross-modality attacks take advantage of cross-relations and dependencies between two (or more) types of data in multimodal systems. Attackers, instead of manipulating one particular modality, strategically modify correlations in images, audio, text, video, or sensor input to evade detection. As an illustration, the attacker can alter the video frames and preserve the audio, inject conflicting sensor information, or align a spofiously made text metadata with the damaged video material. Such discrepancies disorient fusion models and undermine decision-making. The threat is further augmented by cross-modal adversarial examples, coordinated poisoning, and multimodal misinformation campaigns. The types of attacks are hard to identify by the traditional means and require the introduction of state-of-the-art defenses, which are based on ML/DL fusion techniques and detect the intermodal relationships [9].

7.2.3 Data poisoning and adversarial attacks

Adversarial attacks and data poisoning are also a major threat to multimodal systems since they can corrupt data or the models on which they are based. In data poisoning, the attackers use training data to introduce spoofed samples into the training sets, making multimodal models learn the wrong kind of association between images, audio, text, or sensor input data. This compromises precision, allows backdoor attacks, or biases predictions. On the other hand, adversarial attacks apply unperceived perturbations during inference, producing misleading results while maintaining inputs to appear legitimate. Multimodal coordinated adversarial manipulation maximizes stealth and impact. These attacks destroy trust, reliability, and robustness and require a resilient ML/DL defense and secure data pipelines [10].

7.3 Machine learning approaches for cyberattack detection

Multimodal systems with machine learning methods increase attack detection through detecting anomalies, categorizing threats, and discovering patterns in the various types of data (presented in Table 7.2). SVMs, random forests, clustering, and ensemble models are techniques used to identify modality-based or mixed

Table 7.2 ML in cyberattack identification

Approach	Key methods	Main function in cyberattack detection	Advantages	Limitations
Supervised learning techniques	SVM, Random Forest, Decision Trees, Logistic Regression, Gradient Boosting, k-NN	Learn patterns from labeled multimodal data to classify normal vs. malicious behavior such as spoofing, tampering, deepfakes, and adversarial attacks	High detection accuracy, scalability, interpretability	Requires large labeled datasets; limited ability to detect unseen attacks
Unsupervised and semi-supervised learning	Clustering, Anomaly Detection, Autoencoders, Density-Based Models, Self-training, Co-training, Graph-based Learning	Identify unknown or emerging cyberattacks by detecting anomalies in multimodal data with limited labels	Detects new threats, reduces dependence on labeled data, adaptable to dynamic environments	Possible false positives and model tuning complexity
Feature engineering for multimodal data	Tokenization and embeddings (text), visual descriptors (images), spectrograms/ MFCCs (audio), statistical/temporal features (sensor data), PCA, Autoencoders	Transform heterogeneous multimodal inputs into meaningful representations and capture cross-modal relationships	Improves model accuracy, interpretability, and robustness	Requires complex preprocessing and feature design
Multimodal fusion strategies	Early Fusion (feature concatenation), Intermediate Fusion (attention-based weighting), Late Fusion (decision-level integration)	Integrate features from multiple modalities to enhance cyberattack detection	Captures cross-modal correlations and improves detection reliability	Increased computational complexity and fusion design challenges

attacks. They are more accurate, have better scalability, and have real-time threat response in complex environments due to their adaptability and pattern recognition [11].

7.3.1 Supervised learning techniques

Supervised learning methods are a basic part of multimodal database cyberattack detection through the use of labeled data that reflects normal and malicious actions. In a world where the information of text, audio, images, video, and sensors comes together, the supervised models learn the discriminative patterns that distinguish between normal behavior and threats. Popular methods are Support Vector Machines (SVM), Random Forests, Decision Trees, Logistic Regression, Gradient Boosting, and k-Nearest Neighbors (k-NN). These algorithms are useful in detecting the general categories of attacks, including spoofing, tampering, data injection, deepfake materials, and adversarial modifications. The importance of feature extraction and preprocessing is due to the fact that multimodal data should be converted into meaningful representations that do not destroy intermodal relationships. Feature concatenation techniques, attention-based weighting techniques, and statistical fusion techniques improve the capacity of the classifier to extract cross-modal correlations. Supervised models are characterized by high detection accuracy, scalability, and interpretability, which is why they can be used in intrusion detection systems, malware classification, and real-time monitoring. Nonetheless, they may rely on labeled data, which may turn into a weakness when operating in fast-changing cyberspace where new attack patterns are common. To solve this problem, ensemble strategies, multimodal fusion pipelines, and continual learning frameworks are frequently combined with supervised learning in order to enhance adaptability and robustness in Internet of Multimedia Things security ecosystems [12].

7.3.2 Unsupervised and semi-supervised learning

Unsupervised and semi-supervised learning methods play a critical role in cyberattack detection in multimodal systems with few or incomplete labeled data. Unsupervised approaches, including clustering, anomaly detection, autoencoders, and density-based models, learn natural structures and detect abnormalities in text, audio, image, video, or sensor data without being given any labels. These methods are useful in learning the unknown or emerging attack patterns, and therefore, they are useful in dynamic threat environments. Semi-supervised learning helps in filling the gap between a few labeled data and a large population of unlabeled samples. Methods such as self-training, co-training, and graph-based learning use small annotated datasets and large unlabeled datasets to improve detection accuracy. These techniques can use cross-modal consistency to detect anomalies that can be found in more than one type of data in a multimodal setting. Combined, unsupervised and semi-supervised methods enhance flexibility, lessen reliance on expensive labeled information, and enhance robustness against new assaults in Internet of Multimedia Things systems.

7.3.3 Feature engineering for multimodal data

Multimodal data feature engineering plays a vital role in the successful detection of cyberattacks since it converts heterogeneous inputs (text, images, audio, video, and sensor streams) into valuable representations. Each of the modalities needs specific preprocessing: a text is tokenized and embedded, an image is processed with descriptors or deep visual features, audio is modeled with spectrograms or MFCCs, and sensor data is modeled with statistical or temporal features. One of the problematic issues is the ability to capture both modality-specific features and cross-modal relations. Early fusion (feature concatenation), intermediate fusion (attention-based weighting), and late fusion (decision-level integration) are fusion strategies that are used to integrate different features to create a single representation. Additional dimensionality reduction techniques, such as PCA or autoencoders, additionally improve feature spaces and minimize noise. Good feature engineering enhances model interpretability, better model detection, and robust ML/DL pipelines. With multimodal cybersecurity, features that are designed in an effective way allow systems to identify anomalies, adversarial patterns, and cross-modal inconsistencies more effectively and reinforce Internet of Multimedia Things security.

7.4 Deep learning approaches

Deep learning techniques improve the detection of cyberattacks on multimodal databases by automatically identifying advanced and sophisticated features of images, text, audio, video, and sensor data. Such models as CNNs, RNNs, Transformers, and multimodal fusion networks learn cross-modal regularities, which allow them to identify complex threats and adversarial actions in interdependent systems in real-time effectively [13–15].

7.4.1 Convolutional Neural Networks (CNNs)

Convolutional Neural Networks (CNNs) are useful in identifying cyberattacks in the context of multimodal databases, especially when it comes to visual or spatial information. CNNs are not only good at automatically generating image, video frame, and even spectrogram (generated from audio signals) hierarchical features. Their convolutional filters identify edges, textures, patterns, and anomalies that can point to tampering, deepfake manipulation, or adversarial perturbations. CNNs are utilized for image forensics, intrusion detection, facial spoofing detection, and malware classification in the applications of cybersecurity. CNNs can be used to comprehend cross-modal threats by using fusion layers to combine text, audio, or sensor-based models with CNNs applied to multimodal systems. The superior CNNs like ResNet, EfficientNet, and DenseNet enhance the effectiveness of detection because they learn more in-depth and powerful representations. CNNs are very useful in detecting hidden attack patterns, and they can generalize their findings to more complex datasets, which serve as a great contribution to securing the Internet of Multimedia Things environment [16–22].

7.4.2 Recurrent Neural Networks (RNNs) and transformers

Transformers and Recurrent Neural Networks (RNNs) are deep learning models that have high potential in managing sequence and time data in multimodal cybersecurity. RNNs, such as LSTM and GRU, are used to find long-term dependencies in text logs, audio signals, sensor measurements, and video sequences. Their capability to model time-based trends renders them useful in identifying abnormalities like spoofed audio commands, manipulated metadata, and abnormal sensor behavior. Transformers and their self-attention capabilities are good at large-scale multimodal inputs, detecting contextual relationships between sequences without recurrence. They offer better performance on such tasks as intrusion detection, log checking, deepfake text-video consistency, and multimodal correlation modeling. Transformers can also be easily combined with CNNs and other modality-specific networks as single fusion structures. Combined, RNNs and Transformers allow effective identification of advanced, time-sensitive, and cross-modal cyberattacks and contribute to the advancement of the security and resilience of Internet of Multimedia Things settings to a considerable extent.

7.4.3 Autoencoders and generative models for anomaly detection

The use of autoencoders and generative models is important in the detection of anomalies and cyberattacks in multimodal databases through learning compact representations of normal behavior among the various types of data. Autoencoders can be used to reconstruct inputs, i.e., images, text embeddings, audio spectrograms, video frames, sensor sequences, etc., by compressing and decoding them. Reconstruction errors are also enhanced when an attack happens, which allows the system to identify tampered or adversarially altered data. Such variants as Variational Autoencoders (VAEs) and Denoising Autoencoders are more robust to noisy data and fine perturbations. Generative models, especially Generative Adversarial Networks (GANs), are trained to learn underlying multimodal distributions and detect inputs that do not conform to learned distributions. The detectors based on GAN are capable of revealing deepfakes, fabricated sensor signals, and adversarial cross-modal inconsistencies. Also, GANs are used to create artificial training samples to enhance detection in scarce data settings. Autoencoders and generative models together represent an effective unsupervised and semi-supervised framework that can be used to discover hidden threats and allow the detection of anomalies in Internet of Multimedia Things ecosystems early, accurately, and at scale.

7.5 Data fusion and multimodal feature integration

Fusion of data and integration of multimodal features are key to successful detection of cyberattacks in systems with a combination of text, images, audio, video, and sensor data. Fusion methods combine the data of different modalities to extract correlations, minimize redundancy, and improve detection of anomalies. Early fusion joins the raw features; intermediate fusion involves the use of learned representations or attention mechanisms, and late fusion involves the integration of decisions made by modality-specific models. With proper integration, cross-modal attacks, adversarial manipulations, and data inconsistencies are better detected. The use of complementary capabilities of each modality enables the fusion-based strategies to improve the accuracy, resilience, and flexibility of the systems of ML and DL, which improves security in the Internet of Multimedia Things conditions [23–25].

7.5.1 Early fusion, late fusion, and hybrid fusion

Data fusion strategies also have a central role in multimodal cybersecurity, where data of various modalities (text, images, audio, video, sensor streams, etc.) are combined to increase attack detection. Early fusion coalesces rudimentary or preprocessed characteristics across several modalities into one joint representation and inputs them into a machine learning model or deep learning model. The method can identify cross-modal correlations on a feature scale and therefore, can identify fine-grained anomalies and has the disadvantage of high dimensionality and noise sensitivity. Late fusion, in its turn, models each modality separately with dissimilar models and fuses the results at the decision level, e.g., by weighted voting, averaging, or meta-classifiers. Late fusion mitigates noisy modalities and can be flexible in the addition of new types of data without retraining the whole system but could lose fine-grained cross-modal interactions. Hybrid fusion is a fusion that is a combination of early and late fusion. It engages in intermediate integration, where specific representations of the modality are learned, and they are integrated using attention processes, concatenation, or ensemble strategies. This method is a trade-off between cross-modal correlation capture and noise and scale insensitivity. Hybrid fusion is specifically useful in multimodal anomaly detection, adversarial attack detection, and strengthening Internet of Multimedia Things security systems. Various types of data fusion techniques are shown in Figure 7.2.

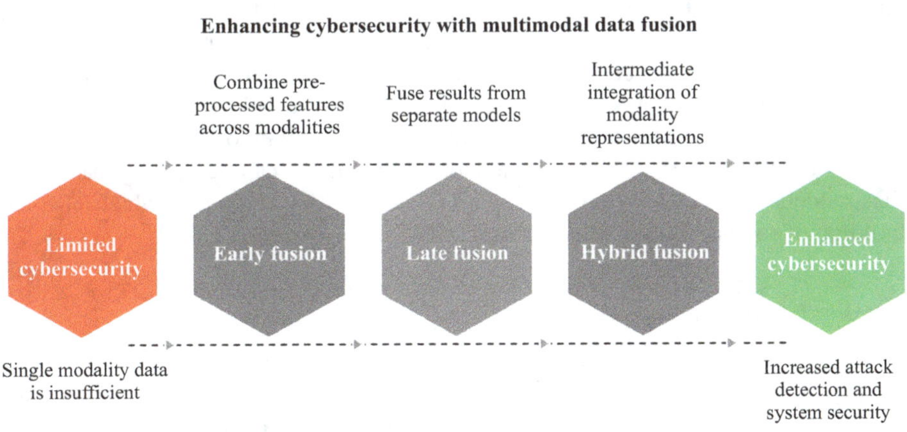

Figure 7.2 Type of fusion for multimodal data

7.5.2 Cross-modality consistency checks

The cross-modality consistency checks are essential in identifying cyberattacks that take advantage of the differences between the various types of data in multimodal systems. These checks detect inconsistencies in text, images, audio, video, sensor streams, and associated correlations and dependencies, as they are attempts to alter content, spoof, or engage in adversarial manipulation. As an example, audio and video lip movements are not aligned, textual metadata and visual data are opposing, sensor data is out of context with the environment, and so on, may be indicators of possible attacks. These cross-modal relationships are quantified and assessed by using the models of machine learning and deep learning, such as attention mechanisms, graph-based networks, and multimodal transformers. Real-time monitoring pipelines or batch analysis systems can be configured with consistency checks to identify anomalies in time. With the help of cross-modality validation, systems are not only able to identify attacks by modality but also identify coordinated manipulations, which would otherwise go undetected by single-modal detection. This will greatly improve the resilience, stability, and safety of Internet of Multimedia Things ecosystems toward advanced cybercrimes.

7.6 Evaluation metrics and benchmarking

In multimodal systems, the effectiveness of the ML and DL models to detect cyberattacks needs a holistic metric and benchmarking protocols. Popular measures are accuracy, precision, recall, F1 score, and area under the receiver operating characteristic curve (AUC-ROC) used to measure the overall detection performance, the ratio between false positives and false negatives, and the reliability of the model. In the context of anomaly detection, reconstruction error, true positive rate, and false alarm rate are essential measures. Benchmarking is the comparison of models in the context of standardized datasets that encompass different modalities, namely, text, images, audio, video, and sensor data, and different attack scenarios, such as spoofing, deepfakes, data poisoning, and cross-modal attacks. The robustness and generalization are commonly tested on public datasets and synthetic multimodal datasets. Moreover, important to real-time applications in the Internet of Multimedia Things environments are computational efficiency, scalability, and latency. Strict assessment and benchmarking can be used to make sure that models are not only correct but also viable to be deployed, which enables building of robust, multimodal cybersecurity frameworks [26,27].

7.6.1 Accuracy, precision, recall, and F1 score

The most basic metrics used to measure the performance of the ML and DL models in detecting cyberattacks on multimodal databases include accuracy, precision, recall, and F1 score. Accuracy is used to gauge the ratio of the correct classification of instances – attack and normal behavior – to the overall count of instances.

Although intuitive, accuracy may be deceiving with unbalanced datasets, where normal events are many as compared to attacks. Precision is used to measure the ratio of correctly recognized attack instances of all the instances that are predicted as attacks. Higher precision means that there will be fewer false alarms, which is essential in working environments to prevent notifications and measures that are not necessary. As mentioned above, the so-called recall, sensitivity, or true positive rate is a measure of the percentage of real attack cases that the model correctly predicted. High recall means that the majority of threats are identified, and there is a low probability of unnoticed violations. F1 score is the harmonic mean of precision and recall, which is a balanced measure that takes into consideration both false positives and false negatives. It can be applied specifically to multimodal cybersecurity environments, where it is important to identify attacks precisely in heterogeneous data streams and trade-offs between over-alerts and non-detection of attacks need to be struck. Multimodal systems often compute these metrics by modality and the system is fused to be able to evaluate the modality-specific and system-wide performance of detection. The process of tracking such measures when training and testing a model provides the robustness, reliability, and successful deployment of Internet of Multimedia Things security solutions.

7.6.2 Robustness and scalability considerations

In multimodal cybersecurity, robustness and scalability are important aspects that require evaluation of the ML and DL models. The concept of robustness is the capability of a model to retain its performance when faced with adversarial conditions, noisy data, or hidden attack patterns. This applies to multimodal systems, where they need to deal with corrupted pictures, manipulated audio, sensor readings that are inconsistent, or cross-modal attacks without causing much reduction in detection accuracy. Adversarial training, data augmentation, and cross-modality validation techniques can be used to increase robustness by training models to respond to a variety of threat cases. Scalability is the ability of the model to handle high amounts of multimodal information in real-time or near real-time. The environment of Internet of Multimedia Things creates high-velocity streams of text, video, audio, and sensor modalities, which require models to manage growing data volumes and modalities, yet without undue computational cost. Scalability is enhanced by approaches such as distributed processing, model compression, incremental learning, and modular architectures. The assessment of robustness and scalability will make detection frameworks more dependable, flexible, and viable to be used within dynamic and large-scale multimodal systems to offer robust cybersecurity to interconnected IoT settings.

7.7 Case studies and applications

Machine learning (ML) and deep learning (DL) methods have proven to be very useful in cyberattack detection with various multimodal systems, which is an indication of real-life applicability in the Internet of Multimedia Things (IoMT) settings. Multimodal electronic health records (medical images, sensor readings, and textual data about the patient) are susceptible to manipulation or unauthorized access in the healthcare industry. CNNs and autoencoder-based models have already been used to observe abnormalities in the imaging data; RNNs and Transformers are used to observe the trends in sensor data and text records to avoid data breaches and protect patient safety. Smart city infrastructure combines video feeds, audio sensors, and video streams of IoT devices. Early and hybrid fusion schemes allow cross-modality anomaly detection where tampered video, spoofed audio commands, or inconsistent traffic sensor data have been discovered. Equally, industrial IoT systems, including factories, use ML-driven intrusion detection to track a combination of sensor, log of operations, and camera data to prevent sabotage and disruption of critical equipment. Multimodal security also applies to financial and e-commerce platforms, in which logs of transactions and behavioral and video verifications are processed with ensemble learning and attention-based DL models to detect fraudulent behavior. These case studies indicate that modality-specific analysis, cross-modality consistency checking, and real-time ML/DL inference are complementary to improve the detection rates and false alarms and provide strong and adaptive protection. The real-life examples illustrate the ability of multimodal cybersecurity solutions to be used in healthcare, smart cities, industrial IoT, and financial applications [28,29].

7.8 Challenges and future research directions

Although the ML and DL methods have potential to secure multimodal databases, a number of challenges still exist, driving the new research. The heterogeneity of data is still a significant barrier since the combination of text, images, video, audio, and sensor streams can be achieved only with the help of complex preprocessing, representation learning, and fusion techniques. It is challenging to process high-dimensional, noisy, and incomplete data without compromising the quality of detection, especially in real-time Internet of Multimedia Things (IoMT) systems. Another problem is limited labeled data, particularly of novel types of attacks like deepfakes, cross-modal adversarial manipulations, and coordinated cyber threats. This requires the creation of unsupervised, semi-supervised, and self-supervised learning methods that are capable of generalizing to undiscovered attacks. Adversarial robustness is also an important requirement, with attackers using more and more vulnerabilities in ML/DL models to go undetected. Scalability and computational efficiency are also of interest to real-time deployment in distributed infrastructures of IoT with massive multimodal data streams. Also, privacy-saving approaches should be incorporated to safeguard sensitive data and allow effective model training and inference. Future research directions are to create adaptive and continuous learning structures to support changing threats, create explainable and interpretable multimodal models to increase trust, and investigate federated learning to enhance collaboration without jeopardizing the privacy of data. Future developments in cross-modal anomaly detection, hybrid fusion models, and the combination of quantum-inspired ML methods may further increase resilience. These issues will be vital in developing strong, scalable, and smart cybersecurity frameworks for multimodal IoMT ecosystems.

7.9 Conclusion

The Internet of Multimedia Things (IoMT) provides multimodal databases with immense possibilities of intelligent applications but difficult cybersecurity challenges because of the heterogeneous data streams, large dimensions, and cross-modal relationships. Conventional security systems that operate on rules are not good enough to detect advanced attacks like deepfakes, adversarial perturbation, and cross-modal data poisoning. Solutions based on machine learning (ML) and deep learning (DL) can be highly effective, as they allow identifying anomalies, detecting items, and monitoring them in real-time, using adaptive methods and data-driven results. Models supervised, unsupervised, and semi-supervised, plus CNNs, RNNs, Transformers, autoencoders, and generative models, are useful in modality-specific and cross-modal threat detection. Resilience is also improved by the data fusion strategies and cross-modality consistency checks, and reliability is ensured by the rigorous assessment based on the accuracy, precision, recall, and F1 score. Although the issues of scalability, robustness, and the availability of labeled data are serious, new studies in hybrid fusion, continual learning, and privacy-preserving ML have the potential to enhance security. In general, ML- and DL-based solutions cannot be neglected to protect multimodal IoMT ecosystems against emerging cyber threats.

References

[1] P. Y. Taşer and M. M. Taşer, "Multimodal machine learning in cybersecurity," *Innovative Artificial Intelligence*, vol. 1, no. 1, pp. 47–55, 2025.

[2] H. Attar, "Joint IoT/ML platforms for smart societies and environments: a review on multimodal information-based learning for safety and security," *ACM Journal of Data and Information Quality*, vol. 15, no. 3, pp. 1–26, 2023.

[3] T. E. Ali, Y.-W. Chong, and S. Manickam, "Comparison of ML/DL approaches for detecting DDoS attacks in SDN," *Applied Sciences*, vol. 13, no. 5, p. 3033, 2023.

[4] S. Nazim, M. M. Alam, S. Rizvi, J. C. Mustapha, S. S. Hussain, and M. M. Su'ud, "Multimodal malware classification using proposed ensemble deep neural network framework," *Scientific Reports*, vol. 15, no. 1, p. 18006, 2025.

[5] F. Yi, B. Jiang, L. Wang, and J. Wu, "Cybersecurity named entity recognition using multi-modal ensemble learning," *IEEE Access*, vol. 8, pp. 63214–63224, 2020.

[6] Xiaofeng Hou, Jiacheng Liu, Xuehan Tang *et al.*, "Architecting efficient multi-modal AIoT systems," in *Proceedings of the 50th Annual International Symposium on Computer Architecture*. 2023, pp. 1–13.

[7] Y. Yan, Y. Xie, Y. Li, Y. Yu, L. Lyu, and Y. Jin, "OutSafe-bench: a benchmark for multimodal offensive content detection in large language models," *arXiv preprint arXiv:2511.10287,* 2025.

[8] A. George and S. Marcel, "Heterogeneous face recognition with prepended domain transformers," in *Face Recognition Across the Imaging Spectrum*. Springer, 2024, pp. 169–204.

[9] S. Fan, A. Ahmed, X. Zeng, R. Xi, and M. Hou, "A personalized multimodal federated learning framework for skin cancer diagnosis," *Electronics*, vol. 14, no. 14, p. 2880, 2025.

[10] Z. Zheng, Z. Li, C. Huang, S. Long, and X. Shen, "Defending data poisoning attacks in DP-based crowdsensing: a game-theoretic approach," *IEEE Transactions on Mobile Computing*, vol. 24, no. 3, pp. 1859–1876, 2024.

[11] U. Inayat, M. F. Zia, S. Mahmood, H. M. Khalid, and M. Benbouzid, "Learning-based methods for cyber attacks detection in IoT systems: a survey on methods, analysis, and future prospects," *Electronics*, vol. 11, no. 9, p. 1502, 2022.

[12] A. K. Kassem, "Intelligent system using machine learning techniques for security assessment and cyber intrusion detection," Université d'Angers, 2021.

[13] A. Al-Abassi, H. Karimipour, A. Dehghantanha, and R. M. Parizi, "An ensemble deep learning-based cyber-attack detection in industrial control system," *IEEE Access*, vol. 8, pp. 83965–83973, 2020.

[14] Y. Zhou, M. Han, L. Liu, J. S. He, and Y. Wang, "Deep learning approach for cyberattack detection," in *IEEE INFOCOM 2018-IEEE Conference on Computer Communications Workshops (INFOCOM WKSHPS)*. IEEE, 2018, pp. 262–267.

[15] J. Zhang, L. Pan, Q.-L. Han, C. Chen, S. Wen, and Y. Xiang, "Deep learning based attack detection for cyber-physical system cybersecurity: a survey," *IEEE/CAA Journal of Automatica Sinica*, vol. 9, no. 3, pp. 377–391, 2021.

[16] S. Rani, A. Kataria, S. Kumar, and V. Karar, "A new generation cyber-physical system: a comprehensive review from security perspective," *Computers & Security*, vol. 148, p. 104095, 2025.

[17] S. Kumar, S. Rani, S. Sharma, and H. Min, "Multimodality fusion aspects of medical diagnosis: a comprehensive review," *Bioengineering*, vol. 11, no. 12, p. 1233, 2024.

[18] S. Rani, P. Bhambri, and M. Chauhan, "A machine learning model for kids' behavior analysis from facial emotions using principal component analysis," in *2021 5th Asian Conference on Artificial Intelligence Technology (ACAIT)*. IEEE, 2021, pp. 522–525.

[19] D. Mittal, H. Singh, and S. Rani, "Exploring explainable artificial intelligence techniques for hate speech detection," in *International Conference On Innovative Computing And Communication*. Springer, 2024, pp. 545–554.

[20] V. Puri, A. Kataria, S. Rani, and P. K. Pareek, "DLT based smart medical ecosystem," in *2023 International Conference on Network, Multimedia and Information Technology (NMITCON)*. IEEE, 2023, pp. 1–6.

[21] M. Chauhan and S. Rani, "Covid-19: a revolution in the field of education in India," in *Learning How to Learn Using Multimedia*. Springer, 2021, pp. 23–42.

[22] S. Rani, A. Kataria, P. Bhambri, P. K. Pareek, and V. Puri, "Artificial intelligence in personalized health services for better patient care," in *Revolutionizing Healthcare: AI Integration with IoT for Enhanced Patient Outcomes*. Springer, 2024, pp. 89–108.

[23] N. Gaw, S. Yousefi, and M. R. Gahrooei, "Multimodal data fusion for systems improvement: a review," *Handbook of Scholarly Publications from the Air Force Institute of Technology (AFIT), Volume 1, 2000–2020*, pp. 101–136, 2022.

[24] D. Lahat, T. Adali, and C. Jutten, "Multimodal data fusion: an overview of methods, challenges, and prospects," *Proceedings of the IEEE*, vol. 103, no. 9, pp. 1449–1477, 2015.

[25] J. Simanek, V. Kubelka, and M. Reinstein, "Improving multi-modal data fusion by anomaly detection," *Autonomous Robots*, vol. 39, no. 2, pp. 139–154, 2015.

[26] Paul Pu Liang, Yiwei Lyu, Xiang Fan *et al.*, "Multibench: multiscale benchmarks for multimodal representation learning," *Advances in Neural Information Processing Systems*, vol. 2021, no. DB1, p. 1, 2021.

[27] P. Bose, P. Rana, and P. Ghosh, "Attention-based multimodal deep learning on vision-language data: models, datasets, tasks, evaluation metrics and applications," *IEEE Access*, vol. 11, pp. 80624–80646, 2023.

[28] J. T. Aparicio, E. Arsenio, and R. Henriques, "Assessing robustness in multimodal transportation systems: a case study in Lisbon," *European Transport Research Review*, vol. 14, no. 1, p. 28, 2022.

[29] K. L. O'Halloran, G. Pal, and M. Jin, "Multimodal approach to analysing big social and news media data," *Discourse, Context & Media*, vol. 40, p. 100467, 2021.

Chapter 8

Privacy-preserving ML to safeguard multimodal data: Internet of Multimedia Things framework

Abstract

Internet of Multimedia Things (IoMMT) is a source of massive volumes of multimodals such as images, audio, text, and sensor streams, which are essential to intelligent applications in healthcare, smart cities, industrial Internet of Things, and autonomous systems. It is not easy to protect such sensitive information as it is heterogeneous and may be leaked during data collection, transmission, and analysis. Federated learning, differential privacy, homomorphic encryption, secure multiparty computation, split learning, and hybrid methods are privacy-preserving machine learning (PPML) techniques that can ensure secure multimodal data without affecting the model performance. The chapter discusses the main PPML techniques, privacy issues, threat models, and metrics of evaluation, as well as its use in practice and the current research trends in the development of powerful, scalable, and privacy-enhanced IoMMT systems.

Keywords: differential privacy; federated learning; homomorphic encryption; multimodal data; privacy-preserving machine learning

8.1 Introduction

The fast evolution of the Internet of Multimedia Things (IoMMT) has changed the ways in which images, videos, audio, sensor streams, and text-based data are captured, relayed, and processed among interconnected intelligent systems. With the emergence of multimodal data being the key to smart healthcare, surveillance, autonomous systems, and industrial monitoring, the question of its safety and privacy has become a burning problem. The traditional security solutions tend to fail in safeguarding large, diverse, and ever-growing data of IoMMT settings. Besides that, new risks are also introduced by the growing use of machine learning and deep learning models, such as model inversion, data leakage, and adversarial manipulation. Privacy-preserving machine learning (PPML) has the potential of providing effective solutions to protect multimodal data without interfering with the model's performance. Differential privacy, secure multiparty computation, federated learning, homomorphic encryption, and trusted execution environments are some of the techniques that enable sensitive data to be processed without violating confidentiality and integrity. The inclusion of these approaches into the structure of the IoMMT enhances data security at all levels, including acquisition, communication, storage, and analytics [1,2]. This chapter discusses the manner in which the PPML strategies can be developed and implemented in relation to the multimodal data security in the IoMMT systems. It outlines some critical challenges, architectural issues, and new research directions to construct secure, privacy-conscious, and intelligent multimedia ecosystems to deploy them in the real world.

8.2 Privacy challenges in multimodal IoMT systems

Multimodal Internet of Multimedia Things (IoMMT) systems gather and analyze various types of data: video, audio, text, biometrics, geolocation, and environmental sensor data. Although this rich data can be used to make smart decisions, it also brings a lot of privacy issues. Every modality has its own identifiers that may expose sensitive information about people even when the explicit personal data is eliminated. In particular, voice messages can tell about feelings or identity, and video frames can reveal the environment, actions, or health status. The high volume, ongoing, and decentralized character of the IoMMT data also contributes to the higher likelihood of malicious access and misuse. Information is frequently created at the edge and sent across networks and stored with cloud systems, creating several points of weakness. Attackers can use such pathways by means of eavesdropping, spoofing, model inversion, or data reconstruction. In addition, multimodal fusion (a combination of various data streams) has the risk of enhancing privacy due to the fact that cross-modal correlations can inadvertently unlock concealed user characteristics [3–5]. The conventional approaches of security, like simple encryption or access control, are not adequate since the Internet of Many Meters and Things applications demand real-time processing, low latency, and high accuracy. The privacy of such dynamic environments is a challenge, and it is hard to guarantee privacy when machine learning models themselves can be confidential sources of information. These issues underscore the necessity of more advanced privacy-aware ML systems that can be used to address multimodal IoMMT ecosystems. Table 8.1 presents various privacy challenges in multimodal IoMMT systems

8.3 Data protection techniques for multimodal data

The security of multimodal information in IoMMT systems needs sophisticated methods that can safeguard and secure assorted and delicate information. Differential privacy introduces controlled noise in order to break down the identification of individuals, and homomorphic encryption allows processing of encrypted data without revealing raw data. Federated learning enables model training on distributed devices and the data remains local limiting the risk of leakage. Secure multiparty computation is a collaboration-based analysis that does

Table 8.1 Summary of privacy challenges in multimodal IoMMT systems

Aspect	Key privacy challenge	Explanation
Data modalities	Modality-specific identifiers	Video, audio, biometrics, and location data can reveal identity, behavior, emotions, or health even without explicit personal data.
Data volume and continuity	Large-scale, continuous data streams	High volume and real-time data collection increase exposure and attack surface.
System architecture	Decentralized edge–cloud pipelines	Data generated at the edge, transmitted over networks, and stored in clouds creates multiple vulnerability points.
Attack vectors	Advanced privacy attacks	Risks include eavesdropping, spoofing, model inversion, and data reconstruction.
Multimodal fusion	Cross-modal privacy leakage	Combining modalities can unintentionally infer hidden or sensitive user attributes.
Traditional security	Insufficient protection	Basic encryption and access control fail to meet real-time, low-latency IoMMT requirements.
Machine learning models	Model-level information leakage	ML models themselves may expose sensitive information through training or inference.
Overall need	Advanced privacy-aware ML	Requires privacy-preserving, adaptive, and multimodal-aware ML frameworks.

not share private inputs. Protection through modalities like video, audio, and sensor streams is further enhanced by access control, blockchain-based authentication, and data anonymization. When combined, these approaches provide confidentiality, integrity, and secure analytics in multimodal settings [2,6,7].

8.3.1 Differential privacy

Differential privacy is a strong method that is aimed at securing sensitive data and still performing an effective analysis of the data. It operates by introducing noise to the data or query outputs in a predefined manner such that the existence or absence of any particular information on an individual cannot be detected. This is to make sure that no attacker with the extra background information can deduce any private information about particular users. The main advantage of differential privacy is that it is mathematically guaranteed, commonly via a parameter in privacy called epsilon (i.e., epsilon (epsilon)). Differential privacy is particularly useful in multimodal IoMMT systems since images, audio, and sensor data as modalities can include recognizable patterns. The use of differential privacy when collecting data, training the model, or inferring the data can minimize the chances of reidentification or leakage. As an illustration, adversaries cannot extract features that are associated with individuals due to the addition of noise to gradient updates during training. Likewise, privatized data aggregation enables analytics at a massive scale without exposing raw data. Nevertheless, it is difficult to keep the model utility high and, at the same time, provide high levels of privacy, especially with more complicated deep learning models. The choice of the right noise levels, the processing of high-dimensional data, and real-time performance are current research problems. Nevertheless, in spite of these obstacles, differential privacy is a pillar of multimodal data protection of sensitive information in smart IoMMT settings [8–10].

8.3.2 Homomorphic encryption

Homomorphic encryption (HE) is an improved cryptographic method that allows computation to be carried out on encrypted data without necessarily decrypting it. This implies that sensitive information is not exposed to any outside parties or abused during the processing pipeline. In HE, the input data and output of computation remain encrypted and only the authorized users who have the appropriate decryption key can obtain the final results in plaintext. HE is a key component in multimodal IoMMT systems to protect data, including images, audio streams, sensor readings, etc., which commonly need real-time or distributed processing. Encrypted data can be handled by cloud servers or edge devices performing tasks such as classification, aggregation, or pattern detection without compromising confidentiality even in untrusted environments. The insider attacks are also inhibited through HE because service providers cannot see or manipulate raw data. The weaknesses of HE include high computational overhead, implementation complexity, and support of deep learning operations, even though it has strong security benefits. Current research works on making the process more efficient by means of optimized schemes and hardware accelerators. Homomorphic encryption has potential to facilitate privacy-preserving analytics of multimodal IoMMT ecosystems [11,12].

8.3.3 Secure multiparty computation

Secure Multiparty Computation (SMPC) is a cryptographic method that allows multiple parties to collaboratively calculate an operation with their inputs but without revealing their inputs at all. The participants provide data that is either encrypted or secret-shared, so no other party is made aware of the data of the other party except for the final agreed outcome. SMPC offers high privacy assurances, which is why it is appropriate in the context of situations when data owners have to cooperate with each other without the possibility of exposing sensitive information. SMPC finds particular application in multimodal IoMMT systems, where there is a need to deal with distributed sensors, healthcare devices, smart cameras, and industrial machines, which produce various streams of data. As an illustration, a number of hospitals can jointly train a diagnostic model with images and sensor data without providing raw patient information. On the same note, collaborative threat detection may be conducted on smart city devices without compromising privacy [13]. SMPC assists in aggregation, inference, and statistical analysis of activities in untrusted or semi-

Table 8.2 Summarization of multimodal data protection techniques

Technique	Core idea	Key advantages	Limitations/ Challenges
Differential privacy	Adds controlled noise to data or query outputs to hide individual information.	Mathematical privacy guarantee, prevents reidentification, supports large-scale analytics.	Balancing privacy and model accuracy, selecting proper noise level, handling high-dimensional multimodal data.
Homomorphic encryption (HE)	Allows computations directly on encrypted data without decryption.	Strong confidentiality, protects against insider attacks, enables secure cloud analytics.	High computational overhead, complex implementation, limited efficiency for deep learning operations.
Secure Multiparty Computation (SMPC)	Multiple parties jointly compute results without revealing their individual inputs.	Strong privacy protection, secure collaboration across organizations, supports distributed analytics.	Computationally expensive, communication overhead, challenges with large-scale deep learning data.
Federated learning	Models are trained locally on devices and only model updates are shared.	Reduces data leakage risk, supports distributed environments, preserves data ownership.	Communication cost, heterogeneous device data, vulnerability to model update attacks.
Blockchain-based authentication and access control	Uses decentralized ledgers and permission systems to control data access.	Transparency, tamper resistance, improved trust among distributed devices.	Scalability issues, latency, and storage overhead.

trusted settings. The method is, however, computationally expensive, particularly when dealing with high-dimensional multimodal data and deep learning architectures. These limitations are being overcome with protocol efficiency and hybrid combinations with federated learning. In general, SMPC provides a powerful solution to privacy-saving analytics within the IoMMT ecosystems [14].

These data protection techniques are summarized in Table 8.2.

8.4 Privacy-preserving machine learning approaches

Privacy-preserving machine learning (PPML) allows training and inference of machine learning models without revealing sensitive multimodal data (shown in Figure 8.1). The most important methods are federated learning, where data is

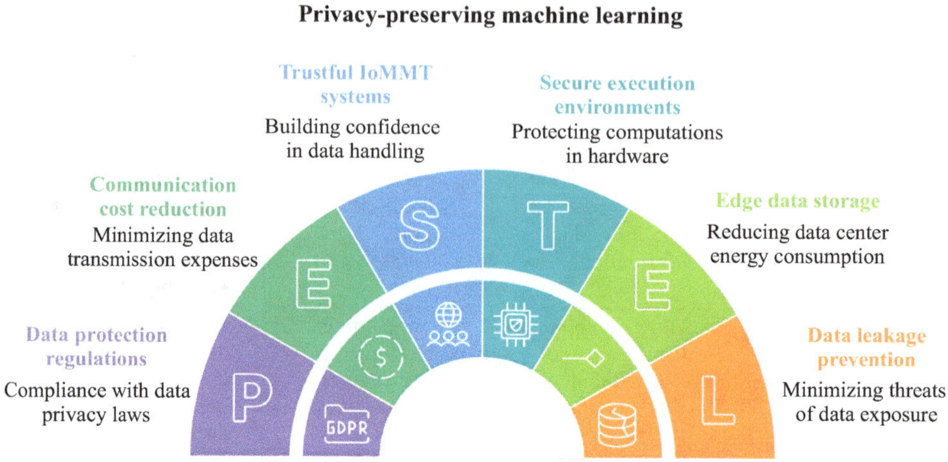

Figure 8.1 Privacy-preserving ML approaches

stored on local devices and only model updates are exchanged; differential privacy, where data is noised to avoid reidentification; and homomorphic encryption or secure multiparty computation, where data is encrypted or secret-shared. Secure execution environments also assure the protection of computations in secure hardware areas. All of these are able to minimize threats of data leakage, ensure safe collaboration, and preserve model utility in video, audio, text, and sensor modalities. The creation of trustful and privacy-conscious IoMMT systems will require the use of PPML [2].

8.4.1 Federated learning

Federated learning (FL) is a machine learning method where two or more devices or institutions can jointly learn using a common model without sharing raw data. Each device does not need to send sensitive multimodal information, like images, audio, and sensor streams, to a central server; instead, every device trains the model on the device and only sends model updates or gradients. The aggregation of these updates is done to enhance the global model without exposing personal information to any other party. FL is especially useful in multimodal IoMMT settings since information is produced by distributed smart devices, medical sensors, surveillance, and industrial equipment. Storing data at the edge, FL minimizes the risk of privacy, decreases the cost of communication, and allows data protection regulations to comply. It also reduces the possibility of data leakage from centralized repositories, which are usually the target of an attack. Non-uniform data distributions, unreliable connectivity, and threat of poisoned or manipulated updates are some challenges of federated learning, though. The combination of FL with differential privacy, secure aggregation, and trusted hardware is associated with enhanced protection. Nevertheless, federated learning continues to be among the most important approaches to secure, scalable, and privacy-sensitive analytics in IoMMT systems [15].

8.4.2 Split learning

Split learning (SL) is a type of machine learning that involves shared training with the model split across client devices and a central server, such that the central server does not receive raw data. In this method, the first layers of a network are executed on the client side and the rest of the layers are executed on the server. Instead of sending the original multimedial information, including images, audio, or sensor measurements, to the server, the client sends only intermediate activations to it. This is an effective way of guarding sensitive data since the features sent across cannot be easily reconstituted back to the original data. Split learning can be used in the multimodal IoMMT setting to the fullest extent of the devices with restricted computational capabilities, including wearables, smart cameras, or industrial sensors. It minimizes the consumption of memory and computations on edge devices and still allows deep learning on powerful backend servers. Split learning can be particularly useful in healthcare, surveillance, and smart home applications where privacy and resource limitations are essential factors. Risks of feature leakage, communication overhead, and gradient-based attack vulnerability are some of the challenges. Split learning can be used together with either differential privacy, encryption, or secure aggregation to increase security. In general, split learning provides a useful and privacy-conscious method of distributed multimodal learning in IoMMT systems.

8.4.3 Hybrid ML approaches

Hybrid machine learning methods are used to facilitate the combination of several privacy-preserving strategies to improve the security, efficiency, and model performance in multimodal IoMMT systems. Such solutions combine concepts of federated learning, split learning, differential privacy, secure multiparty computation, and homomorphic encryption to generate protection in multiple layers in data collection, processing, and model training phases. Hybrid solutions combine techniques that are complementary to each other and overcome the weaknesses of each technique, offering more robust and flexible privacy assurances. Hybrid ML has an especially important place in multimodal settings, where data of various types, including images, audio, text, sensor streams, etc., have specific privacy needs and computational limits. Indicatively, federated learning can be combined with differential privacy to guarantee that local model updates are decentralized and anonymous. Homomorphic encryption and split learning allow sharing encrypted intermediate features and reduce the workload of the devices. In the same manner, federated systems with SMPC enhancements enable different organizations to cooperate safely without disclosing proprietary datasets. Although they have benefits, hybrid approaches present the following challenges: complexity of systems, increased overhead of communication, and difficulty in coordinating distributed devices. These solutions require efficient algorithm development and optimization of protocols to ensure that they are practical. Hybrid ML is a potentially promising future of developing powerful, privacy-conscious multimodal IoMMT systems [2].

8.5 Feature engineering and data anonymization

The feature engineering and the data anonymization are critical to the security of multimodal data in the IoMMT systems. The aim of feature engineering is to encode raw data – images, audio recordings, text, and sensor streams – into valuable, compact representations that enable effective and secure machine learning. It minimizes exposing identifiable information by removing unneeded or sensitive data as well as extracting the appropriate features. Dimensionality reduction, embedding generation, signal filtering, and feature selection are some of the techniques that are applicable in ensuring that analytics are done using only privacy-safe and task-relevant information. Data anonymization is also improved to ensure protection because it eliminates or covers personally identifiable information (PII) prior to sharing or processing [16–22]. Typical ones are k-anonymity, l-diversity, t-closeness, generalization, suppression, and pseudonymization. Anonymization in a multimodal context can include blurring of faces in videos, voice manipulation, metadata removal, or GPS data smoothing. Together with feature engineering, anonymization can be used to minimize the risk of reidentification and still preserve the utility of the data. Nevertheless, multimodal data is problematic, as the correlation between modalities can accidentally or inadvertently identify concealed user characteristics, despite the anonymity. Good anonymization should thus take into consideration cross-modal leakage and balance privacy and model performance. In conclusion, feature engineering and anonymization are important processes in the development of privacy-conscious ML pipelines to ensure safe IoMMT ecosystems [23].

8.6 Threats and attack vectors in multimodal data

The heterogeneity of data processed by multimodal IoMMT systems is associated with a vast array of threats and attack vectors. All the modalities present their own vulnerabilities that can be exploited by attackers. As an example, video and image data can give identifiable attributes that can be used in face recognition attacks, whereas audio data can be targeted by voice cloning or inference of emotions and physiological conditions. Location, identity, or behavioral patterns may be leaked through textual and metadata information. Attackers may also intercept or modify multimodal data in transit at the system level (eavesdropping, spoofing, or man-in-the-middle attacks) [24]. Another threat is adversarial attacks, in which minor distortions are introduced on purpose to multimodal inputs to deceive machine learning algorithms. Model inversion and membership inference attacks are trying to recreate sensitive data or even to understand whether particular users were included in the training set. Cross-modal correlation attacks may also utilize a combination of information in order to reveal concealed interactions or re-identify anonymized users. The physical tampering, malware injection, and side-channel attacks are also prone to edge devices and IoMMT sensors, which are usually

Table 8.3 Summary of threats and attack vectors in multimodal IoMMT systems

Threat category	Attack vector	Description
Modality-specific attacks	Face recognition attacks	Video/image data expose identifiable facial and contextual attributes.
	Voice cloning and emotion inference	Audio data can reveal identity, emotions, and physiological states.
	Text and metadata leakage	Textual and metadata data expose location, identity, and behavior patterns.
Network-level attacks	Eavesdropping	Interception of multimodal data during transmission.
	Spoofing	Impersonation of legitimate devices or data sources.
	Man-in-the-middle (MitM)	Data interception and modification in transit.
ML model attacks	Adversarial attacks	Small crafted perturbations mislead multimodal ML models.
	Model inversion	Reconstruction of sensitive training data from model outputs.
	Membership inference	Identifying whether a user's data was used in training.
Cross-modal attacks	Correlation and reidentification	Fusion of modalities reveals hidden attributes or re-identifies anonymized users.
Device-level attacks	Physical tampering	Direct manipulation of edge devices and sensors.
	Malware injection	Insertion of malicious code into IoMMT devices.
	Side-channel attacks	Leakage through power, timing, or hardware signals.
System weaknesses	Poor authentication	Weak identity verification enables unauthorized access.
	Insecure APIs and encryption	Flawed interfaces and weak cryptography increase attack risk.
Overall impact	End-to-end privacy compromise	Threats span data collection, transmission, processing, and storage stages.

resource-constrained. Poor authentication, poor APIs, and poor encryption increase risks. They are critical in helping to understand the threats that influence the development of strong privacy-protecting mechanisms used to secure multimodal data throughout the entire IoMMT pipeline [25]. Table 8.3 presents various threats and attack vectors in multimodal IoMMT systems.

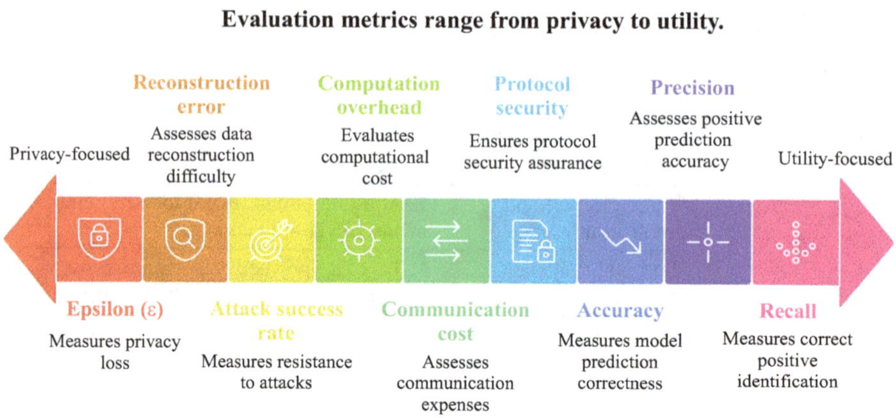

Figure 8.2 Benchmarks for privacy-preserving models

8.7 Evaluation metrics for privacy-preserving models

The assessment of privacy-saving models (shown in Figure 8.2) in multimodal IoMMT systems needs measures that can determine the efficiency of privacy protection and the quality of machine learning processes. Privacy measures are epsilon (ε) in differential privacy as a measure of loss of privacy; reconstruction error, which is the difficulty with which attackers can reconstruct original data; and the attack success rate, which is a measure of resistance to attack types, including model inversion, membership inference, and adversarial attacks. The cryptography methods are evaluated on the basis of computation overhead, communication cost, and protocol security assurance. On the utility side, conventional ML metrics, including accuracy, precision, recall, F1 score, and AUC, ensure that privacy methods do not negatively affect the model quality. In the case of multimodal data, the scores of cross-modal consistency and feature preservation are applied to assess the retention of necessary information between modalities. The metrics of efficiency, such as latency, power usage, and resource utilization, are essential to the IoMMT devices that have limited capabilities. It is necessary to strike a balance between privacy and utility; therefore, privacy–utility trade-off curves are commonly employed to compare various PPML methods. Collectively, these measures give an overall evaluation of the effectiveness of a privacy-preserving model on the safety of sensitive multimodal data and the feasibility of the system.

8.8 Case studies and applications

Privacy-saving methods are becoming more and more widespread in real-life multimodal IoMMT systems that help safeguard sensitive information and facilitate smart analytics. With smart healthcare, wearable sensors, medical imaging equipment, and patient monitoring systems produce continuous multimodal streams. Federated learning and differential privacy allow hospitals to jointly train diagnostic models, e.g., ECG classification or medical image analysis, without the transfer of raw patient data. This will maintain regulation such as HIPAA and enhance clinical decision-making. Smart cities have surveillance cameras, traffic sensors, and environmental monitors that gather video, audio, and geospatial data. Homomorphic encryption and secure multiparty computation enable the authorities to engage in crowd analytics, anomaly detection, and pollution surveillance without any identifiable information. Split learning is implemented in smart camera networks to do local processing of images and offload more complex computations safely to the cloud. Multimodal information from vibration sensors, thermal cameras, and machine logs is utilized in predictive maintenance in industrial IoT. To coordinate the work of factories without disclosing proprietary information, organizations use hybrid privacy-preserving ML, which is a combination of federated learning and secure aggregation. Multimodal fusion models are implemented in autonomous systems, where LIDAR, radar, vision, and GPS signals are used. Privacy-conscious models guarantee the safety of sensitive location and visual information and help to navigate safely and make real-time decisions.

8.9 Challenges and future research directions

Privacy-preserving machine learning of multimodal IoMMT systems has a number of difficulties because they are complicated, large-scale, and varied data. The fact that multimodal data fusion can often augment the threat of privacy leakage is due to the nature of the correlations between modalities in such a way that the presence of the hidden attributes of the user can be detected even when the streams are anonymized. High privacy levels with only slight deterioration of model accuracy are also not easy to achieve, particularly in the case of high-dimensional data, including videos, audio signals, and sensor arrays. Homomorphic encryption, SMPC, and federated learning are many privacy-preserving methods that pose computation and communication overhead, not suitable for resource-constrained IoMMT devices. Also, real-time applications need to be processed quickly and heavy cryptographic operations are difficult to scale. The future study should be aimed at developing light and efficient PPML algorithms specifically for edge devices. New hardware accelerators, secure chip architecture, and energy-conscious learning architecture will play a significant role. It requires new methods to deal with cross-modal privacy threats, learn to identify leakage in the multimodal fusion, and offer formal privacy assurances. A combination of differential privacy, federated learning, and secure computation hybrid methods can provide more protection with more utility. Lastly, the creation of standardized benchmarks, attack simulations, and assessment protocols will help in the establishment of more resilient, scalable, and more reliable privacy-preserving IoMMT ecosystems.

8.10 Conclusions

Privacy-preserving machine learning has come to play a crucial role in ensuring multimodal privacy in the Internet of Multimedia Things, where pictures, sounds, text, and sensor streams are constantly being created and processed. Conventional security protocols cannot be used to safeguard such a wide variety of information that is highly sensitive, particularly as the IoMMT systems are proliferating in healthcare, smart cities, industry, and autonomous platforms. With the combination of methods like federated learning, differential privacy, homomorphic encryption, secure multiparty computation, split learning, and hybrid ML, companies might obtain high privacy guarantees without negatively affecting model performance. Although significant improvement has been made, privacy–utility trade-off, computational overhead, and cross-modal leakage are still issues. The innovation should be sustained to generate lightweight, scalable, and context-driven privacy solutions, which can be used in real-time IoMMT applications. Privacy-preserving machine learning will be the core of constructing safe, viable, and smart multimodal ecosystems that would safeguard user data and undermine the complete potential of IoMMT technologies.

References

[1] H. Sahu, N. Joshi, and S. V. Chande, "Security and privacy preservation of multimedia objects over the Internet of Multimedia of Things (IoMT)," in *International Conference on Emerging Trends in Expert Applications & Security*. Springer, 2024, pp. 1–21.

[2] Qingzhi Liu, Yuchen Huang, Chenglu Jin *et al.*, "Privacy and integrity protection for IoT multimodal data using machine learning and blockchain," *ACM Transactions on Multimedia Computing, Communications and Applications*, vol. 20, no. 6, pp. 1–18, 2024.

[3] A. Mabina, N. Rafifing, B. Seropola, T. Monageng, and P. Majoo, "Challenges in IoMT adoption in healthcare: focus on ethics, security, and privacy," *Journal of Information Systems and Informatics*, vol. 6, no. 4, pp. 3162–3184, 2024.

[4] D. T. Aga and M. Siddula, "Enhanced distributed multimodal federated learning framework for privacy-preserving IoMT applications: E-DMFL," *Electronics*, vol. 14, no. 20, p. 4024, 2025.

[5] Y. Jiao, M. M. Razaq, L. Peng, and P.-H. Ho, "Enhancing IoMT security using large multimodal models," *IEEE Network*, vol. 39, no. 4, pp. 112–119, 2025.

[6] Z. Chen, J. Shuai, F. Tian, W. Li, S. Zang, and X. Zhang, "An improved privacy protection algorithm for multimodal data fusion," *Scientific Programming*, vol. 2022, no. 1, p. 4189148, 2022.

[7] S. Kumar, M. K. Chaube, S. N. Nenavath, S. K. Gupta, and S. K. Tetarave, "Privacy preservation and security challenges: a new frontier multimodal

machine learning research," *International Journal of Sensor Networks*, vol. 39, no. 4, pp. 227–245, 2022.

[8] Z. Lu, B. Wang, and N. Ouyang, "Application of differential privacy technology in multi-modal data sharing," *International Journal of Intelligent Information and Database Systems*, vol. 17, no. 3–4, pp. 340–360, 2025.

[9] C. Cai, Y. Sang, and H. Tian, "A multimodal differential privacy framework based on fusion representation learning," *Connection Science*, vol. 34, no. 1, pp. 2219–2239, 2022.

[10] H. Yang, L. Fu, Q. Lu, Y. Fan, T. Zhang, and R. Wang, "Research on the design of a short video recommendation system based on multimodal information and differential privacy," in *Proceedings of the 2025 4th International Conference on Cyber Security, Artificial Intelligence and the Digital Economy*, 2025, pp. 45–52.

[11] D. K. Vallabhadas and M. Sandhya, "Securing multimodal biometric template using local random projection and homomorphic encryption," *Journal of Information Security and Applications*, vol. 70, p. 103339, 2022.

[12] Z. Li, Y. Sang, X. Deng, and H. Tian, "Lightweight and efficient privacy-preserving multimodal representation inference via fully homomorphic encryption," in *Asian Conference on Intelligent Information and Database Systems*. Springer, 2023, pp. 307–321.

[13] V. S. Naresh, A. Venkata Raju, and O. Srinivasa Rao, "Secure multiparty computation for privacy-preserving machine learning in healthcare: a comprehensive survey," *Wiley Interdisciplinary Reviews: Computational Statistics*, vol. 17, no. 3, p. e70046, 2025.

[14] I. Zhou, F. Tofigh, M. Piccardi, M. Abolhasan, D. Franklin, and J. Lipman, "Secure multi-party computation for machine learning: a survey," *IEEE Access*, vol. 12, pp. 53881–53899, 2024.

[15] C. Feng, D. Feng, G. Huang, Z. Liu, Z. Wang, and X.-G. Xia, "Robust privacy-preserving recommendation systems driven by multimodal federated learning," *IEEE Transactions on Neural Networks and Learning Systems*, vol. 36, no. 5, pp. 8896–8910, 2024.

[16] E. Gachanga, M. Kimwele, and L. Nderu, "Feature based data anonymization for high dimensional data," *Journal of Information Engineering and Applications*, vol. 9, no. 2, pp. 12–21, 2019.

[17] S. Rani, A. Kataria, S. Kumar, and V. Karar, "A new generation cyber-physical system: a comprehensive review from security perspective," *Computers & Security*, vol. 148, p. 104095, 2025.

[18] S. Kumar, S. Rani, S. Sharma, and H. Min, "Multimodality fusion aspects of medical diagnosis: a comprehensive review," *Bioengineering*, vol. 11, no. 12, p. 1233, 2024.

[19] D. Mittal, H. Singh, and S. Rani, "Exploring explainable artificial intelligence techniques for hate speech detection," in *International Conference on Innovative Computing and Communication*. Springer, 2024, pp. 545–554.

[20] V. Puri, A. Kataria, S. Rani, and P. K. Pareek, "DLT based smart medical ecosystem," in *2023 International Conference on Network, Multimedia and Information Technology (NMITCON)*. IEEE, 2023, pp. 1–6.

[21] M. Chauhan and S. Rani, "Covid-19: a revolution in the field of education in India," in *Learning How to Learn Using Multimedia*. Springer, 2021, pp. 23–42.

[22] S. Rani, A. Kataria, P. Bhambri, P. K. Pareek, and V. Puri, "Artificial intelligence in personalized health services for better patient care," in *Revolutionizing Healthcare: AI Integration with IoT for Enhanced Patient Outcomes*. Springer, 2024, pp. 89–108.

[23] E. Shamsinejad, T. Banirostam, M. M. Pedram, and A. M. Rahmani, "A review of anonymization algorithms and methods in big data," *Annals of Data Science*, vol. 12, no. 1, pp. 253–279, 2025.

[24] N. Ghose, L. Lazos, J. Rozenblit, and R. Breiger, "Multimodal graph analysis of cyber attacks," in *2019 Spring Simulation Conference (SpringSim)*. IEEE, 2019, pp. 1–12.

[25] Kavita, G. S. Walia, and R. Rohilla, "A contemporary survey of multimodal presentation attack detection techniques: challenges and opportunities," *SN Computer Science*, vol. 2, no. 1, p. 49, 2021.

Chapter 9

Deep learning with blockchain to deploy secure multimodal smart city applications

Abstract

Smart cities are quickly becoming data-driven environments that are dependent on intelligent technologies to make cities efficient and their citizens happy. In this chapter, the author introduces a comprehensive concept of deep learning and blockchain that will be used to secure and improve multimodal smart city applications. It explores the heterogeneity issues of Internet of Multimedia Things (IoMT) data, such as security, privacy, and trust, and shows how deep learning can facilitate intelligent analysis by means of feature extraction, multimodal fusion, and real-time decision-making. Data integrity and transparency, as well as decentralized governance, are guaranteed by blockchain and secure access control and policy automation through smart contracts. It is also in this chapter that mechanisms of identity and trust management, secure data and model management, and privacy are discussed. Applied benefits are demonstrated by use cases in surveillance, transportation, and energy management, whereas challenges and future research discussions provide a basis for secure, resilient, and intelligent urban ecosystems.

Keywords: artificial intelligence (AI); blockchain technology (BCT); deep learning (DL); Internet of Multimedia Things (IoMT); multimodal data analysis (MDA); smart city applications (SCA)

9.1 Introduction to secure multimodal smart cities

Secure multimodal smart cities combine data of various types, including sensors and cameras, social media, and IoT devices, to provide witty urban services. The Internet of Multimedia Things creates large volumes of heterogeneous data that can be used to build surveillance, transportation, energy management, and public safety applications. Nevertheless, multimodal data is sensitive and distributed, which creates serious security, privacy, and trust issues. Deep learning gives the tool high capabilities in multimodal data analysis and decision-making, whereas blockchain is decentralized, transparent, and resistant to tampering. They can be integrated to provide secure, trustworthy, and scalable smart city ecosystems, which can provide real-time intelligence and resilient data management [1].

9.1.1 Smart cities and IoMT

Smart cities are cities that use the best digital technologies to improve the efficiency, sustainability, and quality of life in the city. The Internet of Multimedia Things (IoMT) is the central concept of smart cities that links heterogeneous devices including cameras, microphones, sensors, wearables, and smart infrastructure. These sensors produce multimodal data such as video, audio, image, and sensor streams continuously to enable smart services, such as traffic tracking, environmental sensing, and the health and safety of the people. IoMT allows situational awareness and data-driven decision-making in distributed cities in real-time. Nevertheless, the scale, heterogeneity, as well as dynamism of the IoMT systems present challenges with regard to interoperability, data management, security, and privacy. To provide reliable operation and trust among citizens, it is necessary to address the challenges. The proper incorporation of IoMT in smart cities is the basis of smart, connected, and responsive cities [2–4].

9.1.2 Motivation for DL–blockchain integration

Deep learning and blockchain are integrated due to the necessity to meet the security, trust, and scalability issues of a multimodal smart city setting. Deep learning is very effective in identifying valuable patterns in high-dimensional, multimodal data, which are complex and thus accurate prediction, recognition, and decision-making are possible. Nevertheless, big data and deep learning models are susceptible to data manipulation, data access control, and model integrity attacks since they are based on extensive amounts of distributed data. Blockchain is a complement of deep learning, as it offers decentralization, data integrity, transparent transactions, and trustless stakeholder coordination. Smart contracts make automated access control and data sharing possible and model validation without the use of centralized authorities. DL and blockchain combined form a safe and reliable system that guarantees data integrity, provenance, and accountability as well as enables real-time intelligent services. This synergy plays a vital role in implementing reliable, privacy-conscious, and scalable smart city applications [5,6].

9.2 Multimodal data and security challenges

There are several sources of multimodal data in smart cities, including video surveillance, audio sensors, text streams, and IoT devices, which can provide complete situational awareness and allow for intelligent decision-making. Although the combination of different data modalities enhances system accuracy and resiliency, it also makes systems more complex and more vulnerable to security attacks. Multimodal data can be sensitive, disseminated, and constantly produced, which can be subject to cyberattacks, data leakage, spoofing, and breaches of privacy. Heterogeneity, scalability, and real-time requirements make it difficult to ensure secure data collection, transmission, storage, and access. These security issues are critical in the establishment of credible and dependable multimodal smart city systems [7,8].

9.2.1 Data modalities in smart cities

Smart cities are based on diverse data modalities to provide intelligent and context-sensitive urban services. Surveillance cameras and traffic surveillance assist in the provision of visual data that aids in protecting the populace, managing congestion, and detecting incidents. Sound information provided by microphones facilitates the use of audio data in noise pollution detection and event detection. Environmental, energy, and infrastructure sensors are sensor data, which give real-time data on the air quality, weather, power use, and the health of the structure [9]. Social media data, reports, and citizen feedback include textual information that can provide information about the mood of the population and current events. Also, GPS-enabled devices provide geospatial and mobility data, which are used in navigation, logistics, and city planning. Situational awareness and decision-making are boosted by the combination of these dissimilar modalities. Nonetheless, to handle a wide range of data types, different sampling rates, and distributed data, more sophisticated data fusion, storage, and processing algorithms are needed to achieve the potential of smart city ecosystems to the full extent [7,10]. Figure 9.1 presents the various types of data modalities in a smart city ecosystem.

9.2.2 Threats and privacy risks

The sheer size of the implementation of interconnected IoMT devices and the constant production of multimodal data expose smart city ecosystems to multifarious security risks, as well as privacy risks. Data tampering, eavesdropping, spoofing, malware injection, and denial-of-service attacks are common cyber threats to sensors,

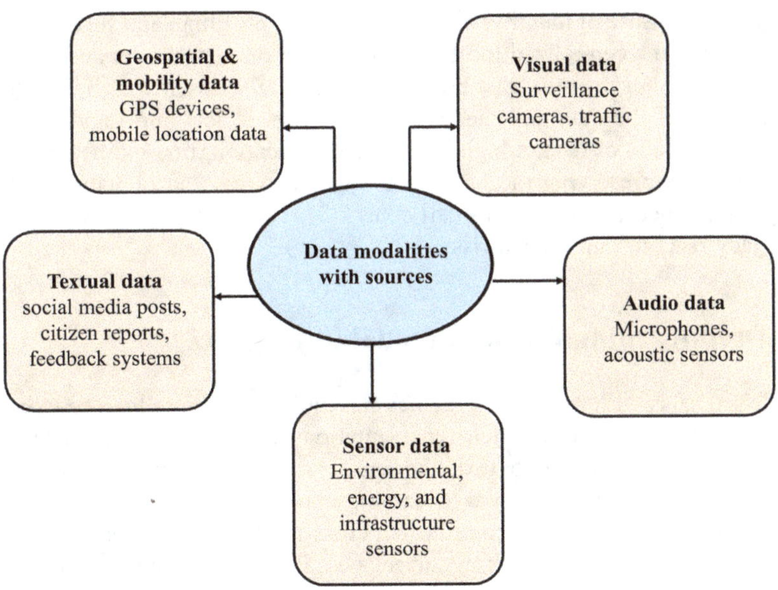

Figure 9.1 Various data modalities in the smart city framework

Table 9.1 Summary of threats and privacy risks

Category	Key issues	Impact on smart cities
Cyber threats	Data tampering, eavesdropping, spoofing, malware, DoS attacks	Incorrect analytics, unsafe decisions in traffic, surveillance, and emergency systems
Device and network vulnerabilities	Compromised sensors, networks, and cloud platforms	Injection of fake data and system disruptions
Privacy risks	Exposure of video, audio, location, and behavioral data	Identity inference, tracking, profiling, and mass surveillance
Centralized data storage	Single point of failure	Large-scale data breaches and loss of control
Lack of transparency	Unclear data usage and model decisions	Ethical concerns and regulatory noncompliance
Security gaps	Weak authentication and access control	Reduced trust and accountability in smart city services

communication networks, and cloud platforms. Hacked machines are able to alter or add fake data, which creates erroneous analytics and potentially harmful decision-making in other applications like traffic control, emergency response, and surveillance. The risk of privacy is also of utmost significance because multimodal data usually include sensitive personal data based on video streams, audio tapes, location history, and behavioral patterns [11]. Lack of authorized access or misuse of data might result in misuse of identity, inference, tracking, profiling, and surveillance. The storage of data in a centralized location and the lack of control over access only add to the probability of massive data breaches. Besides, the absence of transparency in the utilization of the data and model choices brings ethical and regulatory issues. Secure transmission of data, a high level of authentication, fine-grained access control, and privacy-preserving mechanisms to guarantee trust, accountability, and regulatory compliance are needed in smart cities [12]. Table 9.1 presents various threats and privacy risks in multimodal risks.

9.3 Deep learning for multimodal intelligence

Deep learning is at the core of achieving multimodal intelligence (shown in Figure 9.2) through learning rich representations of heterogeneous data streams including images, video, audio, text, and sensor streams. In contrast to conventional machine learning algorithms, deep learning models have the ability to extract hierarchical features and learn complicated cross-modal correlations automatically. Convolutional Neural Networks, recurrent neural networks, and transformers are architectures that enable modality-specific processing and cross-modal fusion. Deep learning is applicable in a smart city setting to provide applications such as

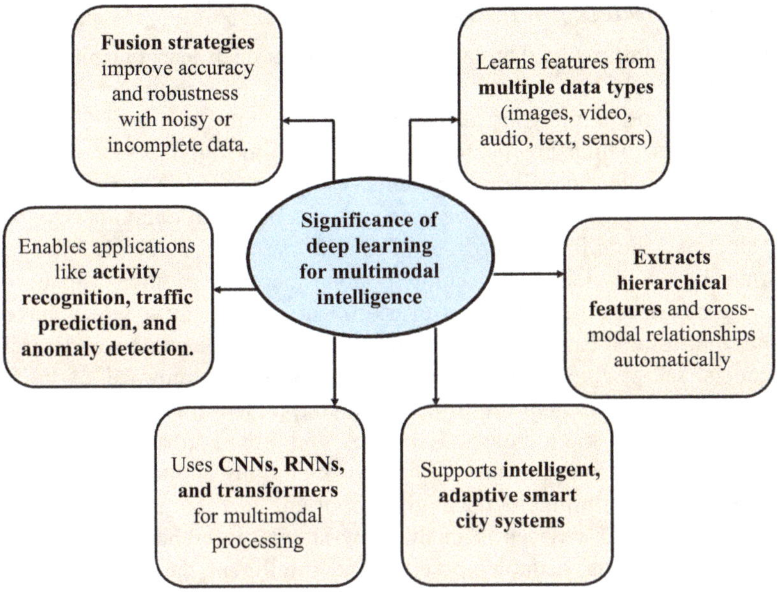

Figure 9.2 Deep learning as a key player in multimodal intelligence

activity recognition, traffic prediction, anomaly detection, and situational awareness. Multimodal fusion strategies at feature, decision, or representation levels enhance robustness and accuracy in the case of noisy or incomplete data. Nonetheless, multimodal intelligence implementation of deep learning takes into account the issues of scalability, real-time processing, data quality, and security. Well-constructed deep learning systems can offer strong intelligence capabilities that are necessary to smart city systems based on data and are flexible and responsive [13,14].

9.3.1 Feature learning and fusion

The key to successful multimodal intelligence is feature learning and fusion because it provides an opportunity to combine heterogeneous sources of data into a single one. To apply deep learning models based on CNNs, RNNs, or transformers and embedding models to extract meaningful and discriminative patterns of each modality, feature learning is performed. These modality-specific features are then fused together to give cross-modal relationships. The typical strategies of fusion are early fusion, occurring at the feature level, and late fusion, occurring at the decision level, or a combination of the two, between deep network layers. Attention processes also improve fusion by prioritizing the significance of various modalities depending on the situation. The use of smart cities demands that feature learning and fusion enhance system robustness, accuracy, and resistance to missing and noisy data. Such methods are critical toward attaining the overall situational awareness and sound decision-making in complicated urban settings [15].

9.3.2 Deep models for IoMT

The Internet of Multimedia Things extensively uses deep learning models to process multimodal data of scale, heterogeneous data, and continuously generated data. Image and video analytics are common tasks with the use of Convolutional Neural Networks, which are useful in traffic monitoring, face recognition, and anomaly detection in surveillance systems. Long Short-Term Memory networks and recurrent neural networks can be used on sequential and temporal data, such as sensor streams, mobility patterns, and audio patterns. Recently, the use of transformer-based models has become popular because of their capabilities to model long-range dependencies and cross-modal relationships, which have been applied to multimodal fusion and real-time analytics. Autoencoders and variational autoencoders are also used in dimensionality reduction, removal of noise, and identification of anomalies in the IoMT data. Graph Neural Networks are a model of relations between interconnected devices and urban infrastructure, allowing spatial-temporal reasoning in smart city networks. Lightweight and edge-optimised deep models are becoming increasingly important for energy-efficient and fast resource-limited IoMT devices to enable low-latency inference. Combined, these deep models allow the scalable, precise, and intelligent data processing of the multimedia information in smart cities [16–19].

9.4 Blockchain for security and trust

The blockchain offers a decentralized and unalterable system of maintaining security and trust in distributed smart cities (summarized in Table 9.2). Through its unalterable record of transactions, blockchain eliminates the potential of

Table 9.2 Blockchain for secure smart cities

Aspect	Description
Purpose	Provides a decentralized and tamper-resistant system to ensure security and trust in smart city environments.
Key feature	Immutable transaction records prevent unauthorized data manipulation and improve transparency.
Security mechanisms	Uses cryptography for data integrity, authentication, and non-repudiation.
Consensus mechanism	Enables trustless coordination among distributed nodes without centralized control.
Applications in IoMT	Supports secure data sharing, device authentication, and access control across heterogeneous networks.
Smart contracts	Automate security policies and trust management processes.
Overall benefit	Establishes a secure, transparent, and reliable foundation for multimodal smart city applications.

inappropriate manipulation of data and improves transparency between various interested parties. Cryptographic schemes guarantee data integrity, authentication, and non-repudiation, and consensus schemes allow trustless coordination without the use of centralized authorities. The blockchain is also used to facilitate the secure sharing of data, authentication of devices, and access control in heterogeneous networks. Smart contracts also automate the security policies and trust management. Consequently, blockchain creates a stable basis for creating secure, transparent, and trustworthy multimodal smart city applications [20].

9.4.1 Blockchain architecture

A blockchain architecture is a decentralized architecture that is aimed at secure, transparent, and tamper-resistant data management. It is made up of a distributed registry that is stored in several nodes, with each block holding a list of transactions, a timestamp, and a cryptographic hash connecting it to the preceding block. This chain of structure makes it immutable, and any change in any block cannot be made by the majority of the nodes. Transactions are validated by consensus mechanisms, which include Proof of Work, Proof of Stake, or Practical Byzantine Fault Tolerance, and do not require a centralized authority. Cryptographic methods, such as the use of public–private key encryption and digital signatures, offer authentication, data integrity, and non-repudiation. There are some other layers like peer-to-peer networks, smart contracts, and permissioned access control that increase scalability, automation, and security. The blockchain architecture is used in smart city applications to share data among IoMT devices safely, implement traceability, and decentralize trust management, which is the basis of resilient and transparent multimodal intelligence systems.

9.4.2 Smart contracts and access control

Smart contracts are self-executing applications that are implemented on blockchain networks, which automatically apply pre-established rules and agreements and do not need intermediaries. They deliver a secure access control mechanism, data sharing as well as automated transactions between IoMT devices, service providers, and stakeholders in smart city settings. Multimodal data integrity and privacy are guaranteed since only authorized parties can access or manipulate smart contracts containing security policies and authorization rules. As an example, a smart contract may control the access of surveillance images, sensor measurements, or citizen information and provide access permissions based on roles, attributes, or preset conditions. Fine-grained, dynamic, and auditable policies implemented in access control frameworks with the aid of smart contracts are essential to heterogeneous and distributed IoMT networks [21]. The permissioned blockchains are selective, and only trusted nodes can validate transactions or access sensitive data. Smart contracts and blockchain make it transparent, accountable, and resistant to tampering, with each request to access and any transaction being stored in the ledger in a way that cannot be altered. This will decrease the need to use centralized authorities, control insider threats, and improve trust among various stakeholders. All in all, smart contracts are an automated, secure, and scalable solution to access control enforcement and data governance in multimodal smart city applications [22,23].

9.5 Integrated DL–blockchain framework

A decentralized framework of deep learning and blockchain is used to integrate the predictive intelligence of deep learning with the decentralized security of blockchain to support trustworthy multimodal smart city applications. The analysis of heterogeneous data in IoMT can be used to perform the following tasks: anomaly detection, traffic prediction, and situational awareness with the use of deep learning models, whereas blockchain can guarantee the integrity, provenance, and unauthorized sharing of data among distributed devices and stakeholders. Smart contracts also help to automate access control and enforce policies, which minimizes the use of centralized authorities. The integration tackles the issues of data tampering, privacy violations, and model integrity and offers a scalable, transparent, and resilient platform to enable real-time decision-making in secure and intelligent urban settings [24,25].

9.5.1 System architecture

An integrated deep learning-blockchain system architecture is developed to integrate intelligent data processing with decentralized security of smart city applications. At the data layer, heterogeneous multimodal data is gathered, including images, video, audio, sensor measurements, and textual information, which are the outputs of IoMT devices that are distributed in urban areas. These data are preprocessed and sent on secure communication channels to edge or cloud computing nodes to undergo real-time analysis. The deep learning layer is used to extract features, process each modality in a specific way, and combine different modalities with models like CNNs, RNNs, transformers, or Graph Neural Networks. Projections, anomaly identification, or decision results are produced to serve applications such as traffic control, community safety, energy control, and environmental surveillance. The blockchain layer ensures the integrity of the data, its transparency, and trust as the transactions, model updates, and access logs are registered on a distributed ledger. Smart contracts provide automatic access control, authorization policies, and secure data sharing among the various stakeholders. The validation of transactions is done by consensus mechanisms, and authenticity and non-repudiation of data are guaranteed by the use of cryptographic techniques. Such an architecture enables a secure, scalable, and auditable framework, which enables deep learning models to run on reliable data and allows decentralized governance. It guarantees end-to-end security, real-time intelligence, and accountability in multimodal smart cities.

9.5.2 Secure data and model management

An integrated DL–blockchain framework that ensures the confidentiality, integrity, and availability of multimodal smart city data and AI models is provided through secure data and model management. IoMT device data is encrypted throughout transmission and storage, and blockchain logs have incontrovertible provenance and access history, which can be used to trace and hold accountable. Smart contracts provide access control on a more fine-grained level, with only authorized users or devices being able to read, write, or update data. In the case of deep learning models, secure management is to prevent tampering or adversarial attacks on model parameters, updates, and training datasets. Blockchain can be used to integrate federated learning or edge-based model updates that can be trusted to ensure integrity of distributed nodes and decentralized model training. The audit trails in the ledger enable the stakeholders to monitor the provenance and performance of the models and minimize the chances of malicious modifications. Altogether, a secure data and model management system combines encryption, access control, blockchain immutability, and decentralized learning to create a strong base of reliable, privacy-sensitive, and resilient smart city applications.

9.6 Security and privacy mechanisms

Multimodal smart cities employ security and privacy mechanisms, which involve the use of cryptography, access control, and trust management to safeguard sensitive IoMT data. These are encryption, anonymization, verification of identities, and role-based or attribute-based access control. Smart contracts carry out secure policies automatically, blockchain provides immutability and transparency, and blockchain technologies are utilized to secure contracts. Collectively, these systems ensure data integrity, prevent unauthorized access, and maintain privacy, which allows trustworthy, robust, and compliant deep learning-based smart city application operation [1,26].

9.6.1 Identity and trust management

Identity and trust management: This is an essential element of securing multimodal smart city applications. Identity management is a method that guarantees that all IoMT devices, users, and stakeholders are uniquely authenticated to gain access to data or services. Digital certificates, public–private key encryption, and decentralized identifiers (DID) are some of the techniques that guarantee efficient authentication and eliminate impersonation attacks. Trust management is a method of analyzing the behavior and reliability of devices, nodes, and network participants. Blockchain is important as it keeps records of interactions, transactions, and updates in the model, which are immutable and allow verifiable trust measurements. The reputation systems and consensus mechanisms also increase trust by punishing bad participants and rewarding good behavior. In combined DL–blockchain systems, identity and trust management collaboratively regulate access and data integrity and help in collaborative decision-making. These mechanisms will form a trustworthy, auditing, and robust base to deploy intelligent and privacy-aware smart city applications in distributed and heterogeneous IoMT networks by offering secure authentication, continuous monitoring, and transparent verification.

9.6.2 Data protection techniques

The security and reliability of multimodal smart city systems largely rely on data protection, especially in IoMT setting, where sensitive information is constantly being produced by cameras, sensors, audio equipment, and textual data. Good protection methods guarantee confidentiality, integrity, and availability, which reduce threats of unauthorized access, tampering, and breach of privacy. One of such key mechanisms is encryption, which involves converting data into non-readable forms by using symmetric or asymmetric cryptographic keys. End-to-end encryption secures the data when transmitting between the IoMT devices, edge nodes, and cloud servers, and storage encryption secures the datasets at rest. Homomorphic encryption also enables computations to be done on encrypted data without exposing raw data, which makes privacy-preserving analytics possible. Anonymization and pseudonymization methods minimize the chance of identity disclosure due to the removal or obscuration of personally identifiable information, especially in video, audio, or location-based data. Differential privacy adds controlled noise to the data or the output of the model, which offers statistical privacy guarantees but preserves analytical utility. These are access control mechanisms that are usually implemented through smart contracts in a blockchain that govern the entities that can read, write, or modify data depending on the roles, attributes, or contextual policies. Audit trails and unchangeable blockchain records are also a source of transparency and accountability, allowing one to verify each access or change. Moreover, secure model management such as federated learning is used to make sure sensitive local data is not sent to the edge device, but only the model updates are sent in an encrypted and verifiable form. Together, these methods form a multimodal defense architecture that prevents cyberattacks on multimodal data and helps maintain privacy regulations, as well as fosters trust in the smart city applications.

Various data protection techniques are summarized in Table 9.3.

9.7 Smart city applications and use cases

Applications of smart cities make use of multimodal data and intelligent technologies to improve life in cities and make them efficient and safer. Cities are able to monitor, analyze, and act in line with real-time occurrences in various areas by incorporating IoMT devices, deep learning, and blockchain. Its uses include smart surveillance as a measure of safety in the community, traffic control to enable efficient transportation, energy control to help in efficient consumption, and environmental sensors to monitor pollution. Multimodal data fusion enhances the accuracy of the decision made, and blockchain guarantees the integrity of the data along with its secure sharing and trustworthiness of the stakeholders. These applications show how safe, fact-based, and smart systems can deliver urban management to ensure cities are more responsive, resilient, and citizen-oriented [3,27–29].

Table 9.3 Various data protection techniques

Technique	Purpose	Key features/benefits
Encryption (symmetric and asymmetric)	Ensure data confidentiality	Converts data into unreadable form; protects data in transit and at rest
End-to-end encryption	Secure data transmission	Protects data between IoMT devices, edge nodes, and cloud servers
Homomorphic encryption	Privacy-preserving computation	Enables computation on encrypted data without revealing raw data
Anonymization and pseudonymization	Prevent identity disclosure	Removes or masks personally identifiable information (PII)
Differential privacy	Statistical privacy protection	Adds controlled noise while preserving analytical utility
Access control (blockchain-based)	Regulate data access	Smart contracts enforce role-, attribute-, and context-based permissions
Audit trails and immutable logs	Transparency and accountability	Blockchain records enable traceability and tamper resistance
Federated learning	Secure model management	Keeps data local; only encrypted model updates are shared
Multimodal defense architecture	Overall system security	Integrates multiple techniques to ensure confidentiality, integrity, and availability

9.7.1 Surveillance and public safety

The smart city surveillance and public safety applications are based on the multimodal data of CCTV cameras, drones, microphones, sensors, and social media to track the urban areas in real time. Deep learning models are used to check video and audio streams to detect anomalies, crowds, faces, and suspicious behaviors and detect emergency situations. Blockchain guarantees integrity and provenance of collected data and avoids tampering and unauthorized access, and smart contracts ensure secure and auditable access control by various stakeholders. Such combined technologies will allow prompt alerts, effective resource distribution, and coordinated response in case of an emergency, which will improve the overall level of safety of the population, the effectiveness of law enforcement, and urban security.

9.7.2 Transportation and energy

Smart cities use multimodal IoMT data in transportation and energy to achieve efficient transportation and cost-cutting and enhance sustainability. In the transport sector, traffic prediction, congestion, route optimization, and autonomous vehicle coordination are traffic forecasting tasks run through deep learning on traffic data gathered by traffic cameras, GPS, sensors, and social media. In the case of energy systems, smart meters, renewable energy, and IoT-enabled infrastructure, data can be used to monitor data in real-time, balance the demand and supply, and identify faults. Blockchain also provides secure, transparent, and tamper-proof sharing of data among the stakeholders, and smart contracts facilitate billing, access control, and energy trading. Combined, these technologies allow smart, resilient, and energy-efficient urban transport and energy control, in favor of sustainable and adaptable urban processes.

9.8 Challenges and future directions

The introduction of multimodal smart city applications using integrated deep learning-blockchain solutions has a number of challenges. One of its major issues is scalability because IoMT networks create large, heterogeneous, and high-velocity data that need to be processed in real-time. The edge devices have resource limitations such as limited computational power, storage, and energy, which are challenges to deploying complex deep learning models. The applications that are sensitive to latency, like traffic control or emergency response, require optimized communication and processing pipelines. Privacy and regulation are also under the spotlight as sensitive multimodal data needs to be preserved and collaborative analytics should be allowed. The other challenge is to ensure interoperability of heterogeneous devices, networks, and standards, especially in integrating varied data sources and blockchain platforms. Moreover, the computation and latency costs of blockchain can be incompatible with real-time needs, and lightweight consensus algorithms or hybrid designs are necessary. The future research directions entail the development of scalable, energy-efficient, and privacy-preserving deep learning models, which are specific to the edge and IoMT settings. Trust and security will be improved by advanced blockchain protocols that have lower latency, dynamically programmed smart contracts, and cross-chain interoperability. Federated learning, differential privacy, and explainable AI can also be further integrated to enhance model transparency, resilience, and ethical compliance. By solving these issues, one will be able to have secure, intelligent, and sustainable smart city ecosystems that can deliver real-time multimodal decision-making.

9.9 Conclusions

This chapter discussed how deep learning and blockchain can be integrated to allow secure, intelligent, and resilient multimodal smart city applications. Deep learning offers effective mechanisms of heterogeneous IoMT data analysis that can be used to make real-time decisions in the areas of surveillance, transportation, and energy management. Blockchain augments these features with data integrity, transparency, decentralized trust, and access control, and policy enforcement is automated by smart contracts. They constitute a strong framework that will tackle the security, privacy, and reliability concerns arising when using IoMT networks on a large scale in cities. Other important mechanisms that were brought out in the chapter include feature learning, multimodal fusion, secure data and model management, identity and trust management, and privacy-preserving techniques. The possible benefits of these technologies to enhance the safety of the population, streamline the urban flow, and make the functioning of organizations energy-efficient were proven in practice. Although there are still challenges concerning the scalability, latency, interoperability, and compliance with the regulatory requirements, the current research in lightweight deep learning models, federated learning, and more advanced blockchain protocols will help to make the smart city ecosystems secure, smarter, and more citizen-centric.

References

[1] A. Sureshkumar, M. Sathyamoorthy, R. K. Dhanaraj, S. Aanjanadevi, and V. Palanisamy, "Secure facial biometric authentication in smart cities using multimodal methodology," *Scientific Reports*, vol. 15, no. 1, p. 44839, 2025.

[2] C. Mangla, S. Rani, and N. Herencsar, "An energy-efficient and secure framework for IoMT: an application of smart cities," *Sustainable Energy Technologies and Assessments*, vol. 53, p. 102335, 2022.

[3] T. Sadiq and C. W. Omlin, "Sensing in smart cities: a multimodal machine learning perspective," *Smart Cities*, vol. 9, no. 1, p. 3, 2025.

[4] D. K. J. B. Saini, K. Lakshmi, S. Kolekar, and L. Monish, "Federated blockchain intelligence: a multi-modal AI framework for cyber-resilient smart cities," in *2025 International Conference on NexGen Networks and Cybernetics (IC2NC)*. IEEE, 2025, pp. 129–137.

[5] Y. Afaq and A. Manocha, "Blockchain and deep learning integration for various application: a review," *Journal of Computer Information Systems*, vol. 64, no. 1, pp. 92–105, 2024.

[6] G. M. Zebari and N. Al Musalhi, "A comprehensive review of integrating AI and blockchain security: innovations, challenges, and future directions," *Security and Privacy*, vol. 8, no. 5, p. e70094, 2025.

[7] D. Lahat, T. Adali, and C. Jutten, "Multimodal data fusion: an overview of methods, challenges, and prospects," *Proceedings of the IEEE*, vol. 103, no. 9, pp. 1449–1477, 2015.

[8] P. Nanjundan, L. Thomas, P. Indu, and S. Eslamian, "Challenges and opportunities in multimodal learning research," *Multimodal Learning Using Heterogeneous Data*, pp. 239–246, 2026.

[9] Anas Al-Rahamneh, José Javier Astrain, Jesús Villadangos *et al.*, "Enabling customizable services for multimodal smart mobility with city-platforms," *IEEE Access*, vol. 9, pp. 41628–41646, 2021.

[10] W. Lin, "Design of a multimodal network data security detection model based on self-supervised learning," *Security and Privacy*, vol. 8, no. 5, p. e70062, 2025.

[11] J. H. Ziegeldorf, O. G. Morchon, and K. Wehrle, "Privacy in the Internet of Things: threats and challenges," *Security and Communication Networks*, vol. 7, no. 12, pp. 2728–2742, 2014.

[12] G. F. AlMudahi, L. K. AlSwayeh, S. A. AlAnsary, and R. Latif, “Social media privacy issues, threats, and risks,” in *2022 Fifth International Conference of Women in Data Science at Prince Sultan University (WiDS PSU)*. IEEE, 2022, pp. 155–159.

[13] Haewon Byeon, Vikas Raina, Mukta Sandhu *et al.*, “Artificial intelligence-enabled deep learning model for multimodal biometric fusion,” *Multimedia Tools and Applications*, vol. 83, no. 33, pp. 80105–80128, 2024.

[14] T. Zubatiuk and O. Isayev, “Development of multimodal machine learning potentials: toward a physics-aware artificial intelligence,” *Accounts of Chemical Research*, vol. 54, no. 7, pp. 1575–1585, 2021.

[15] Z. Ye and J. Yu, “Multi-level features fusion network-based feature learning for machinery fault diagnosis,” *Applied Soft Computing*, vol. 122, p. 108900, 2022.

[16] K. Datta Gupta, D. K. Sharma, S. Ahmed, H. Gupta, D. Gupta, and C.-H. Hsu, “A novel lightweight deep learning-based histopathological image classification model for IoMT,” *Neural Processing Letters*, vol. 55, no. 1, pp. 205–228, 2023.

[17] M. Chauhan and S. Rani, “Covid-19: a revolution in the field of education in India,” in *Learning How to Learn Using Multimedia*. Springer, 2021, pp. 23–42.

[18] S. Rani, A. Kataria, P. Bhambri, P. K. Pareek, and V. Puri, “Artificial intelligence in personalized health services for better patient care,” in *Revolutionizing Healthcare: AI Integration with IoT for Enhanced Patient Outcomes*. Springer, 2024, pp. 89–108.

[19] A. Kumar, R. Gupta, S. Kumar, K. Dutta, and M. Rani, “Securing IoMT-based healthcare system: issues, challenges, and solutions,” *Artificial Intelligence and Cybersecurity in Healthcare*, pp. 17–56, 2025.

[20] Y. Ma, Y. Sun, Y. Lei, N. Qin, and J. Lu, “A survey of blockchain technology on security, privacy, and trust in crowdsourcing services,” *World Wide Web*, vol. 23, no. 1, pp. 393–419, 2020.

[21] Syed Yawar Abbas Zaidi, Munam Ali Shah, Hasan Ali Khattak *et al.*, “An attribute-based access control for IoT using blockchain and smart contracts,” *Sustainability*, vol. 13, no. 19, p. 10556, 2021.

[22] L. Bindra, K. Eng, O. Ardakanian, and E. Stroulia, “Flexible, decentralised access control for smart buildings with smart contracts,” *Cyber-Physical Systems*, vol. 8, no. 4, pp. 286–320, 2022.

[23] T. Alam, “Blockchain and big data-based access control for communication among IoT devices in smart cities,” *Wireless Personal Communications*, vol. 132, no. 1, pp. 433–456, 2023.

[24] Ahamed Aljuhani, Prabhat Kumar, Rehab Alanazi, Turki Albalawi, Okba Taouali, and A. K. M. Najmul Islam, “A deep-learning-integrated blockchain framework for securing industrial IoT,” *IEEE Internet of Things Journal*, vol. 11, no. 5, pp. 7817–7827, 2023.

[25] K. Swathi, Putta Durga, K. Venkata Prasad *et al.*, “Secure blockchain integrated deep learning framework for federated risk-adaptive and privacy-preserving IoT edge intelligence sets,” *Scientific Reports*, vol. 15, no. 1, p. 41133, 2025.

[26] L. Cui, G. Xie, Y. Qu, L. Gao, and Y. Yang, "Security and privacy in smart cities: challenges and opportunities," *IEEE Access*, vol. 6, pp. 46134–46145, 2018.

[27] S. Rani, A. Kataria, S. Kumar, and V. Karar, "A new generation cyber-physical system: a comprehensive review from security perspective," *Computers & Security*, vol. 148, p. 104095, 2025.

[28] S. Kumar, S. Rani, S. Sharma, and H. Min, "Multimodality fusion aspects of medical diagnosis: a comprehensive review," *Bioengineering*, vol. 11, no. 12, p. 1233, 2024.

[29] V. Puri, A. Kataria, S. Rani, and P. K. Pareek, "DLT based smart medical ecosystem," in *2023 International Conference on Network, Multimedia and Information Technology (NMITCON)*. IEEE, 2023, pp. 1–6.

Chapter 10

Secure ML and DL systems for intelligent traffic monitoring and management

Abstract

The emergence of smart cities is supported by the fast development of the Internet of Multimedia Things and data-centric technologies, making intelligent transportation systems a new pillar of a smart city. This chapter discusses safe machine learning and deep learning architectures for intelligent traffic monitoring and management with a special focus on the role of multimodal data analytics in improving traffic efficiency and safety. It reviews important machine learning (ML) and deep learning (DL) methods of traffic analysis and prediction with the security threats and attack models attacking data, models, and infrastructure. They include secure system architecture, privacy-preserving learning strategies like federated and distributed learning, trust, and authentication and access control measures. Practical applications can be demonstrated in real-world case studies and explained by the necessity to incorporate security and privacy into smart traffic solutions. The chapter further recognizes the existing issues and future research opportunities and highlights the necessity to have strong, scalable, and reliable learning-based traffic management systems in smart transportation systems of the next generation.

Keywords: authentication; federated learning; Internet of Multimedia Things; intelligent traffic monitoring; secure machine learning

10.1 Introduction

Intelligent traffic monitoring has become a vital implementation of the Internet of Multimedia Things (IoMT) that allows real-time monitoring, analysis, and control of complicated transport systems. Multimodal data is continuously produced by heterogeneous multimedia sensors, including surveillance cameras, acoustic sensors, LiDAR, GPS-enabled vehicles, and roadside units, in the context of an IoMT-based traffic environment. The data offers a lot of contextual information regarding the traffic flow, traffic congestion, incidents, and the environment, enabling the use of data-driven decision-making to achieve smart mobility. The algorithms of machine learning (ML) and deep learning (DL) are at the center of converting raw multimodal traffic data into actionable intelligence [1,2]. Computer vision models are useful in vehicle detection, tracking, and classification of video streams, whereas deep neural networks can be used to estimate traffic density, detect anomalies, and predict accidents. These models enable low-latency and scalable traffic monitoring of urban and highway networks when combined with edge and cloud computing infrastructures. Nevertheless, the use of data-heavy ML and DL models poses severe security and privacy issues. Traffic monitoring systems are susceptible to data poisoning, adversarial attack, manipulation of their models, and unauthorized access to sensitive multimedia information. Thus, safe ML and DL systems are needed in order to guarantee data integrity, model robustness, and reliable system behavior. In the context of the IoMT, intelligent traffic surveillance not only results in increased transport efficiency and safety but also requires robust security measures that ensure multimodal data and decision-making based on learning [3–6].

This chapter is intended to provide the overall picture of secure machine learning and deep learning systems in the context of intelligent traffic monitoring and management of the Internet of Multimedia Things. It aims at combining multimodal data analytics with powerful security and privacy measures to provide trustworthy, resilient, and reliable traffic surveillance, prediction, and decision-making in smart transportation settings.

10.2 Multimodal traffic data sources and security requirements

Smart traffic surveillance systems within the Internet of Multimedia Things are based on various multimodal data sources to provide the correct situational awareness and dynamic decision-making. Typical traffic data sources are video data of roadside and overhead surveillance cameras, audio data of incident-detecting acoustic sensors, LiDAR and radar data of vehicle ranges and speed estimates, GPS tracks of connected vehicles, and contextual data of traffic lights and environmental sensors [6–8]. These heterogeneous data modalities combine to improve traffic flow analysis, predict congestion, detect violations, and respond to emergencies. Nonetheless, multimodal traffic systems have stringent security requirements due to the distributed and data-intensive nature of the system. The confidentiality of the data is paramount since the traffic videos and paths of vehicles can disclose sensitive information about a person and a location. Data integrity should be ensured to avoid manipulation of sensor inputs that may confuse ML and DL models, making wrong judgments on traffic. Authentication and access control are necessary so that one can only allow trusted devices and users to add or get traffic data. Moreover, availability is also a major condition, as traffic infrastructure denial-of-service attacks may also interfere with real-time monitoring and control. The transmission of data, strong storage systems, and ability to resist adversarial attacks on learning models are thus the pillars of trustworthy and reliable multimodal traffic monitoring in IoMT settings [9]. Various multimodal traffic data sources are presented in Figure 10.1.

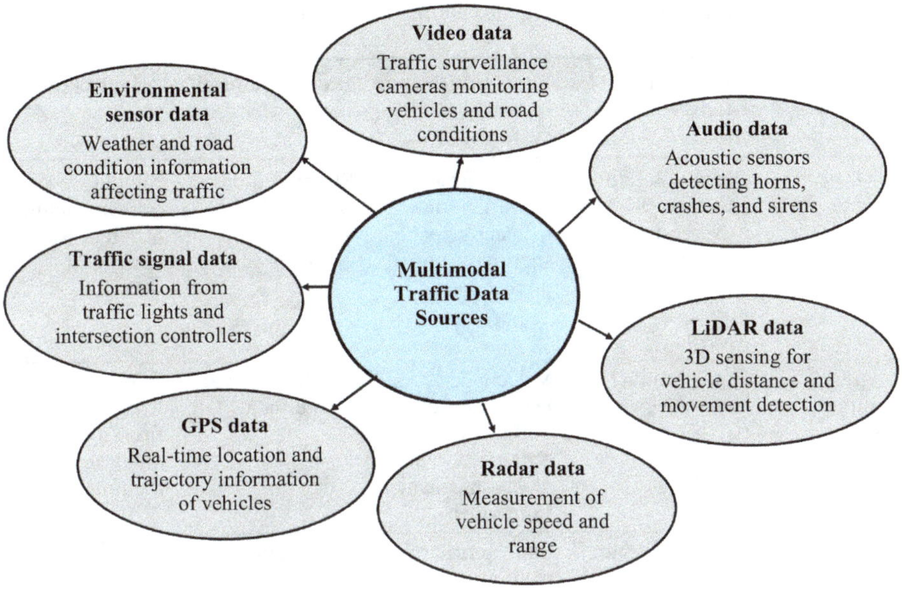

Figure 10.1 Multimodal traffic data sources

10.3 ML and DL techniques for traffic analysis and prediction

The analytical core of intelligent traffic monitoring and management systems in the Internet of Multimedia Things is based on the use of machine learning (ML) and deep learning (DL) methods (**summarized in** Table 10.1). These methods allow extracting meaningful patterns of large-scale multimodal traffic data automatically and help analyze and predict traffic information in dynamic urban settings correctly. The support vector machine, k-nearest neighbors, random forests, and Bayesian models are traditional ML models that have been extensively applied in traffic flow classification, incident detection, and short-term traffic prediction using structured information like speed, volume, and occupancy. As multimedia data of high dimensionality continue to become more and more accessible, DL models have become increasingly popular, as they are more effective at learning features. Convolutional Neural Networks (CNNs) are widely used in traffic video analytics to identify vehicles and lanes, estimate traffic densities, and detect violators. Recurrent Neural Networks (RNNs) (and especially Long Short-Term Memory (LSTM) and Gated Recurrent Unit (GRU) networks) are useful in capturing the temporal correlations in traffic flow data, permitting short- and medium-term traffic prediction to be accurate. Graph Neural Networks (GNNs) also improve traffic modeling by learning spatial correlations between intersections and road segments connected with each other. Multimodal and hybrid learning methods use a combination of several ML and DL models to integrate information from cameras, sensors, and linked cars.

Table 10.1 ML and DL techniques for traffic assessment

Technique category	Algorithms/ Models	Key applications in traffic systems	Data type used	Advantages
Machine learning	Support Vector Machine (SVM), k-Nearest Neighbors (KNN), Random Forest, Bayesian Models	Traffic flow classification, incident detection, short-term traffic prediction	Structured data (speed, traffic volume, occupancy)	Simple implementation, efficient for structured datasets
Deep learning – CNN	Convolutional Neural Networks (CNN)	Vehicle detection, lane identification, traffic density estimation, violation detection from video	Traffic video and image data	Automatic feature extraction from high-dimensional multimedia data
Deep learning – RNN	Recurrent Neural Networks (RNN), LSTM, GRU	Short-term and medium-term traffic flow prediction	Time-series traffic data	Captures temporal dependencies effectively
Graph-based deep learning	Graph Neural Networks (GNN)	Modeling spatial relationships among road segments and intersections	Traffic network graph data	Learns spatial correlations in transportation networks
Multimodal/ hybrid learning	Combination of ML and DL models	Integration of data from cameras, sensors, and connected vehicles	Multimodal traffic data	Improved prediction accuracy and comprehensive analysis
Transformer-based models	Attention mechanisms, Transformer architectures	Enhanced spatial-temporal traffic prediction	Large-scale multimodal traffic datasets	Focus on important features and complex dependencies
Reinforcement learning	RL-based traffic control agents	Adaptive traffic signal control, route optimization	Real-time traffic environment data	Learns optimal policies through interaction

The attention mechanisms and transformer-based models enhance the accuracy of prediction by emphasizing important spatial-temporal modalities [10]. Adaptive traffic signal control and route optimization Reinforcement Learning (RL) methods are increasingly being applied to learn optimal policies where agents interact with the traffic environment. Irrespective of their performance, ML and DL models are associated with scalability, robustness, and interpretability problems. To achieve accurate and reliable traffic analysis and prediction in the intelligent transportation system based on IoMTs, it is necessary to address these challenges by designing an efficient model, providing the security of training, and trusting the deployment [11].

10.4 Security threats and attack models in traffic monitoring systems

The distributed architecture, the use of wireless communication, and the intensive use of data-driven ML and DL models make intelligent traffic monitoring systems deployed in the Internet of Multimedia Things vulnerable to a vast majority of security threats (shown in Figure 10.2). The first is data-level attacks such as data poisoning, false data injection, and so on, where attackers modify sensor measurements or training data to reduce the performance of a model or cause it to make erroneous decisions on traffic. False alarms about congestion or missed incident detection and unsafe traffic control measures can be the result of such attacks. Another severe threat is model-level attacks. Adversarial attacks on ML and DL models are designed with well-defined inputs that result in false classification or false predictions, including mistaking vehicles or traffic lights in surveillance videos. Attack on model inversion and extraction may also affect confidentiality of the system by exposing sensitive training information or model parameters. Moreover, the malicious behavior can be induced in particular conditions due to the backdoor attacks that are introduced in the course of model training. Traffic

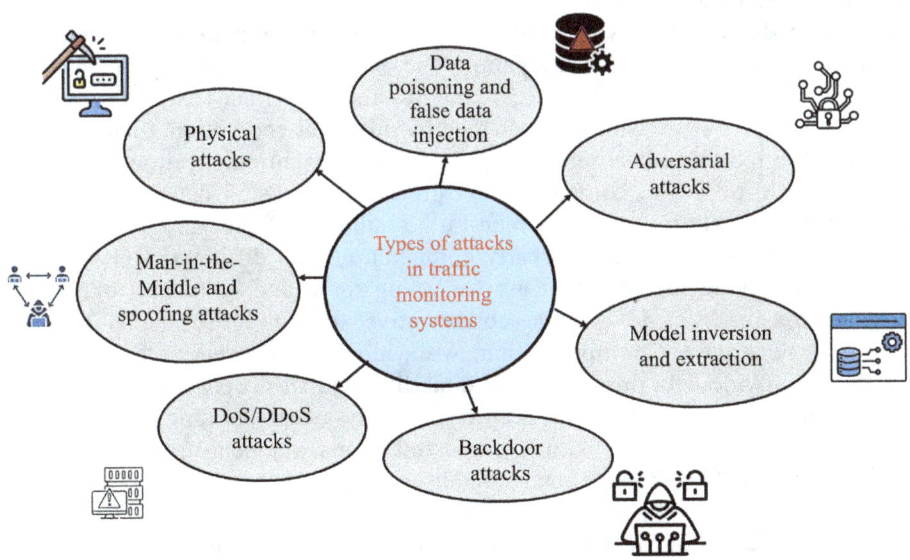

Figure 10.2 Types of attacks in traffic monitoring systems

monitoring infrastructures are also vulnerable to network and system-level attacks. DoS and distributed DoS attacks have the capability of interrupting real-time data transmission and processing, which has a significant impact on system availability. Data confidentiality and integrity can be destroyed by man-in-the-middle attacks and spoofing as well as unauthorized access to edge or cloud nodes. Security risks are also increased by physical assaults on roadside units and sensors. These security threats and attack models are crucial to know in order to create a powerful and secure traffic monitoring system based on ML and DL. Threat modeling can be effectively used to design proactive defense systems to provide reliable, resilient, and trustworthy monitoring of traffic in smart transportation environments.

10.5 Secure architectures for ML-/DL-based traffic management

To deploy ML- and DL-based traffic management systems in the Internet of Multimedia Things, where massive amounts of sensitive multimodal data are being generated and processed in real time, secure architectures are needed. A standard secure architecture follows a layered architecture that consists of sensing, communication, edge, cloud, and application layers, which have specific security mechanisms. On the sensing layer, there are trusted hardware, secure boot, and device authentication to guarantee the integrity of the data obtained by cameras, sensors, and connected vehicles. The concept of edge computing has been instrumental in protecting traffic because it allows processing and inference of data near the data sources. ML and DL models based on edges minimize time and maximum exposure of raw multimedia data, which improves privacy. Models and intermediate data are safeguarded against tampering and unauthorized use by secure enclaves, lightweight encryption, and access control at edge nodes. The cloud layer is used to train large-scale models and store long-term data and analytics of global traffic, which is protected by powerful encryption, identity management, and secure updating of models. Inter-layer communication is ensured with the help of secure communication protocols, intrusion detection systems, and constant monitoring to avoid man-in-the-middle and eavesdropping attacks. Federated learning, secure multiparty computation, and differential privacy are privacy-preserving methods that are becoming more and more part of system architecture in order to provide collaborative training of a model without revealing sensitive traffic information. Also, blockchain-based systems are discussed to provide data provenance, auditability, and trust between two or more parties. Integrating architectural security, privacy-aware learning, and resilient system design, the secure ML/DL-based traffic management architectures can provide dependable, scalable, and reliable intelligent transportation services in the IoMT setup [12–19].

Security layers of ML/DL-based traffic management architecture in IoMT are summarized in Table 10.2.

Table 10.2 Security layers/techniques of ML/DL-based traffic management architecture in IoMT

Architecture layer/ component	Security mechanisms	Role in traffic management systems	Key benefits
Sensing layer	Trusted hardware, secure boot, device authentication	Ensures integrity of data collected from cameras, sensors, and connected vehicles	Prevents device tampering and unauthorized access
Communication layer	Secure communication protocols, intrusion detection systems (IDS), continuous monitoring	Protects data transmission between sensors, edge, and cloud layers	Prevents eavesdropping and man-in-the-middle attacks
Edge layer	Edge computing, secure enclaves, lightweight encryption, access control	Processes traffic data near data sources and runs ML/DL inference	Reduces latency, improves privacy, limits exposure of raw multimedia data
Cloud layer	Strong encryption, identity management, secure model updates	Large-scale model training, global traffic analytics, and long-term data storage	High computational power and secure centralized management
Privacy-preserving learning	Federated learning, secure multiparty computation, differential privacy	Enables collaborative model training without sharing sensitive traffic data	Enhances privacy protection and secure data utilization
Trust and data integrity	Blockchain-based frameworks	Maintains data provenance, auditability, and trust among stakeholders	Improves transparency and tamper-resistant recordkeeping
System-level security design	Integration of architectural security, privacy-aware learning, and resilient system design	Supports reliable ML/DL-based intelligent traffic management	Provides scalable, dependable, and secure IoMT transportation services

10.6 Privacy-preserving learning for traffic data (federated and distributed approaches)

The need to protect privacy has been one of the critical concerns of smart traffic monitoring systems in the Internet of Multimedia Things because traffic data can be sensitive information, including vehicle identities, routes traveled, and behavioral patterns. Federated Learning (FL) is a popular solution that can be used to train models collaboratively across distributed edge devices and traffic nodes without exchanging raw data. In FL-based traffic systems, models are trained on-device (either on camera feeds, sensor measurements, or vehicle data), and only updates made to models are sent to a central server to aggregate them. This helps a great deal in minimizing the risk of privacy and overhead in communication and allows scalable learning. Distributed learning methods also go further to preserve privacy since they decentralize data storage and model training. Peer-to-peer learning, split learning, and hierarchical learning are some of the methods that distribute model components between edge and cloud layers to reduce exposure of data at a single point. The confidentiality and integrity of shared model parameters are improved through the use of secure aggregation protocols, gradient encryption, and trusted execution environments. Mechanisms of differential privacy are frequently added to avoid the inference of sensitive data as a result of updates to the models. Such privacy-preserving learning systems are also resilient to the system since they minimize reliance on centralized data stores, which also helps to curb massive data breaches. Non-independent data distributions, communication efficiency, and resistance to poisoning attacks are, however, the issues that are under active research. These concerns are key to the implementation of credible and privacy-conscious ML and DL applications to analyze traffic data in intelligent transportation systems based on IoMT [20].

10.7 Trust, authentication, and access control in smart traffic systems

Secure smart traffic systems used in the Internet of Multimedia Things have their basic elements, such as trust, authentication, and access control. Because of the high density of heterogeneous and resource-limited devices, it is necessary to build trust among the sensors, roadside units, vehicles, edge nodes, and cloud services. Trust management systems are used to assess the behavior of devices, reliability of data, and past interactions to dynamically determine the reliability of the parties in the traffic network. Authentication measures are used to restrict access to traffic data and system services for legitimate devices and users. Cryptographic authentication, use of digital certificates, and identity-based schemes are all used in order to enhance real-time traffic applications with low latency. In highly dynamic networks like vehicular networks, there is also the need to have fast and scalable authentication protocols to accommodate frequent mobility of devices and handovers. Two-way authentication between infrastructure and devices also helps to stop impersonation and spoofing attacks. The access control policies determine the interaction of the authenticated entities with the traffic data and ML/DL services. Role-based and attribute-based access control models are very common in order to implement fine-grained permissions according to device roles, user attributes, and contextual conditions. The combination of access control and safe logging and auditing systems increases responsibility and adherence to data protection policies. Trust evaluation, strong authentication, and adaptive access control can be combined to ensure a secure platform for reliable and resilient smart traffic monitoring and management in IoMT environments [21].

10.8 Case studies and real-world implementations

The real-life implementation of secure machine learning and deep learning-based traffic monitoring systems in the Internet of Multimedia Things demonstrates their revolutionary effect on the contemporary transportation infrastructure [22]. Many intelligent cities globally have joined intelligent traffic surveillance systems with multiple multimedia sensing, edge computing, and advanced DL models to enhance traffic efficiency and safety. Multimodal data is continuously obtained by high-resolution cameras, LiDAR, and roadside sensors and processed with convolutional neural networks to detect vehicles and their classification, monitor the lanes, and estimate traffic density. To resolve the security issues, such systems use encrypted data transmission, device authentication, and data storage that is controlled by access control, and this would guarantee confidentiality and integrity of sensitive traffic information. An interesting practical application is the application of video analytics based on edges to manage traffic congestion. In these, DL models are deployed on edge nodes at the intersection of roads to process live video feeds and predict the length of queues and speeds of vehicles in real time. Local processing of data minimizes latency and raw video streams are not sent to central servers, improving privacy. The edge devices are secured against tampering and unauthorized access using secure model deployment mechanisms such as trusted execution environments and secure boot procedures. These solutions have proved to be able to optimize traffic flow and congestion during the peak hours [23]. Another notable case study is the federated learning-based traffic prediction system. Traffic information gathered at various intersections and linked cars is very diffuse and private in big urban centers. Federated learning enables models of local traffic prediction to be trained locally, and only encrypted model updates are exchanged with a central aggregator. Such a solution keeps the data confidential and allows network-wide collaborative learning. Experiments in the field have demonstrated that federated models are capable of matching the accuracy of prediction of a centralized method and significantly lowering the probability of data leakage and mass breaches. In integrated and independent car systems, reliable vehicle-to-infrastructure communication systems are being implemented to facilitate intelligent traffic control. ML-based models process data that is exchanged between vehicles and roadside units to predict congestion, optimize signal timing, and improve route planning [24]. There is strong authentication, trust management, and an intrusion detection system that is incorporated to curb spoofing, false data injection, and denial-of-service attacks. Such secure implementations are involved in safer and more reliable real-time traffic coordination. Intelligent traffic monitoring is also important in terms of security as evident in emergency response and incident detection systems. Anomaly detection models built using deep learning that run on the edge are able to quickly detect accidents, stalled vehicles, or abnormal traffic patterns based on the video and sensor data. Upon detection, alerts are safely sent to traffic control centers and emergency services, which allows responding faster and enhances the safety of people. In general, these case studies demonstrate that the effective practical implementation of intelligent traffic monitoring in IoMT systems is not only possible with the help of sophisticated ML and DL methods but also with the help of effective security, privacy, and trustworthy architecture.

10.9 Challenges and future research directions

Nevertheless, the implementation of secure ML- and DL-based intelligent traffic monitoring systems in the Internet of Multimedia Things has a number of challenges despite the considerable improvements. Scalability is one of the key problems because the traffic systems need to handle large amounts of heterogeneous multimodal data in real time, with low latency and high reliability. The strength of ML and DL models against adversarial attacks, data poisoning, and concept drift due to dynamic traffic patterns is a fundamental issue. Another issue is privacy preservation, especially in the trade-off between the model performance and the high requirements of data protection in the setting of distributed and federated learning. The constraint of resources in the edge devices further restricts the implementation of sophisticated deep learning models, which leads to the desire to have lightweight and energy-efficient AI models that are explainable. System integration and security control are also challenges due to interoperability of heterogeneous devices and standards. In the context of future research, it is necessary to create adaptive security-conscious learning models that are able to efficiently optimize accuracy, privacy, and resilience. The contributions of trustful AI, safe model updating, trust management with blockchain, and next-generation vehicle networks are likely to have a significant role. By tackling these issues, it will be possible to have scalable, secure, and sustainable intelligent traffic monitoring systems in intelligent cities in the future.

10.10 Conclusion

Modern transportation is being revolutionized by intelligent traffic monitoring and management systems that are fueled by machine learning and deep learning in the Internet of Multimedia Things. These systems make it possible to analyze multimodal data of distributed sensors, cameras, and connected vehicles in real time, predict and control the traffic, and adapt. Nevertheless, the combination of ML and DL provides vital security and privacy solutions to issues such as manipulation of data, adversarial attacks, and unsanctioned access. This chapter has identified secure architectures, privacy-sensitive learning strategies, and trust management mechanisms that can deal with these obstacles and increase system reliability. Real-life case studies indicate that the integration of advanced models of learning and efficient security models results in efficient, scalable, and reliable traffic solutions. With the further development of smart cities, the future traffic systems should focus on safe, privacy-conscious, and robust ML and DL architectures to provide safe, efficient, and sustainable transportation systems.

References

[1] A. Hazarika, N. Choudhury, M. M. Nasralla, S. B. A. Khattak, and I. U. Rehman, "Edge ML technique for smart traffic management in intelligent transportation systems," *IEEE Access*, vol. 12, pp. 25443–25458, 2024.

[2] O. Aouedi, K. Piamrat, and B. Parrein, "Intelligent traffic management in next-generation networks," *Future Internet*, vol. 14, no. 2, p. 44, 2022.

[3] H. Khan and J. S. Thakur, "Smart traffic control: machine learning for dynamic road traffic management in urban environments," *Multimedia Tools and Applications*, vol. 84, no. 12, pp. 10321–10345, 2025.

[4] Umesh Kumar Lilhore, Agbotiname Lucky Imoize, Chun-Ta Li *et al.*, "Design and implementation of an ML and IoT based adaptive traffic-management system for smart cities," *Sensors*, vol. 22, no. 8, p. 2908, 2022.

[5] Elmustafa Sayed Ali, Mohammad Kamrul Hasan, Rosilah Hassan *et al.*, "Machine learning technologies for secure vehicular communication in internet of vehicles: recent advances and applications," *Security and Communication Networks*, vol. 2021, no. 1, p. 8868355, 2021.

[6] H. Almukhalfi, A. Noor, and T. H. Noor, "Traffic management approaches using machine learning and deep learning techniques: a survey," *Engineering Applications of Artificial Intelligence*, vol. 133, p. 108147, 2024.

[7] D. Wittenberg, A. Paschke, A. Kukuk, and J. Pannek, "Information requirements and legal framework for multimodal transport system coordination," *Logistics*, vol. 8, no. 4, p. 123, 2024.

[8] S. Godhbani, S. Elkosantini, S. M. Lee, and W. Suh, "A new multimodal and spatio-temporal dataset for traffic control: development, analysis, and potential applications," in *2024 IEEE International Conference on Advanced Systems and Emergent Technologies (IC_ASET)*. IEEE, 2024, pp. 1–5.

[9] A. Al Sabouni, A. Freiberger, B. Grosse, A.-K. Hübers, S. Kamenz, and S. Kaser, "Drivers for multimodal traffic management," *Transportation Research Procedia*, vol. 72, pp. 2347–2354, 2023.

[10] O. Aouedi, V. A. Le, K. Piamrat, and Y. Ji, "Deep learning on network traffic prediction: recent advances, analysis, and future directions," *ACM Computing Surveys*, vol. 57, no. 6, pp. 1–37, 2025.

[11] Alfonso Navarro-Espinoza, Oscar Roberto López-Bonilla, Enrique Efrén García-Guerrero *et al.*, "Traffic flow prediction for smart traffic lights using machine learning algorithms," *Technologies*, vol. 10, no. 1, p. 5, 2022.

[12] R. Taheri, H. Ahmed, and E. Arslan, "Deep learning for the security of software-defined networks: a review," *Cluster Computing*, vol. 26, no. 5, pp. 3089–3112, 2023.

[13] R. Singh and N. Soni, “Enhancing cloud security against DDoS attacks: a comprehensive review of ML and DL-based defence mechanisms,” in *2024 International Conference on Communication, Computing and Energy Efficient Technologies (I3CEET)*. IEEE, 2024, pp. 1642–1645.

[14] I. Rakine, K. El Guemmat, S. Ouahabi, I. Atouf, and M. Talea, “IoT intrusion detection: a review of ML and DL-based approaches,” in *2024 4th International Conference on Innovative Research in Applied Science, Engineering and Technology (IRASET)*. IEEE, 2024, pp. 1–7.

[15] N. Niknami and J. Wu, “Advanced ML/DL-based intrusion detection systems for software-defined networks,” in *Network Security Empowered by Artificial Intelligence*. Springer, 2024, pp. 121–146.

[16] S. Rani, A. Kataria, S. Kumar, and V. Karar, “A new generation cyber-physical system: a comprehensive review from security perspective,” *Computers & Security*, vol. 148, p. 104095, 2025.

[17] S. Kumar, S. Rani, S. Sharma, and H. Min, “Multimodality fusion aspects of medical diagnosis: a comprehensive review,” *Bioengineering*, vol. 11, no. 12, p. 1233, 2024.

[18] S. Rani, P. Bhambri, and M. Chauhan, “A machine learning model for kids’ behavior analysis from facial emotions using principal component analysis,” in *2021 5th Asian Conference on Artificial Intelligence Technology (ACAIT)*. IEEE, 2021, pp. 522–525.

[19] V. Puri, A. Kataria, S. Rani, and P. K. Pareek, “DLT based smart medical ecosystem,” in *2023 International Conference on Network, Multimedia and Information Technology (NMITCON)*. IEEE, 2023, pp. 1–6.

[20] Y. Liu, J. James, J. Kang, D. Niyato, and S. Zhang, “Privacy-preserving traffic flow prediction: a federated learning approach,” *IEEE Internet of Things Journal*, vol. 7, no. 8, pp. 7751–7763, 2020.

[21] M. Asif, Z. Aziz, M. Bin Ahmad, A. Khalid, H. A. Waris, and A. Gilani, “Blockchain-based authentication and trust management mechanism for smart cities,” *Sensors*, vol. 22, no. 7, p. 2604, 2022.

[22] K. Saini and S. Sharma, “Smart road traffic monitoring: unveiling the synergy of IoT and AI for enhanced urban mobility,” *ACM Computing Surveys*, vol. 57, no. 11, pp. 1–45, 2025.

[23] R. Iqbal, F. Doctor, B. More, S. Mahmud, and U. Yousuf, “Big data analytics and computational intelligence for cyber–physical systems: recent trends and state of the art applications,” *Future Generation Computer Systems*, vol. 105, pp. 766–778, 2020.

[24] Rafah Kareem Mahmood, Ans Ibrahim Mahameed, Noor Q. Lateef *et al.*, “Optimizing network security with machine learning and multi-factor authentication for enhanced intrusion detection,” *Journal of Robotics and Control (JRC)*, vol. 5, no. 5, pp. 1502–1524, 2024.

Chapter 11

Security of multimodal healthcare data: importance, techniques, and challenges

Abstract

Internet of Medical Things (IoMT) is rapidly growing and it has revolutionized the sphere of healthcare by allowing real-time surveillance, distance diagnostics, and customized therapy due to the connection of devices and multimodal information. This chapter discusses the paramount role of ensuring multimodal healthcare data, comprising electronic health records, medical images, biosignals, genomic data, and patient-generated information. It discusses the nature of this type of data, the most critical security and privacy needs, and possible threats, vulnerabilities, and attack patterns. Advanced machine learning and deep learning methods are mentioned to detect anomalies, prevent infections, and analyze behavior, whereas privacy-preserving frameworks, federated learning, and architecture that is compliant with regulations can guarantee the security of data sharing and analysis. Challenges, open research issues, and future directions are also discussed in the chapter, and the necessity of scalable, adaptive, and intelligent security solutions is also mentioned. On the whole, it offers in-depth information about the protection of sensitive healthcare data, patient trust, and empowering the IoMT-based healthcare ecosystems to be resilient and privacy-conscious.

Keywords: anomaly detection; deep learning; healthcare security; IoMT; privacy-preserving

11.1 Introduction

The spread of the Internet of Medical Things (IoMT) has revolutionized the medical system and allowed real-time tracking, diagnosis, and personal treatment using interconnected devices and sensors. Multimodal healthcare data, which includes medical images, electronic health records, genomic data, biosignals, and information provided by patients, is one that provides a complete understanding of health in patients. Nonetheless, such information is highly confidential and thus it is an ideal target of cyberattacks, such as data breaches, ransomware, and unauthorized access. It is important to ensure that multimodal healthcare data are kept confidential, intact, and available to ensure patient safety and compliance with regulations and to retain trust in healthcare systems. The security mechanisms should support the heterogeneity of the data, high-volume transmission, and real-time processing needs and provide the opportunity to share information safely across hospitals, research centers, and cloud environments. Encryption, access control, blockchain, and machine learning-based anomaly detection are becoming more popular and advanced methods of ensuring the protection of this vital information against emerging threats and privacy-preserving analytics in the current healthcare ecosystems [1–3].

The purpose of the chapter is to investigate the essential role of multimodal healthcare data protection in the Internet of Medical Things (IoMT). It reviews the main security and privacy issues, outlines possible threats and vulnerabilities, and offers more sophisticated approaches to machine learning and deep learning to protect the data. Privacy-saving frameworks, secure architectures, and regulatory compliance are also addressed in the chapter, and it provides insights regarding successful techniques of protecting sensitive healthcare information in the current interconnected systems.

11.2 Characteristics of healthcare multimodal data in IoMT

The multimodal data in Internet of Medical Things (IoMT) is by nature heterogeneous and includes various types of data, including electronic health records (EHRs), medical imaging (MRI, CT, X-ray), biosignals (ECG, EEG), genomic sequences, and patient-generated data in wearable devices [4,5]. This data has high dimensions, and it is usually large and generated at high velocity, and it needs real-time collection and processing. It is complicated by the fact that it has different formats, resolutions, and temporal aspects that are difficult to integrate, analyze, and store. The data on multimodal healthcare is very sensitive and confidential since this type of data includes personally identifiable information (PII) and vital health information (shown in Figure 11.1), and it is prone to stringent regulatory standards such as HIPAA and GDPR. Moreover, it is frequently interdependent, in that the knowledge is obtained through the correlation of various modalities to enhance the diagnosis, prognosis, and individual treatment. The information is also dynamic as it is constantly updated with clinical intervention and patient monitoring. The nature of these features requires highly effective security, interoperability, and privacy controls to guarantee secure, trustworthy, and useful applications in the IoMT-based healthcare systems [6–8].

11.3 Security and privacy requirements in healthcare systems

The multimodal data of healthcare systems are strongly sensitive to security and privacy needs because of the sensitive nature of patient data (summarized in Table 11.1). Confidentiality is the most important feature to eliminate unauthorized access to personal health data and to ensure that only authorized personnel or systems can see or edit the records. Integrity makes sure that the data is correct and no alterations have been made when storing and transmitting data, a factor that is

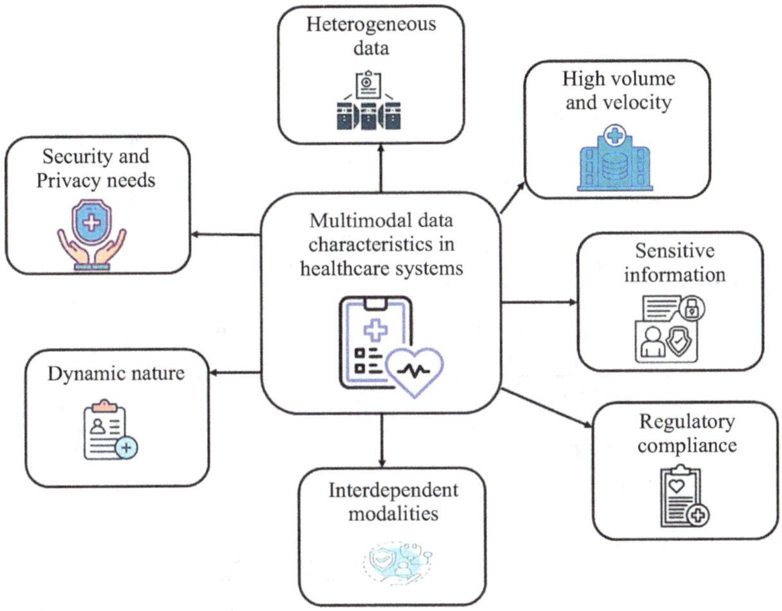

Figure 11.1 Healthcare multimodal data characteristic – IoMT framework

especially important in the process of reliable diagnosis and treatment. Availability ensures that healthcare information and services are available whenever needed by authorized users in real time, especially during emergency or critical care situations. Privacy needs require adherence to acceptable regulations like HIPAA, GDPR, and local healthcare data protection legislation and focus on patient consent, anonymization, and limited data sharing [9–16]. The use of authentication and access control measures is necessary to confirm the identity of the user and assign roles based on permission, and encryption secures data both at rest and in transit. Auditability and traceability assist in tracking the access patterns, identifying the anomalies, and ensuring accountability. Also, the contemporary IoMT setting requires resiliency to cyberattacks, such as ransomware, phishing, and data breaches, which may negatively affect privacy and patient safety. It is important to establish trust, regulatory adherence, and integrity of multimodal healthcare ecosystems by implementing a combination of technical, administrative, and organizational safeguards [6,17].

11.4 Threats, vulnerabilities, and attack models

The sensitive nature of multimodal healthcare data and the interrelated nature of devices and systems in IoMT expose it to various threats and vulnerabilities. The risks are cyberattacks (ransomware, phishing, distributed denial-of-service (DDoS) attacks, and malware). Insider threats, where a person who is supposed to possess access privileges abuses his or her privileges, are also a great threat. Weak authentication schemes, insecure communication, outdated software, and absence

Table 11.1 Summarization of security and privacy requirements in multimodal healthcare systems

Security/privacy requirement	Description	Importance in healthcare systems
Confidentiality	Protects patient data from unauthorized access and ensures only authorized users can view or modify records	Safeguards sensitive personal and medical information
Integrity	Ensures that healthcare data remains accurate and unaltered during storage and transmission	Essential for reliable diagnosis and treatment decisions
Availability	Guarantees timely access to healthcare information and services for authorized users	Critical for emergency care and real-time medical decision-making
Regulatory compliance	Adherence to healthcare regulations such as HIPAA, GDPR, and local data protection laws	Ensures legal compliance and protects patient rights
Authentication and access control	Verifies user identity and assigns role-based permissions for system access	Prevents unauthorized system usage and data manipulation
Data encryption	Secures data during storage (at rest) and transmission (in transit)	Protects patient information from interception and breaches
Auditability and traceability	Tracks data access, usage patterns, and system activities	Helps detect anomalies and ensures accountability
Resilience to cyberattacks	Protection against threats such as ransomware, phishing, and data breaches	Maintains patient safety and system reliability

of encryption are some of the vulnerabilities. The IoMT devices are frequently characterized by poor computational power and are likely to be vulnerable to security breaches and lack of updates. The lack of interoperability between the heterogeneous devices and systems may create holes that can be used by attackers. Attack models explain the way attackers exploit these vulnerabilities. Passive attacks entail intercepting data communications in order to obtain sensitive data without modifying data. Active attacks involve data alteration, data injection, or data deletion, which affect integrity and system reliability. Replay attacks are attacks in which the captured data is resent to influence system functionality, whereas man-in-the-middle attacks are attacks in which the communication between devices has been intercepted and modified. Knowledge of such threats, vulnerabilities, and model attacks is essential in the design of powerful defense mechanisms, the deployment of efficient intrusion detection mechanisms, and the creation of safe architectures that will protect the confidentiality, integrity, and availability of healthcare multimodal data in IoMT ecosystems. Various types of threats and attacks are summarized in Table 11.2.

Table 11.2 Various types of threats, vulnerabilities, and attack models in multimodal healthcare systems

Category	**Threat/vulnerability/ attack model**	**Description**
Cyber threat	Ransomware	Malicious software encrypts healthcare data and demands payment for access restoration.
Cyber threat	Phishing	Fraudulent messages trick users into revealing login credentials or sensitive information.
Cyber threat	DDoS attack	Overloads networks or servers to disrupt healthcare services and system availability.
Cyber threat	Malware	Harmful software that damages systems or steals healthcare data.
Insider threat	Privilege misuse	Authorized individuals misuse their access rights to manipulate or leak sensitive data.
Vulnerability	Weak authentication	Poor authentication mechanisms allow unauthorized system access.
Vulnerability	Insecure communication	Unprotected data transmission between IoMT devices can be intercepted.
Vulnerability	Outdated software	Lack of updates or patches exposes systems to security exploits.
Vulnerability	Lack of encryption	Sensitive healthcare data remains exposed during storage or transmission.
Vulnerability	Limited device resources	IoMT devices often have low computational power, limiting strong security implementation.
Vulnerability	Interoperability issues	Heterogeneous devices and systems may create exploitable security gaps.
Attack model	Passive attack	Attackers intercept communication to obtain sensitive data without altering it.
Attack model	Active attack	Data is modified, injected, or deleted, affecting system integrity and reliability.
Attack model	Replay attack	Previously captured data packets are retransmitted to manipulate system behavior.
Attack model	Man-in-the-middle attack	Attackers intercept and alter communication between devices.

11.5 Machine learning-based security techniques

In the IoMT systems, machine learning (ML) has become an effective tool to improve the security of multimodal healthcare data (shown in Figure 11.2). The ML algorithms have the ability to identify patterns, anomalies, and possible threats in large and complex data automatically and offer proactive defense mechanisms.

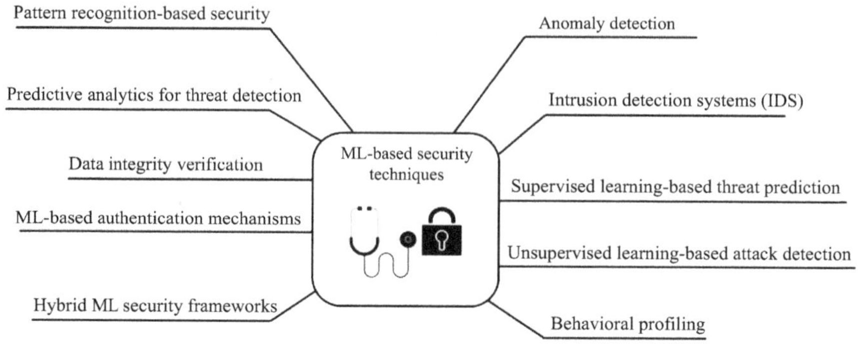

Figure 11.2 ML-based security techniques for multimodal healthcare data

Support vector machine (SVM), k-nearest neighbors (KNN), and random forests are examples of anomaly detection models, which detect abnormal behavior in the network traffic, device activity, or user access that can be used to indicate a cyberattack or data breach. ML-driven intrusion detection systems (IDS) are able to categorize network traffic as malicious or benign to allow real-time mitigation of threats. Supervised learning models use past attack information to forecast the occurrence of vulnerabilities, whereas unsupervised learning can be used to detect attack patterns that have not been seen before. Behavioral profiling also uses ML methods by monitoring the actions of users or their devices and sending warnings in case of an insider threat. Moreover, pattern recognition and predictive analytics can be used in ML to increase data integrity and authentication so that sensitive healthcare data is not changed. ML-based security systems are dynamic and scalable since they keep adapting to new attack tactics by constantly learning about the threats. These methods are becoming more and more combined with conventional security mechanisms, and they become hybrid solutions, which enhance the resilience of healthcare IoMT settings overall [18].

11.6 Deep learning approaches for healthcare data protection

Deep learning (DL) methods provide superior solutions to securing multimodal healthcare data in IoMT systems by automatically learning complicated patterns and relationships in high-dimensional data. To detect anomalies in medical images and sensor-generated data and identify tampering or unauthorized changes, convolutional neural networks (CNNs) are used. RNNs and long short-term memory (LSTM) networks can be useful in the analysis of time-series biosignals to identify unusual patterns that can suggest cyber threats or malfunctioning device behavior. The intrusion detection systems based on DL use large-scale network and system logs to categorize attacks with a high level of accuracy including the zero-day exploits, which would not be detected by the traditional rule-based systems. Autoencoders have been commonly applied in the detection of anomalies, where the input data is reconstructed in order to detect anomalies that represent a possible security breach. Moreover, DL models support privacy-sensitive approaches, including federated learning, under which sensitive patient data is kept locally, whereas models are trained using a decentralized approach across institutions. Deep learning methods offer scalable, dynamic, and robust protection to multimodal healthcare systems by continually learning about changing attack patterns. The combination of encryption, access control, and blockchain technologies enhances the overall data security, which guarantees confidentiality, integrity, and availability in the healthcare systems using the IoMT [19].

11.7 Privacy-preserving and regulatory-compliant frameworks

In order to secure multimodal healthcare data in an IoMT environment, it is important to ensure privacy and regulatory compliance. Privacy-preserving frameworks are designed to maintain sensitive information about the patients and facilitate the analysis and sharing of data. Differential privacy, homomorphic encryption, and secure multiparty computation are some of the techniques that can perform computation on encrypted data without revealing actual data on patients. Federated learning also promotes privacy because it allows joint learning of models in institutions without centralizing sensitive information. Data collection, storage, transmission, and consent management have requirements that are established by regulatory compliance frameworks, including HIPAA, GDPR, and local healthcare regulations. These models impose rigid access control, audit logs, and anonymization protocols to ensure that patient identities are not disclosed. Role-based access control (RBAC) and attribute-based access control (ABAC) will make sure that only authorized individuals can access particular subsets of data and reduce exposure. Combination of privacy-preserving mechanisms with regulatory-compliant practices allows sharing of multimodal healthcare data across hospitals, research centers, and cloud platforms in a secure manner. These frameworks alleviate data breach and unauthorized usage risks, as well as increase trust, collaborative research, and patient-centric, ethical healthcare analytics in the current IoMT environment [20,21].

11.8 Secure architectures for IoMT-based healthcare applications

The security architectures in the IoMT-based healthcare systems are intended to safeguard multimodal data during its life cycle, which includes both the acquisition and transmission stages as well as the storage and analysis stages. Such architectures are usually designed with layered security models, which means they have device, network, and cloud protection. Lightweight encryption, secure boot, and firmware integrity checks at the device level are used to make IoMT sensors and wearables resistant to tampering and unauthorized access. Secure communication protocols like TLS/SSL, VPN, and blockchain-based ledgers protect data in transit and avoid eavesdropping, man-in-the-middle attacks, and data interception at the network level. To safeguard aggregated healthcare data, cloud-level security incorporates strong access control, rest encryption, intrusion detection, and anomaly detection. The architecture of edge computing is becoming popular to compute sensory information on the edges to minimize exposure on the way to the cloud and to take advantage of real-time analytics. Standardized protocols and privacy-preserving APIs are used to ensure interoperability and secure data exchange between heterogeneous devices and systems. Secure IoMT architectures achieve confidentiality, integrity, and availability by integrating these layers, which allows the delivery of healthcare safely, efficiently, and reliably and ensures compliance with regulatory requirements and preserves trust of patients [22–24].

11.9 Challenges, open issues, and future research directions

Various technical and organizational issues are associated with securing multimodal healthcare data in the Internet of Things settings because the information is heterogeneous, large-volume, and sensitive. A significant difficulty is in securing IoMT devices with limited computational resources, memory, and power, and it is not always possible to provide strong encryption, authentication, and intrusion detection tools. Another important concern is to ensure interoperability between different devices, sensors, and platforms and keep the data safe. Also, the speed and volume of real-time healthcare data demand efficient and low-latency security systems that do not jeopardize patient care and system performance. The fact that the system design is increasingly complicated by the necessity to comply with the constantly changing regulations, including but not limited to HIPAA, GDPR, and the laws of the specific country in which the healthcare facility operates, also complicates the situation with multi-institutional and cross-border data sharing. The open issues involve balancing privacy and analytics and research data utility. Although privacy-preserving approaches such as differential privacy, federated learning, and homomorphic encryption have potential, they can cause computation overheads and can lower the accuracy of the model. Multimodal healthcare data security frameworks have not yet been standardized, and similar to heterogeneous systems, it is challenging to guarantee uniform security measures. Also, there are no scalable solutions that are adaptive and can identify advanced cyberattacks, insider threats, and zero-day exploits in real time. The future research directions are to exploit advanced machine learning and deep learning models to come up with adaptive and context-based security systems, which will adapt to the new threats. The federated and edge learning methods can reduce the weaknesses of centralization and collaborative analytics. Data integrity, transparency, and trust can be improved through integration of blockchain, secure multiparty computation, and quantum-resistant cryptography. Transparency and accountability in automated security decisions can also be explained by methods of explainable AI. All these directions are intended to develop smart, resilient, and privacy-conscious IoMT healthcare ecosystems, which would allow sharing data safely, provide patient-centric services, and make reliable clinical decisions in an ever-interconnected healthcare setting.

11.10 Conclusion

This chapter highlights that the need to ensure the safety of multimodal healthcare data in the Internet of Medical Things (IoMT) is critical. The sensitivity and variety of data, such as medical images, biosignals, electronic health records, and information created by patients, pose challenges to ensuring confidentiality, integrity, and availability. Cyberattacks, insider misuse, and data breaches are the threats that may be reduced with the help of effective, adaptable security mechanisms. Machine learning and deep learning can be used as effective solutions to anomaly detection, intrusion prevention, and behavioral profiling, whereas privacy-preserving frameworks, federated learning, and regulatory-compliant architectures can be used to conduct secure, collaborative data analytics. Although these improvements have been made, there are still problems like device constraints, lack of interoperability, and privacy versus data utility. It will be a critical move in future research on intelligent, context-aware, and scalable security solutions, combined with blockchain, edge computing, and explainable AI. All in all, these strategies are necessary in the implementation of protective measures of sensitive healthcare information, preserving patient trust, and facilitating privacy-protected, reliable, and secure IoMT-powered healthcare services.

References

[1] S. Chaabene, A. Boudaya, B. Bouaziz, and L. Chaari, "An overview of methods and techniques in multimodal data fusion with application to healthcare," *International Journal of Data Science and Analytics*, vol. 20, pp. 3093–3117, 2025.

[2] H. Singh, M. Deshmukh, and L. K. Awasthi, "Secure healthcare data management using multimodal image fusion and dual watermarking," *Scientific Reports*, vol. 15, no. 1, p. 9047, 2025.

[3] K. N. Singh, N. Baranwal, A. K. Singh, A. K. Agrawal, and H. Zhou, "Using multimodal biometrics, data hiding and encryption for secure healthcare imaging system," *IEEE Transactions on Consumer Electronics*, vol. 71, no. 2, pp. 6711–6718, 2025.

[4] R. Arul, Y. D. Al-Otaibi, W. S. Alnumay, U. Tariq, U. Shoaib, and M. J. Piran, "Multi-modal secure healthcare data dissemination framework using

blockchain in IoMT," *Personal and Ubiquitous Computing*, vol. 28, no. 1, pp. 3–15, 2024.

[5] H. Ghayvat, M. Awais, R. Geddam, P. Tiwari, and W. Löwe, "Revolutionizing healthcare: IoMT-enabled digital enhancement via multimodal ADL data fusion," *Information Fusion*, vol. 111, p. 102518, 2024.

[6] Wei Ping, Qihang Sun, Qi Wang *et al.*, "Dynamic multimodal fusion for real-time lung cancer diagnostics in IoMT-enabled healthcare," *IEEE Internet of Things Journal*, vol. 12, pp. 46083–46092, 2025.

[7] A. Saha, R. Sil, A. Chatterjee, S. Saha, and M. Malhotra, "A comprehensive survey of emerging AI paradigms: data fusion, multimodal analytics, and IoMT in healthcare," *Feature Fusion for Next-Generation AI: Building Intelligent Solutions from Medical Data*, pp. 157–165, 2025.

[8] T. M. Ghazal, M. K. Hasan, S. N. H. Abdullah, K. A. Abubakkar, and M. A. Afifi, "IoMT-enabled fusion-based model to predict posture for smart healthcare systems," *Computers, Materials, & Continua*, vol. 71, no. 2, p. 2579, 2022.

[9] T. Ermakova, B. Fabian, M. Kornacka, S. Thiebes, and A. Sunyaev, "Security and privacy requirements for cloud computing in healthcare: elicitation and prioritization from a patient perspective," *ACM Transactions on Management Information Systems (TMIS)*, vol. 11, no. 2, pp. 1–29, 2020.

[10] A. Algarni, "A survey and classification of security and privacy research in smart healthcare systems," *IEEE Access*, vol. 7, pp. 101879–101894, 2019.

[11] S. Rani, A. Kataria, S. Kumar, and V. Karar, "A new generation cyber-physical system: a comprehensive review from security perspective," *Computers & Security*, vol. 148, p. 104095, 2025.

[12] S. Kumar, S. Rani, S. Sharma, and H. Min, "Multimodality fusion aspects of medical diagnosis: a comprehensive review," *Bioengineering*, vol. 11, no. 12, p. 1233, 2024.

[13] D. Mittal, H. Singh, and S. Rani, "Exploring explainable artificial intelligence techniques for hate speech detection," in *International Conference on Innovative Computing and Communication*. Springer, 2024, pp. 545–554.

[14] V. Puri, A. Kataria, S. Rani, and P. K. Pareek, "DLT based smart medical ecosystem," in *2023 International Conference on Network, Multimedia and Information Technology (NMITCON)*. IEEE, 2023, pp. 1–6.

[15] M. Chauhan and S. Rani, "Covid-19: a revolution in the field of education in India," in *Learning How to Learn Using Multimedia*. Springer, 2021, pp. 23–42.

[16] S. Rani, A. Kataria, P. Bhambri, P. K. Pareek, and V. Puri, "Artificial intelligence in personalized health services for better patient care," in *Revolutionizing Healthcare: AI Integration with IoT for Enhanced Patient Outcomes*. Springer, 2024, pp. 89–108.

[17] J. JPC Rodrigues, I. De La Torre, G. Fernández, and M. López-Coronado, "Analysis of the security and privacy requirements of cloud-based electronic health records systems," *Journal of Medical Internet Research*, vol. 15, no. 8, p. e186, 2013.

[18] S. Kim and K.-J. Park, "A survey on machine-learning based security design for cyber-physical systems," *Applied Sciences*, vol. 11, no. 12, p. 5458, 2021.

[19] Y. Liu, U. R. Acharya, and J. H. Tan, "Preserving privacy in healthcare: a systematic review of deep learning approaches for synthetic data generation," *Computer Methods and Programs in Biomedicine*, vol. 260, p. 108571, 2025.

[20] Naween Kumar, Akansha Singh, Vaibhav Saini *et al.*, "Harnessing federated learning for smart city data management in cloud environments," *Integration of Federated Learning and Blockchain for Smart Cities*, pp. 289–323, 2025.

[21] L. Chen, N. Zhang, H.-M. Sun, C.-C. Chang, S. Yu, and K.-K. R. Choo, "Secure search for encrypted personal health records from big data NoSQL databases in cloud," *Computing*, vol. 102, no. 6, pp. 1521–1545, 2020.

[22] L. Lodha, V. S. Baghela, J. Bhuvana, and R. Bhatt, "A blockchain-based secured system using the Internet of Medical Things (IOMT) network for e-healthcare monitoring," *Measurement: Sensors*, vol. 30, p. 100904, 2023.

[23] A. Kumar, R. Gupta, S. Kumar, K. Dutta, and M. Rani, "Securing IoMT-based healthcare system: issues, challenges, and solutions," in: R. Agrawal, P. S. Rathore, G. G. Devarajan, and R. R. Divivedi (eds.), *Artificial Intelligence and Cybersecurity in Healthcare*, pp. 17–56. Beverly, MA: Scrivener Publishing; 2025.

[24] N. Sharma and P. G. Shambharkar, "Multi-layered security architecture for IoMT systems: integrating dynamic key management, decentralized storage, and dependable intrusion detection framework," *International Journal of Machine Learning and Cybernetics*, vol. 16, pp. 6399–6446, 2025.

Chapter 12

ML facilitated encrypted smart home systems in the Internet of Multimedia Things

Abstract

The swift development of smart home technologies has transformed contemporary life by making smart, interconnected, and multimedia-enhanced spaces of the Internet of Multimedia Things possible. In this chapter, the authors provide an overview of machine learning- and deep learning-based methods to secure encrypted smart home systems. It examines the special security issues brought about by heterogeneous devices, continuous multimedia data generation, and changing cyber threats. The chapter tells about the role of machine learning (ML) and deep learning (DL) models in improving intrusion detection, authentication, access control, and adaptive threat response without violating user privacy. The state-of-the-art encryption methods that can be applied to resource-constrained Internet of Multimedia Things (IoMT) devices are discussed, as is how they can be combined with intelligent security solutions. Practical implementation is pointed out in real-world case studies in the areas of surveillance, energy management, and healthcare monitoring, as well as access control. Lastly, the chapter outlines the most important challenges and directions of future research, which are lightweight, privacy-preserving, and scalable solutions. The knowledge brought forward should help in building robust, reliable, and safe smart home systems in future multimedia IoMT systems.

Keywords: deep learning; encryption; Internet of Multimedia Things; machine learning; smart home security

12.1 Introduction

The fast development of smart home technologies has changed the conventional living space into smart, connected environment moving under the influence of the Internet of Multimedia Things (IoMT). These systems combine various multimedia streams of data, including audio, video, sensor data, and user behavior patterns, to allow automation, comfort, energy saving, and improved quality of life. Nevertheless, the ubiquitous gathering and transmission of sensitive multimodal data also bring about great security and privacy issues, such as unauthorized access, data leakage, and cyberattacks on smart home infrastructures. Machine learning (ML) and deep learning (DL) have become potent tools to ensure the security of smart home systems through the provision of intelligent encryption, intrusion detection, anomaly identification, and adaptive access control. ML- and DL-based security mechanisms have the potential to dynamically react to the changing threats by learning the complex patterns of heterogeneous multimedia data without negatively affecting the system performance and user convenience. Smart home systems with encrypted smart homes powered by intelligent models provide a high level of protection against known and unknown attacks, confidentiality, integrity, and availability of data in highly dynamic IoMT environments [1,2].

This chapter discusses the application of ML-supported encrypted smart home systems in the wider Internet of Multimedia context. It has identified the main security requirements, elaborated on enhanced learning-based encryption and authentication methods, and considered the real-life issues and future research trends. The chapter is meant to bring into view a holistic insight into the manner in which intelligent learning paradigms can enhance trust, resilience, and privacy in next-generation smart home ecosystems.

12.2 Security challenges in smart homes

The Internet of Multimedia Things (IoMT) environment of smart homes presents complex security challenges because they are highly interconnected, data-intensive, and heterogeneous. These systems combine multimedia gadgets like smart cameras, voice assistants, sensors, and appliances, all of which capture and transfer sensitive user information at all times. The great number of Internet-connected devices makes the attack surface large and, therefore, makes it very vulnerable to cyber threats. Data privacy and confidentiality is one of the challenges. Smart homes process personal data, such as audio records, video feeds, daily activities, and habits. The data can leak, be surveilled, or be stolen due to weak encryption, weak communication channels, or poor key management. It is challenging to provide end-to-end protection of multimodal data and be responsive in real time. Another challenge is the heterogeneity and interoperability of the devices [1,3,4]. Smart homes are systems composed of equipment from different vendors with different levels of security and computing power. Most low-cost or resource-constrained devices do not have strong security provisions, and they are simple targets for an attacker. Poorly maintained firmware release and patch control also contribute to these risks. There are also unauthorized access and authentication vulnerabilities. The improperly implemented access control, default credentials, and ineffective authentication schemes may enable attackers to take control of smart devices, alter system behavior, or cause disruption to the required services. This danger is increased in common resources where there are several users and visitors. Also, attacks over the network like Distributed Denial of Service (DDoS), man-in-the-middle attacks, and spoofing endanger system availability and reliability. The compromised smart devices can be used as one of the large botnets that affect individual homes and networks in general. Lastly, the issue of user awareness and security management is always a problem. The nontechnical users can fail to securely update their devices or can even set them

Table 12.1 Summary of security challenges in smart home ecosystems

Challenge category	Description	Impact
Data privacy and confidentiality	Continuous collection of audio, video, and behavioral data with weak encryption and key management	Data leakage, surveillance, identity and privacy breaches
Large attack surface	Numerous interconnected smart devices	Increased vulnerability to cyberattacks
Device heterogeneity	Devices from multiple vendors with varying security and computing capabilities	Inconsistent security, difficult interoperability
Resource constraints	Low-cost devices lack strong security mechanisms	Easy targets for attackers
Firmware and patch issues	Poor update and patch management	Exploitation of known vulnerabilities
Authentication and access control	Default credentials, weak authentication, improper access control	Unauthorized device control and service disruption
Network-based attacks	DDoS, Man-in-the-Middle, spoofing attacks	Reduced availability, reliability, and trust
Botnet exploitation	Compromised devices used in large-scale attacks	Threats beyond individual homes
User awareness and management	Nontechnical users misconfigure or fail to update devices	Persistent security weaknesses

up incorrectly, exposing them to threats. To counter such challenges, smart homes in dynamic IoMT settings need smart security solutions that are intelligent, adaptive, and automated to protect such homes. Summary of various security challenges in smart homes is presented in Table 12.1.

12.3 Machine learning for smart home security

Machine learning (ML) has an important role to play in improving the level of security in smart home settings, as it facilitates intelligent, adaptive, and data-driven protection systems. ML models can discover complicated patterns in large amounts of multimodal data (generated by smart home devices, such as network traffic, sensor readings, audiovisual streams, and user interaction logs), unlike traditional rule-based security solutions. This feature enables smart home systems to identify minor anomalies and emerging threats as they happen. Intrusion and anomaly detection can be considered one of the most important uses of ML in smart home security. Controlled and uncontrolled learning methods have the ability to detect anomalies in the normal functioning of the devices, which are indicative of cyberattacks, unauthorized access, or compromised devices. As an illustration, unusual traffic on a network or abnormal activity of a device can be identified early, before any massive security breach. Intelligent authentication and access control are also commonly performed with the help of ML. Continuous and nonintrusive user authentication can be achieved through behavioral biometrics including voice recognition, facial recognition, and usage patterns. Knowing the user profiles, ML-based systems will be able to dynamically change access privileges and minimize the risks of stolen credentials or impersonation attacks [5–7]. Adaptive threat prediction and response is another useful application. The ML models will be able to process attack history and system logs and anticipate possible vulnerabilities and actively reinforce the security. Such predictability enhances the ability to withstand zero-day attacks and advanced enemies. Although the benefits are evident, the ML-based security systems have issues of quality of data, model comprehension, and computational complexity. However, used together with encryption and secure communication protocols, ML-based solutions provide a potent model for developing strong, scalable, and privacy-conscious smart home security systems within the Internet of Multimedia Things ecosystem [5,8,9]. Table 12.2 summarizes the various contributions of ML algorithms in smart home security.

Table 12.2 ML applications in smart home security

Application area	ML role	Key benefits	Challenges
Multimodal data analysis	Learns patterns from network traffic, sensors, audiovisual data, and user logs	Intelligent, data-driven security monitoring	Data quality and high data volume
Intrusion and anomaly detection	Detects abnormal device behavior and network activity using supervised/unsupervised learning	Early detection of cyberattacks and compromised devices	False positives, model tuning
Intelligent authentication	Uses behavioral biometrics (voice, face, usage patterns)	Continuous, nonintrusive, dynamic access control	Privacy concerns, computational cost
Adaptive access control	Adjusts privileges based on learned user behavior	Reduced risk of credential theft and impersonation	Model interpretability
Threat prediction and response	Analyzes logs and attack history to predict vulnerabilities	Proactive defense against zero-day and advanced attacks	Training complexity
Integrated security framework	Combined with encryption and secure communication	Scalable, robust, and privacy-aware security	Resource constraints in IoMT devices

12.4 Deep learning approaches for encrypted smart homes

Deep learning (DL) methods have received considerable focus in securing encrypted smart homes because of their aptitude to model multimedia data that are intricate, high-dimensional, and produced within the Internet of Multimedia Things (IoMT). Smart houses generate encrypted audio, video, image, and sensor data in a continuous manner, and DL models are highly recommended to identify meaningful patterns in such heterogeneous data and maintain data confidentiality. Privacy-preserving intrusion detection is one of the most outstanding uses of DL in encrypted smart homes. Deep neural networks, including convolutional neural networks (CNNs) and recurrent neural networks (RNNs), have the capability to use encrypted or partially encrypted traffic patterns to detect malicious activities without necessarily having access to raw content [10–12]. This will allow ongoing tracking and still keep privacy of the user. Anomaly detection is also done using autoencoders and deep belief networks to learn normal system behavior and indicate anomalies. DL techniques also differentiate secure authentication and authorization. Encrypted data storage and transmission can be supplemented with biometric-based authentication based on deep learning, i.e., face recognition, voice recognition, and gait analysis, to provide secure and reliable access control [13,14]. Such models are more accurate and resistant to spoofing attacks than their conventional counterparts. Also, encryption control with the aid of deep learning enhances key creation, distribution, and smart encryption plans. DL models have the ability to dynamically allocate encryption levels with perception of threat, capability of the device, and sensitivity of the information, balancing system efficiency and security. Although they are effective, the challenges associated with the use of DL-based solutions include computational complexity, energy usage, and model transparency. Nevertheless, the development of edge intelligence, lightweight neural networks, and federated learning is facilitating scalable and secure operation of deep learning methods on encrypted smart home systems through contemporary IoMT systems [15]. Table 12.3 presents the role of various DM techniques in securing smart homes.

Table 12.3 DL for the security of smart homes

Aspect	**Key techniques/ models**	**Benefits**	**Challenges**
Privacy-preserving intrusion detection	CNNs, RNNs	Maintains user privacy, real-time monitoring	High computation cost
anomaly detection	Autoencoders, Deep Belief Networks	Early threat detection	Model interpretability
Authentication and authorization	Face, voice, gait recognition (DL-based)	High accuracy, spoof resistance	Energy consumption
Encryption control	DL-based optimization models	Balance security and efficiency	Complexity in deployment
Deployment enablers	Edge AI, lightweight DL, federated learning	Reduced latency, privacy-aware learning	Resource constraints

12.5 Encryption techniques in IoMT smart homes

Encryption is a key element to ensure data security and privacy in IoMT-based smart homes, where sensitive multimedia and sensor data are produced in large volumes that are constantly generated, transferred, and stored. Such data are video streams and surveillance cameras, voice commands of smart assistants, health and environmental sensors, and user histories. Efficient encryption methods are necessary to ensure that such information does not fall into the wrong hands, eavesdropping, or computer attacks. Symmetric encryption algorithms like Advanced Encryption Standard (AES) are very common in smart homes because they are very efficient with minimal calculation load [16–21]. They can be used in real-time data security, especially with IoMT devices with limited resources. Nevertheless, one of the critical issues is secure key management, particularly in dynamic multi-device settings. Secure key exchange, device authentication, and access control are typically carried out using asymmetric encryption, such as RSA and Elliptic Curve Cryptography (ECC). ECC is also quite appealing to smart homes since it provides high security with smaller key lengths, which is suitable for low-power and embedded applications. In order to increase the level of security, hybrid encryption schemes are used, where the efficiency of symmetric encryption is exploited, along with the safety of the key distribution of asymmetric cryptography. Further, the end-to-end encryption (E2EE) will provide protection to data during its lifecycle, between the device and cloud interfaces, and user interfaces. Lightweight cryptography, attribute-based encryption, and homomorphic encryption are emerging methods of interest to provide a means of access control on a fine-grained basis and privacy-preserving data processing. These encryption approaches, combined with security systems that are implemented by machine learning, create a strong base of secure, scalable, and reliable smart homes in the Internet of Multimedia Things [22–24]. Table 12.4 summarizes the role of encryption techniques in IoMT smart homes.

12.6 Case studies and applications

Practical applications and case studies in real-life scenarios have shown that machine learning-based and encryption-based security systems are effective in IoMT-based smart home systems. Among them are smart surveillance systems, where the encrypted video streams of the cameras inside and outside the building are processed with the help of ML and DL models to identify intrusion, suspicious activity, or unauthorized presence. Privacy-conscious analytics means that threat detection can be achieved without showing raw video content, which guarantees security and privacy of the users [25]. There is another significant case study of voice-controlled smart assistants. Voice recognition that is performed with the help of deep learning and encrypted audio data allows secure user authentication and command verification. ML models have the capability to differentiate between

Table 12.4 Encryption techniques for IoMT smart homes

Encryption aspect	Techniques used	Purpose in smart homes	Key advantages	Limitations/ Notes
Symmetric encryption	AES	Real-time protection of multimedia and sensor data	High efficiency, low computation	Secure key management required
Asymmetric encryption	RSA, ECC	Key exchange, device authentication, access control	Secure key distribution	Higher computational cost
Lightweight cryptography	Lightweight AES, ECC variants	Resource-constrained IoMT devices	Low power and memory usage	Limited algorithm strength options
Hybrid encryption	Symmetric + asymmetric schemes	Secure and efficient data encryption	Balances security and performance	Increased system complexity
End-to-end encryption (E2EE)	Device-to-cloud encryption	Protects data throughout lifecycle	Prevents eavesdropping	Key handling complexity
Advanced encryption models	Attribute-Based, Homomorphic Encryption	Fine-grained access control, privacy-preserving analytics	Enhanced privacy and flexibility	High computational overhead
ML-integrated security	Encryption + ML systems	Adaptive and intelligent security	Scalable, resilient protection	Integration complexity

authorized and spoofed or replayed voice attacks and minimize the threat of unauthorized device control. Smart energy management systems use ML algorithms on encrypted sensor data provided by smart meters and appliances to detect abnormal patterns of energy usage that can be interpreted to mean device tampering or cyber intrusion. These systems enhance efficiency in operations and security in addition to safeguarding delicate consumption information. Smart home applications like remote patient monitoring are healthcare-oriented and depend on a secure transmission of data. ML-assisted encryption will provide the confidentiality of health-related multimedia data and provide the ability to detect anomalies in real time in case of emergency situations. Federated and edge learning methods also contribute to more privacy as sensitive data is stored at home. Also, biometric authentication and encrypted communication are included in access control and smart locking systems to prevent unauthorized access. The case studies presented here point to the fact that the integration of machine learning, deep learning, and advanced encryption methods can be used to create secure, reliable, and privacy-conscious smart home applications in the Internet of Multimedia Things ecosystem. Various ML applications for securing smart homes are shown in Figure 12.1.

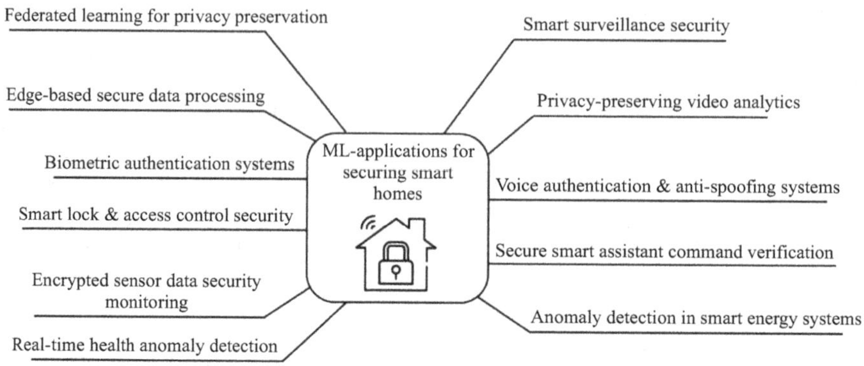

Figure 12.1 ML applications for securing smart homes

12.7 Challenges and future directions

Although machine learning- and deep learning-based security of encrypted smart homes has made great progress, there are still some challenges that restrict their extensive implementation and success in the context of IoMT. Resource constraints are one of the biggest problems. Numerous smart home devices have low computational capabilities, storage, and energy, which complicates the deployment of high-level ML/DL models and sophisticated encryption algorithms without negatively impacting their performance and latency. Privacy of information and confidentiality are also major issues. Though ML models need large amounts of data to be trained, collecting data continuously poses more risk of privacy exposure. Secure data sharing, reliable model training, and inference/poisoning attacks remain an unsolved problem in research. In addition, model interpretability and transparency are also restricted and it is hard to comprehend or have faith in automated security decisions made by the system administrators and users. Scalability and interoperability are other forms of challenge. Smart homes are made up of heterogeneous devices of various vendors, which may be based on incompatible communication protocols and security standards [26]. The development of coherent, flexible security systems that can be smoothly used in a variety of devices and platforms is complicated. Also, the changing cyber threat, including adversarial attacks on ML models, is a new risk that cannot be easily mitigated by conventional security mechanisms. The future research directions include lightweight and explainable AI models, edge and federated learning, and privacy-preserving methods of computation, including secure multiparty computation and homomorphic encryption. Adaptive encryption coupled with real-time threat intelligence integration and standardization of IoMT security architecture will also contribute to resilience. The goals of these directions are to develop scalable, reliable, and user-friendly smart home security systems to support next-generation multimedia IoMT systems [27].

12.8 Conclusion

The chapter discussed how machine learning and deep learning can be used in ensuring encrypted smart home systems in the Internet of Multimedia Things environment. With the rise in the use of smart homes, which depend on interconnected multimedia devices, the concern of data confidentiality, integrity as well as availability has become a priority. The discussion identified the main security issues, how ML and DL are implemented to detect intrusions, authenticate, and respond to threats ad hoc, and the significance of strong encryption solutions to safeguard sensitive multimodal data. Real-life case studies and examples were used to illustrate the way in which smart home intelligent security solutions could be implemented in practice and keep users' privacy simultaneously. Although the current state of affairs has some limitations concerning resource scarcity, interoperability, and the changing cyber threats, the solutions to the problem are available in the form of emerging technologies like edge intelligence, federated learning, and privacy-preserving computation. In general, the chapter highlights that intelligent learning models and high-grade encryption should be combined to ensure resilience, trustworthiness, and future-proof smart home systems in the Internet of Multimedia Things.

References

[1] A. Rego, P. L. G. Ramírez, J. M. Jimenez, and J. Lloret, "Artificial intelligent system for multimedia services in smart home environments," *Cluster Computing*, vol. 25, no. 3, pp. 2085–2105, 2022.

[2] M. S. Farooq, S. Khan, A. Rehman, S. Abbas, M. A. Khan, and S. O. Hwang, "Blockchain-based smart home networks security empowered with fused machine learning," *Sensors*, vol. 22, no. 12, p. 4522, 2022.

[3] C. Lee, L. Zappaterra, K. Choi, and H.-A. Choi, "Securing smart home: technologies, security challenges, and security requirements," in *2014 IEEE Conference on Communications and Network Security*. IEEE, 2014, pp. 67–72.

[4] R. Al Mogbil, M. Al Asqah, and S. El Khediri, "IoT: security challenges and issues of smart homes/cities," in *2020 International Conference on Computing and Information Technology (ICCIT-1441)*. IEEE, 2020, pp. 1–6.

[5] O. Taiwo, A. E. Ezugwu, O. N. Oyelade, and M. S. Almutairi, "Enhanced intelligent smart home control and security system based on deep learning model," *Wireless Communications and Mobile Computing*, vol. 2022, no. 1, p. 9307961, 2022.

[6] S. Ramapatruni, S. N. Narayanan, S. Mittal, A. Joshi, and K. Joshi, "Anomaly detection models for smart home security," in *2019 IEEE 5th Intl Conference on Big Data Security on Cloud (BigDataSecurity), IEEE Intl Conference on High Performance and Smart Computing,(HPSC) and IEEE*

Intl Conference on Intelligent Data and Security (IDS). IEEE, 2019, pp. 19–24.

[7] N. Sarwar, I. S. Bajwa, M. Z. Hussain, M. Ibrahim, and K. Saleem, "IoT network anomaly detection in smart homes using machine learning," *IEEE Access*, vol. 11, pp. 119462–119480, 2023.

[8] V. K. Sharma, S. K. Mohapatra, S. Shitharth, S. Yonbawi, A. Yafoz, and S. Alahmari, "An optimization-based machine learning technique for smart home security using 5G," *Computers and Electrical Engineering*, vol. 104, p. 108434, 2022.

[9] Mehrbakhsh Nilashi, Rabab Ali Abumalloh, Sarminah Samad *et al.*, "Factors impacting customer purchase intention of smart home security systems: social data analysis using machine learning techniques," *Technology in Society*, vol. 71, p. 102118, 2022.

[10] W. A. Alonazi, H. HAMDI, N. A. Azim, and A. Abd El-Aziz, "SDN architecture for smart homes security with machine learning and deep learning," *International Journal of Advanced Computer Science and Applications*, vol. 13, no. 10, pp. 917–927, 2022.

[11] L. Almuqren, K. Mahmood, S. S. Aljameel, A. S. Salama, G. P. Mohammed, and A. A. Alneil, "Blockchain-assisted secure smart home network using gradient-based optimizer with hybrid deep learning model," *IEEE Access*, vol. 11, pp. 86999–87008, 2023.

[12] P. Wang, F. Ye, X. Chen, and Y. Qian, "DataNet: deep learning based encrypted network traffic classification in SDN home gateway," *IEEE Access*, vol. 6, pp. 55380–55391, 2018.

[13] Abbas Acar, Hossein Fereidooni, Tigist Abera *et al.*, "Peek-a-boo: I see your smart home activities, even encrypted!" in *Proceedings of the 13th ACM Conference on Security and Privacy in Wireless and Mobile Networks*, 2020, pp. 207–218.

[14] F. F. Alruwaili, "Blockchain-powered deep learning for internet of things with cloud-assisted secure smart home networks," *IEEE Access*, 2024.

[15] G. Vardakis, G. Tsamis, E. Koutsaki, K. Haridimos, and N. Papadakis, "Smart home: deep learning as a method for machine learning in recognition of face, silhouette and human activity in the service of a safe home," *Electronics*, vol. 11, no. 10, p. 1622, 2022.

[16] N. Garg, M. Wazid, J. Singh, D. P. Singh, and A. K. Das, "Security in IoMT-driven smart healthcare: a comprehensive review and open challenges," *Security and Privacy*, vol. 5, no. 5, p. e235, 2022.

[17] S. Rani, A. Kataria, S. Kumar, and V. Karar, "A new generation cyber-physical system: a comprehensive review from security perspective," *Computers & Security*, vol. 148, p. 104095, 2025.

[18] S. Kumar, S. Rani, S. Sharma, and H. Min, "Multimodality fusion aspects of medical diagnosis: a comprehensive review," *Bioengineering*, vol. 11, no. 12, p. 1233, 2024.

[19] S. Rani, P. Bhambri, and M. Chauhan, "A machine learning model for kids' behavior analysis from facial emotions using principal component analysis,"

in *2021 5th Asian Conference on Artificial Intelligence Technology (ACAIT)*. IEEE, 2021, pp. 522–525.

[20] V. Puri, A. Kataria, S. Rani, and P. K. Pareek, "DLT based smart medical ecosystem," in *2023 International Conference on Network, Multimedia and Information Technology (NMITCON)*. IEEE, 2023, pp. 1–6.

[21] S. Rani, A. Kataria, P. Bhambri, P. K. Pareek, and V. Puri, "Artificial intelligence in personalized health services for better patient care," in *Revolutionizing Healthcare: AI Integration with IoT for Enhanced Patient Outcomes*. Springer, 2024, pp. 89–108.

[22] L. Khan and F. Kabir, "Security and privacy analysis of Internet of Medical Things (IoMT) based smart care homes," in *International Conference on Signal and Data Processing*. Springer, 2023, pp. 243–250.

[23] A. Akram, J. Akram, A. Alabdultif, A. Anaissi, and R. H. Jhaveri, "Secure and interoperable IoMT-based smart homes," *IEEE Consumer Electronics Magazine*, 2025.

[24] T. Vaiyapuri, A. Binbusayyis, and V. Varadarajan, "Security, privacy and trust in IoMT enabled smart healthcare system: a systematic review of current and future trends," *International Journal of Advanced Computer Science and Applications*, vol. 12, no. 2, pp. 731–737, 2021.

[25] L. Liu, M. Gao, Y. Zhang, and Y. Wang, "Application of machine learning in intelligent encryption for digital information of real-time image text under big data," *EURASIP Journal on Wireless Communications and Networking*, vol. 2022, no. 1, p. 21, 2022.

[26] Badraddin Alturki, Qasem Abu Al-Haija, Rayan A. Alsemmeari *et al.*, "IoMT landscape: navigating current challenges and pioneering future research trends," *Discover Applied Sciences*, vol. 7, no. 1, p. 26, 2024.

[27] Sumit Majumder ID, Emad Aghayi, Moein Noferesti *et al.*, "Smart homes for elderly healthcare—recent advances and research challenges," *Sensors*, vol. 17, no. 11, p. 2496, 2017.

Chapter 13

Machine learning with blockchain for securing agriculture-based applications

Abstract

The security, integrity, and trustworthiness of heterogeneous data have become a burning issue in the rapidly changing smart agriculture environment. This chapter discusses how machine learning (ML) and blockchain technologies can be integrated to ensure the security of agriculture-based applications in the Internet of Multimedia Things (IoMT). It explains how multimodal agricultural data, including sensor measurements, satellite pictures, videos taken by drones, and farmer feedback, can be smartly analyzed with the help of ML and deep learning algorithms and safely stored and shared with the help of blockchain systems. The chapter brings to the fore ML-based methods in detecting anomalies, predicting yields, detecting diseases, and decision support and blockchain capabilities of decentralization, immutability, smart contracts, and traceability. The proposals of the architectural models of ML–blockchain-based agricultural systems are introduced with a focus on secure data exchange, access management, and trust management. Practical use cases such as supply chain monitoring, precision farming, and sustainable resource management are also discussed in the chapter and end with the main challenges, limitations, and future research directions.

Keywords: agricultural IoMT; blockchain security; deep learning; machine learning; multimodal data; smart agriculture

13.1 Introduction to smart agriculture in IoMT

Smart agriculture in the Internet of Multimedia Things (IoMT) is the merging of state-of-the-art sensing, communication, and intelligent data analytics to convert the conventional farming method into information-based, secure, and automated systems. Smart agriculture will allow monitoring the health of crops, soil health, irrigation patterns, pest activity, and environmental factors in real-time due to the integration of multimedia sensors, including cameras, drones, soil sensors, and weather stations. These mixed streams of data give a lot of contextual data, which can be used in precision farming, better utilization of resources, and better crop productivity. The IoMT-based agriculture systems enable real-time decision-making capability based on wireless networks, cloud computing, and edge devices to enable farmers to react to the changing conditions of the field in real-time. Nevertheless, the vast gathering and transfer of sensitive farming information present major challenges in security, privacy, and data integrity. Machine learning applications improve smart farming by providing predictive analytics, anomaly detection, and smart automation, and blockchain technology provides decentralized trust, resistant storage of data, and open management of transactions. IoMT, machine learning, and blockchain can be used to build a solid digital farming ecosystem infrastructure on which modern agricultural applications can be built to be secure, scalable, and sustainable [1–3].

13.2 Multimodal agricultural data and security requirements

Multimodal agricultural data is the term used to denote the combination of heterogeneous data produced by a variety of devices in smart farming and includes soil sensors, weather stations, satellite pictures, drones, surveillance cameras, livestock wearables, and farm management records. The data modalities include numbers of readings, images, videos, audio signals, and geospatial information, which offer a holistic picture of the agricultural activities. Combination of multimodal data facilitates proper crop tracking, future yield forecasting, disease identification, irrigation scheduling, and livestock control. Nevertheless, the decentralized and distributed character of Internet of Multimedia Things (IoMT)-based agriculture presents some essential security issues [4–6]. The type of agricultural data can be quite sensitive, as it can divulge production on the farm, confidential cultivation methods, economic data, and supply chain information. The wrong decision-making, losses in the economy, and lack of confidence in digital farming systems may be caused by unauthorized access, data alteration, sensor data spoofing, and denial-of-service attacks. As such, it requires strong security specifications such as data confidentiality to avoid its leakage, integrity to guarantee its accuracy and authenticity, availability to ensure continuous operations, and authentication to identify legitimate devices and users. Also, it is crucial to ensure secure data exchange, accessibility, data privacy, and cyberattack resistance to safeguard multimodal agricultural information and assure the reliability and sustainability of the smart agriculture ecosystems [7–12]. Table 13.1 summarizes the key characteristics and security requirements of multimodal agricultural data.

13.3 Role of machine learning in precision agriculture

Machine learning is important to facilitate precision agriculture (shown in Figure 13.1) through converting vast amounts of heterogeneous agricultural data into meaningful information and decision support systems [13,14]. Machine

Table 13.1 Characteristics and security requirements of multimodal agricultural data

Aspect	Description
Definition of multimodal agricultural data	Combination of heterogeneous data generated from multiple smart farming devices such as soil sensors, weather stations, satellites, drones, cameras, livestock wearables, and farm management systems.
Types of data modalities	Numerical sensor readings, images, videos, audio signals, and geospatial data.
Purpose/Applications	Crop monitoring, yield prediction, disease detection, irrigation management, and livestock monitoring.
Benefits of multimodal data integration	Provides a comprehensive view of farm conditions and improves decision-making in precision agriculture.
Security challenges in IoMT-based agriculture	Distributed and decentralized systems increase risks of cyber threats and vulnerabilities.
Sensitive nature of agricultural data	May reveal farm productivity, cultivation techniques, financial details, and supply chain information.
Potential cyber threats	Unauthorized access, data manipulation, sensor spoofing, and denial-of-service (DoS) attacks.
Impact of security breaches	Wrong agricultural decisions, financial losses, and reduced trust in digital farming systems.
Key security requirements	Data confidentiality, integrity, availability, and authentication.
Additional security measures	Secure data sharing, access control, data privacy protection, and resilience against cyberattacks to maintain reliable smart agriculture ecosystems.

learning models can be used to detect more complex patterns and correlations that cannot be observed through traditional means by analyzing data obtained with the help of soil sensors, weather stations, satellite images, drones, and farm equipment. The models assist in proper prediction of crop yields, soil nutrients, and ideal planting times. Machine learning, including classification and image recognition, is applied in crop health management, where early detection of plant diseases, pest infestation, and nutrient deficiencies is performed, and timely intervention and less use of chemicals are implemented [13,15–17]. Predictive models are also effective in managing irrigation through predicting the crop water needs using weather forecasts, moisture content in the soil, and crop development stage, resulting in effective use of water. Machine learning in livestock farming can be used to analyze behaviors, monitor health conditions, and optimize productivity using wearable and video-based data. Moreover, anomaly detectors assist in detecting machine malfunctions, inconsistent sensor measurements, and environmental hazards. In summary, machine learning can enhance resource efficiency, lower the cost of operation, boost agricultural productivity, and improve sustainability of agricultural practices through precise, adaptive, and data-driven agricultural

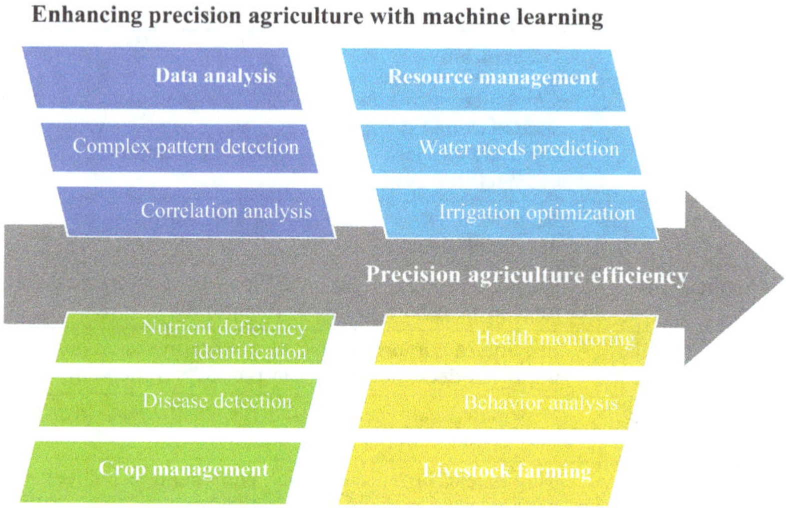

Figure 13.1 Machine learning for precision agriculture

management systems [17]. The role of ML techniques in precision agriculture is depicted in Figure 13.1.

13.4 Blockchain fundamentals for agricultural security and trust

Blockchain is a distributed registry technology that offers a decentralized, transparent, and resistant framework for securing data and establishing trust in digital systems. Blockchain basics are crucial in the agricultural scenario in solving security, data integrity, and trust concerns that are emerging as a result of the growing use of Internet of Multimedia Things (IoMT) and data-driven farming apps. A blockchain is a series of blocks, with each block holding a list of transactions, a timestamp, and a cryptographic hash of the preceding block, making records unalterable and traceable. Proofs of work or Proofs of stake are consensus mechanisms that allow distributed parties to agree on the validity of transactions without the help of a central authority. To achieve agricultural security, blockchain will provide the integrity of data in that the sensor readings, records of crops, and transactions cannot be altered by an unauthorized entity. It aids in sharing data between farmers, suppliers, regulators, and consumers with transparency without violating trust and accountability. Smart contracts are self-executing programs stored on the blockchain that are used to automate agricultural operations like crop insurance claims, subsidy payments, and payment of suppliers according to

and smart supply chain management are beneficial in improving trust, accountability, and sustainability in agriculture-based digital ecosystems [25].

13.7 Use cases and case studies in agriculture-based applications

The use of sophisticated technologies in agriculture-based applications (summarized in Table 13.2) is on the rise to deal with the issue of productivity, sustainability, and security. A notable application is the case of precision crop monitoring, where IoMT sensors, drones, and satellite images are used to gather multimodal data that is used to determine the health of crops, soil moisture, and nutrient levels. This data is used by machine learning models to identify diseases, forecast yields, and prescribe the best irrigation and fertilization techniques. Blockchain is a secure method of storing and tracking data collected, which increases the trust of interested parties. The other significant application is supply chain traceability, whereby blockchain-based platforms trace agricultural products from the farm to market. The examples of food safety cases indicate that immutable records can be used to

Table 13.2 Advanced technologies in agriculture-based applications

Application area	Technologies used	Purpose	Key benefits
Precision crop monitoring	IoMT sensors, drones, satellite imagery, machine learning	Monitor crop health, soil moisture, and nutrient levels	Disease detection, yield prediction, optimized irrigation, and fertilization
Agricultural data management	Blockchain	Secure storage and tracking of agricultural data	Data integrity, transparency, increased stakeholder trust
Supply chain traceability	Blockchain platforms	Track agricultural products from farm to market	Improved food safety, contamination tracing, fraud prevention
Smart contract-based logistics	Blockchain, smart contracts	Automate payments and logistics after delivery validation	Faster transactions, reduced manual intervention, transparency
Livestock management	Wearable sensors, machine learning, blockchain identity systems	Monitor animal health and behavior	Early disease prediction, productivity improvement, secure livestock records
Agricultural insurance and subsidy management	Machine learning, blockchain	Risk assessment and automated claim processing	Transparent fund transfer, efficient subsidy, and insurance management

determine the sources of contamination, prevent fraud, and enforce regulations. Smart contracts are automated payments and logistics that are recorded according to validated delivery terms. Wearable sensors and ML algorithms can be used in livestock management to track animal health and behavior, predict diseases early, and enhance productivity. Identity management based on blockchain ensures the livestock records and history of ownership. Also, the use of ML–blockchain in agricultural insurance and subsidy management allows proper risk assessment, automatic claim processing, and open blockchain fund transfer. These applications and case studies underscore the role of intelligent, secure, and decentralized technologies in enhancing the efficiency of operations, trust, and resilience of the current agriculture-based application [26].

13.8 Challenges, open issues, and future research directions

Although there has been major progress, machine learning and blockchain technology applications in agriculture-based applications have various challenges and unresolved questions. Another significant issue is the heterogeneity and quality of data because multimodal agricultural data is usually incomplete, noisy, and recorded in different environmental conditions, which impacts the accuracy of machine learning models. Scalability and latency are the problems that occur in the implementation of resource-intensive ML algorithms and blockchain protocols with large-scale deployments of the Internet of Multimedia Things (IoMT), especially in rural locations with sparse connectivity and the lack of computational resources. Security and privacy are also important issues as agricultural information can provide sensitive data on the production of the farm and business model. The research question of how to ensure privacy-preserving data analytics while being transparent on blockchain platforms, remains an open topic of research. There are also no standardized architectures and protocols of interoperability between various IoMT devices, ML models, and blockchain frameworks. Future work involves light- and energy-efficient ML models in edge and fog computing settings and scalable blockchain consensus mechanisms in the case of agriculture. Decentralized and privacy-sensitive models trained using federated learning and blockchain have potential solutions. Also, explainable agriculture AI will enhance trust and adoption by increasing the transparency of ML decisions. Regulatory, ethical, and socioeconomic concerns will also be addressed to make sure that intelligent agriculture systems are deployed in a sustainable, inclusive, and secure way.

13.9 Conclusion

Agriculture is experiencing a digital transformation at a fast rate due to the necessity of increased productivity, sustainability, and trust in food systems. The chapter has given a holistic perspective of how machine learning and blockchain technologies can be collectively utilized to improve security, transparency, and efficiency in agriculture-related applications in the Internet of Multimedia Things ecosystem. The chapter has identified the complementary capabilities of the technologies through the analysis of multimodal agricultural data, the functions of machine learning in precision farming, and the principles of blockchain to manage the safety of data. Machine learning facilitates intelligent analysis, prediction, and automation, whereas blockchain provides integrity, traceability, and decentralized trust to data. ML/blockchain models are integrated into secure data sharing, effective supply chain management, and automated processes based on smart contracts. They demonstrated their usefulness in crop and livestock management, food, and agricultural insurance in practical use cases. The challenges that existed, including scalability, quality of data, privacy, and interoperability, were also discussed in the chapter, and further research is necessary. In general, the intersection of machine learning and blockchain provides a powerful basis for creating safe, open, and sustainable smart agriculture platforms.

References

[1] N. Mahalingam and P. Sharma, "An intelligent blockchain technology for securing an IoT-based agriculture monitoring system," *Multimedia Tools and Applications*, vol. 83, no. 4, pp. 10297–10320, 2024.

[2] R. Fu, X. Ren, Y. Li, Y. Wu, H. Sun, and M. A. Al-Absi, "Machine-learning-based UAV-assisted agricultural information security architecture and intrusion detection," *IEEE Internet of Things Journal*, vol. 10, no. 21, pp. 18589–18598, 2023.

[3] R. Chaganti, V. Varadarajan, V. S. Gorantla, T. R. Gadekallu, and V. Ravi, "Blockchain-based cloud-enabled security monitoring using internet of things in smart agriculture," *Future Internet*, vol. 14, no. 9, p. 250, 2022.

[4] Ranjan Sapkota, Rizwan Qureshi, Muhammad Usman Hadi *et al.*, "Multimodal LLMs in agriculture: a comprehensive review," *IEEE Transactions on Automation Science and Engineering*, vol. 22, pp. 22510–22540, 2025.

[5] D. Jiang, Z. Shen, Q. Zheng, T. Zhang, W. Xiang, and J. Jin, "Farm-Light-Seek: an edge-centric multimodal agricultural IoT data analytics framework with lightweight LLMs," *IEEE Internet of Things Magazine*, vol. 8, pp, 72–79, 2025.

[6] L. Li, L. Liu, Y. Peng, Y. Su, Y. Hu, and R. Zou, "Integration of multimodal data for large-scale rapid agricultural land evaluation using machine learning and deep learning approaches," *Geoderma*, vol. 439, p. 116696, 2023.

[7] M. El Sakka, M. Ivanovici, L. Chaari, and J. Mothe, "A review of CNN applications in smart agriculture using multimodal data," *Sensors*, vol. 25, no. 2, p. 472, 2025.

[8] S. Rani, A. Kataria, P. Bhambri, P. K. Pareek, and V. Puri, "Artificial intelligence in personalized health services for better patient care," in

Revolutionizing Healthcare: AI Integration with IoT for Enhanced Patient Outcomes. Springer, 2024, pp. 89–108.

[9] V. Puri, A. Kataria, S. Rani, and P. K. Pareek, "DLT based smart medical ecosystem," in *2023 International Conference on Network, Multimedia and Information Technology (NMITCON)*. IEEE, 2023, pp. 1–6.

[10] S. Kumar, S. Rani, S. Sharma, and H. Min, "Multimodality fusion aspects of medical diagnosis: a comprehensive review," *Bioengineering*, vol. 11, no. 12, p. 1233, 2024.

[11] A. Kumar, R. Gupta, S. Kumar, K. Dutta, and M. Rani, "Securing IoMT-based healthcare system: issues, challenges, and solutions," *Artificial Intelligence and Cybersecurity in Healthcare*, pp. 17–56, 2025.

[12] S. Rani, A. Kataria, S. Kumar, and V. Karar, "A new generation cyber-physical system: a comprehensive review from security perspective," *Computers & Security*, vol. 148, p. 104095, 2025.

[13] A. Sharma, A. Jain, P. Gupta, and V. Chowdary, "Machine learning applications for precision agriculture: a comprehensive review," *IEEE Access*, vol. 9, pp. 4843–4873, 2020.

[14] T. A. Shaikh, T. Rasool, and F. R. Lone, "Towards leveraging the role of machine learning and artificial intelligence in precision agriculture and smart farming," *Computers and Electronics in Agriculture*, vol. 198, p. 107119, 2022.

[15] G. Mohyuddin, M. A. Khan, A. Haseeb, S. Mahpara, M. Waseem, and A. M. Saleh, "Evaluation of machine learning approaches for precision farming in smart agriculture system: a comprehensive review," *IEEE Access*, vol. 12, pp. 60155–60184, 2024.

[16] D. Radočaj, M. Jurišić, and M. Gašparović, "The role of remote sensing data and methods in a modern approach to fertilization in precision agriculture," *Remote Sensing*, vol. 14, no. 3, p. 778, 2022.

[17] R. Akhter and S. A. Sofi, "Precision agriculture using IoT data analytics and machine learning," *Journal of King Saud University-Computer and Information Sciences*, vol. 34, no. 8, pp. 5602–5618, 2022.

[18] S. Hu, S. Huang, J. Huang, and J. Su, "Blockchain and edge computing technology enabling organic agricultural supply chain: a framework solution to trust crisis," *Computers & Industrial Engineering*, vol. 153, p. 107079, 2021.

[19] Y. Chen, Y. Li, and C. Li, "Electronic agriculture, blockchain and digital agricultural democratization: origin, theory and application," *Journal of Cleaner Production*, vol. 268, p. 122071, 2020.

[20] Y. Bai, K. Fan, K. Zhang, X. Cheng, H. Li, and Y. Yang, "Blockchain-based trust management for agricultural green supply: a game theoretic approach," *Journal of Cleaner Production*, vol. 310, p. 127407, 2021.

[21] Chengliang Zheng, Xiangzhen Peng, Ziyue Wang *et al.*, "A review on blockchain applications in operational technology for food and agriculture critical infrastructure," *Foods*, vol. 14, no. 2, p. 251, 2025.

[22] Vikas Hassija, Siddharth Batra, Vinay Chamola *et al.*, "A blockchain and deep neural networks-based secure framework for enhanced crop protection," *Ad Hoc Networks*, vol. 119, p. 102537, 2021.

[23] I. Kaushik, N. Prakash, and A. Jain, "An AI-blockchain-assisted smart agriculture framework for enabling secure and efficient data transaction: a hybrid approach," *Knowledge and Information Systems*, vol. 67, no. 11, pp. 10087–10135, 2025.

[24] Y. LekhanRaj, M. Rudresh, and C. Shadaksharaiah, "SmartAgriChain: an integrated ML and IoT framework for sustainable precision agriculture," in *2025 Third International Conference on Networks, Multimedia and Information Technology (NMITCON)*. IEEE, 2025, pp. 1–5.

[25] M. H. Abidi, H. Alkhalefah, U. Umer, and M. K. Mohammed, "Blockchain-based secure information sharing for supply chain management: optimization assisted data sanitization process," *International Journal of Intelligent Systems*, vol. 36, no. 1, pp. 260–290, 2021.

[26] Redmond R. Shamshiri, Barbara Sturm, Cornelia Weltzien *et al.*, "Digitalization of agriculture for sustainable crop production: a use-case review," *Frontiers in Environmental Science*, vol. 12, p. 1375193, 2024.

Chapter 14

Leveraging ML and DL for safeguarding multimodal data in Industrial IoT environments

Abstract

In the age of fast industrial digitalization, securing the heterogeneous and high-volume data produced by the Industrial IoT systems is a basic need. The chapter is dedicated to the application of machine learning and deep learning methods in the process of securing multimodal data within the context of Industrial Internet of Things (IIoT). It includes a detailed discussion of multimodal sources of data and the corresponding cyber threat environment, and then it introduces the machine learning (ML)-based and deep learning (DL)-based anomaly detection and intrusion prevention techniques. The chapter reviews the secure architectural designs, which combine edge, fog, and cloud intelligence and privacy-sensitive and trust management schemes like federated learning and blockchain. The practical applicability of such approaches is pointed out by the real-life industrial applications and case studies. The main implementation issues and the performance evaluation metrics are examined to ensure a successful implementation. The chapter ends by highlighting the future directions and new trends, focusing on adaptive, explainable, and resilient intelligent security solutions in next-generation IoT systems of the industrial world.

Keywords: anomaly detection; deep learning; Industrial IoT security; machine learning; multimodal data; privacy preservation

14.1 Introduction to Industrial IoT and multimodal data security

The Industrial Internet of Things (IIoT) is a revolutionary paradigm whereby linked sensors, machines, controllers, and cyber-physical systems work together to facilitate intelligent and automated as well as data-driven industrial processes. The IIoT is used to increase productivity, efficiency, predictive maintenance, and operational safety of industries in manufacturing, energy, oil and gas, transportation, and smart factories due to the combination of advanced communication technologies with real-time monitoring and control. The environments of the modern IIoT create large amounts of heterogeneous data that are produced by various sources, such as sensor signals, machine logs, images, videos, audio streams, and operational metadata, which are all known as multimodal data. This multimodal data is a very important issue to secure because of its volume, velocity, variety, and sensitivity. Industrial data is usually an important target of cyberattacks, data corruption, and unauthorized access due to the presence of proprietary information, safety-sensitive parameters, and mission-critical knowledge. Conventional security controls do not usually have the capacity to manage the complexity and dynamism of IIoT systems. As a result, there has been an increasing demand for intelligent security solutions, adaptable security solutions, and scalable security solutions. Machine learning (ML) and deep learning (DL) solutions provide potential opportunities in anomaly detection, intrusion detection, integrity, and context-aware security of distributed IIoT networks [1–3].

14.2 Multimodal data sources in IIoT and threat landscape

The multimodal data sources in Industrial IoT (IIoT) systems are provided by different and interrelated elements (shown in Figure 14.1) that observe, regulate, and optimize industrial procedures. Such sources can be numerical sensor data (temperature, pressure, vibration, flow), machine logs, control signals of PLCs and SCADA systems, camera and thermal imaging data, audio fault and acoustic signals, and contextual data (timestamps, location, operator input). A combination of these diverse modalities facilitates the overall situational awareness, predictive maintenance, quality control, and intelligent decision-making in intelligent industrial systems. Nevertheless, multimodal data is also quite rich, which increases the threat space. Data injection, spoofing, replay attacks, ransomware, insider threats, model poisoning, and adversarial manipulation of sensor and visual data are examples of cyber threats to IIoT systems. Weakly secured communication channels, devices compromised, and outdated industrial protocols are also additional problems as far as security risks are concerned. Cyber attacks on a single data modality can spread throughout the interconnected systems, causing erroneous analytics, unsafe control measures, and operational failures. Thus, to develop resilient, intelligent, and robust IIoT security mechanisms, it is crucial to comprehend multimodal sources of data and the dynamic threat environment [4–12].

14.3 Machine learning techniques for IIoT security

Machine learning methods are critical in reinforcing security in Industrial IoT (IIoT) systems through intelligent, adaptive automation of threat detection and response (summarized in Table 14.1). Support vector machines, decision trees, random forests, and k-nearest neighbors are commonly applied as supervised learning techniques to intrusion detection, malware classification, and attack

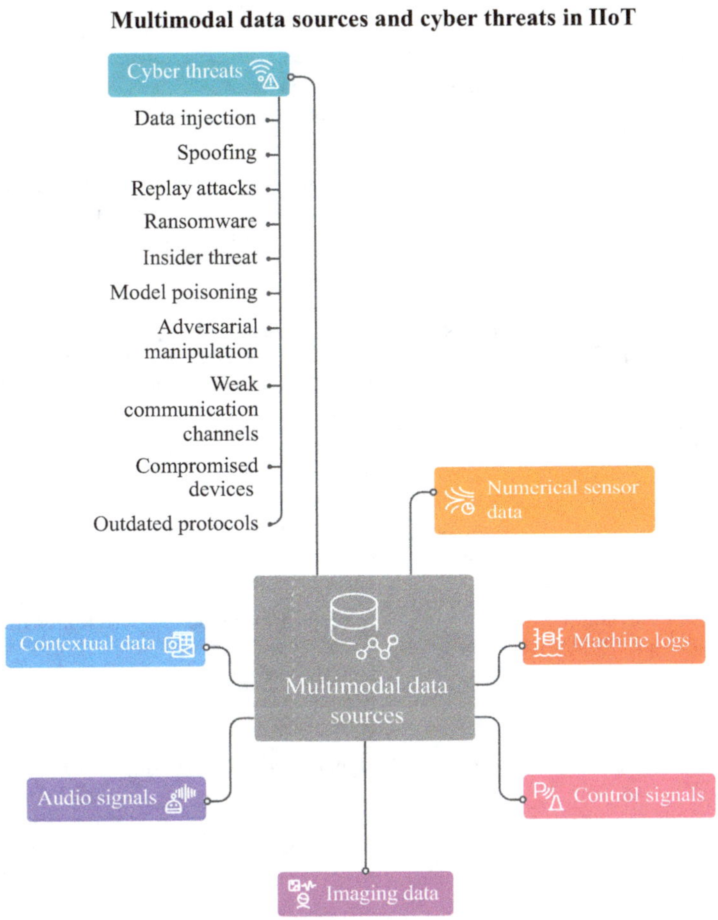

Figure 14.1 Multimodal data sources in IIoT landscape

pattern recognition of labeled network traffic and system logs. Unsupervised learning methods such as k-means clustering, DBSCAN, and autoencoders are useful in detecting anomalies through deviation from normal operation behavior without any prior knowledge of attack patterns. Deep learning methods also enhance the security of IIoT because they model high-dimensional and complex data. Convolutional neural networks are used to process visual image data of industrial cameras and spectrograms to detect faults and intrusions, whereas recurrent neural networks and long short-term memory models are used to analyze temporal relationships among sensor streams and network traffic. Hybrid and ensemble models enhance reliability and performance, as they involve a combination of multiple learners. Also, reinforcement learning advocates adaptive security policies, dynamic access control, and automated response policies. Altogether, machine learning allows implementing proactive, scalable, and

Table 14.1 Summarization of ML techniques for IIoT security

ML technique category	Algorithms/models	Key security applications in IIoT	Advantages
Supervised learning	Support Vector Machine (SVM), Decision Trees, Random Forest, k-Nearest Neighbors (KNN)	Intrusion detection, malware classification, attack pattern recognition using labeled network traffic and logs	High accuracy when labeled data is available; effective for known attack detection
Unsupervised learning	K-means Clustering, DBSCAN, Autoencoders	Anomaly detection by identifying deviations from normal operational behavior	Detects unknown or zero-day attacks without prior labeling
Deep learning	Convolutional Neural Networks (CNN), Recurrent Neural Networks (RNN), Long Short-Term Memory (LSTM)	CNN: analysis of visual/ industrial camera data and spectrograms; RNN/ LSTM: temporal analysis of sensor streams and network traffic	Handles complex, high-dimensional, and sequential IIoT data
Hybrid / Ensemble models	Combination of multiple ML algorithms	Improved intrusion detection and system security through integrated learning approaches	Higher reliability, robustness, and performance
Reinforcement learning	RL-based adaptive models	Dynamic access control, adaptive security policies, automated threat response	Enables intelligent and adaptive security management

contextual security solutions that address the dynamic and heterogeneous character of IIoT systems [13–17].

14.4 Deep learning models for anomaly and intrusion detection

The capacity of deep learning models to acquire intricate patterns with extensive, high-dimensional, and multimodal information has made them highly efficient in detecting anomalies and intrusions in the Industrial IoT (IIoT) environment. Unsupervised anomaly detection autoencoders and variational autoencoders find extensive use in detecting abnormal system behavior, with differences between reconstructed and original data suggesting abnormal behavior. These models have found application in particular dynamic industrial applications when it comes to monitoring sensor data, network traffic, and machine logs. Long short-term memory (LSTM) and gated recurrent unit models are recurrent neural networks that can be useful in learning time dependencies in time-series data, facilitating the early detection of stealthy and evolving attacks. Convolutional neural networks are used on both spatial and visual representations like surveillance images, thermal maps, and traffic flow representations and on transformed network data matrices. In complex IIoT systems, the hybrid architecture, which involves CNNs and LSTMs, is better in detection accuracy as it learns both the spatial and temporal features. Besides, the graph neural networks can depict the relationships between the devices and communication flows, enhancing the detection of coordinated and distributed intrusions. These deep learning models offer adaptive, high-precision, and scalable security mechanisms to the contemporary IIoT systems [18–20].

14.5 Secure architectures for ML/DL-enabled IIoT systems

Machine learning and deep learning-based Industrial IoT (IIoT) systems have secure architectures, which are aimed at securing heterogeneous data, intelligent models, and distributed infrastructures against various cyber threats (depicted in Figure 14.2). These architectures are usually layered and they include a perception layer, edge layer, fog layer, and cloud layer. At the perception layer, lightweight authentication, encryption, and secure boot mechanisms are used to protect the sensor, actuators, and industrial devices so that the authenticity of data is guaranteed at the point of creation. The edge layer is of high importance since it does local data preprocessing and real-time ML/DL inference to minimize latency and minimize exposure of raw sensitive data. This level often includes secure enclaves, hardware-implemented trusted execution environments, and model integrity checks

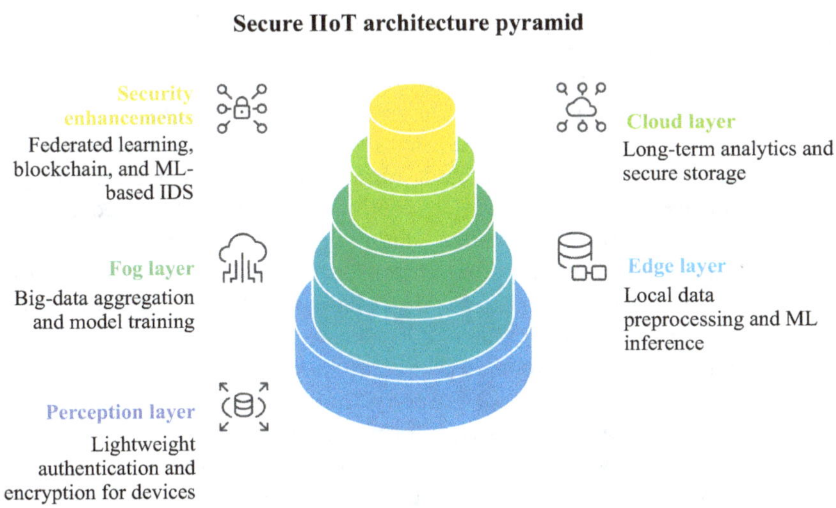

Figure 14.2 Elements of secure IIoT architecture

to ensure that deployed models are not tampered with and reverse engineered. Mist and cloud layers will assist in big data aggregation, training of models, and long-term analytics, which will be implemented using access control policies, secure APIs, and encrypted storage to protect data and trained parameters. Federated learning is also becoming a part of secure IIoT architectures where it is necessary to train a model together without a centralized exchange of data, thus maintaining privacy and minimizing attack surfaces. Distributed ledger technologies and blockchain are also interconnected to offer immutable logging, data provenance, decentralized trust management, and automated enforcement of policies via smart contracts. Also, persistent monitoring modules based on ML-based intrusion detection systems are implemented at all layers to support adaptive threat detection and response. Altogether, secure IIoT architectures based on ML/DL focus on defense-in-depth, scalability, and resilience to provide reliable intelligent processes in the framework of complex industrial conditions without compromising the confidentiality, integrity, and availability of data [21,22].

14.6 Privacy-preserving and trust management mechanisms

The privacy and trust management mechanisms should be used to guarantee secure and reliable working of the Industrial IoT (IIoT) systems that are based on machine learning and deep learning. Privacy-preserving methods are designed to safeguard sensitive industrial information, proprietary workflow, and operational intelligence without being limited to intelligent analytics. Data sharing and model training are some of the methods that are employed to avoid revealing sensitive information; these methods are data anonymization, pseudonymization, and differential privacy. Federated learning also improves privacy principles as ML/DL models can be trained on edge or fog nodes, and only model updates are transferred rather than raw data. Trust management mechanisms are aimed at creating a sense of confidence between IIoT devices, services, and the stakeholders in highly distributed environments. The identity and access management systems make sure that only identities that are authorized and authenticated are allowed to engage in data exchange and model execution. Trust models based on blockchains can be used to offer decentralized authentication, audit trails that cannot be changed, and policy enforcement that is transparent with the help of smart contracts. Reputation-based systems assess the behavior of devices over time in order to detect compromised or malicious nodes. Besides, model watermarking, integrity check, and secure update models are secure model management methods that prevent tampering and intellectual property theft of ML/DL models. Privacy-saving and trust management systems form a platform of resilience, accountability, and transparency that allows secure cooperation and reliable intelligence over IIoT ecosystems [23]. Various privacy-preserving mechanisms for IIoT are summarized in Table 14.2.

Table 14.2 Privacy-preserving mechanisms for IIoT

Mechanism category	Techniques/methods	Purpose in IIoT systems	Key benefits
Privacy-preserving data techniques	Data anonymization, pseudonymization, differential privacy	Protect sensitive industrial data, proprietary workflows, and operational information during analytics and sharing	Maintains confidentiality while enabling data analysis
Federated learning	Distributed ML/DL model training on edge or fog nodes with only model updates shared	Prevents raw industrial data from leaving local devices	Enhances privacy, reduces data leakage risks
Identity and Access Management (IAM)	Authentication systems, access control policies	Ensures that only authorized devices and users participate in data exchange and model execution	Strengthens system security and controlled access
Blockchain-based trust models	Decentralized authentication, immutable audit trails, smart contracts	Establish trust among distributed IIoT devices and stakeholders	Transparency, tamper-proof records, decentralized control
Reputation-based trust systems	Behavioral monitoring of devices and nodes	Detects compromised, malicious, or unreliable devices over time	Improves reliability and trustworthiness of the network
Secure model management	Model watermarking, integrity verification, secure model updates	Protects ML/DL models from tampering, theft, or unauthorized modification	Preserves model integrity and intellectual property
Overall outcome	Integrated privacy and trust mechanisms	Enables secure collaboration and reliable intelligence in IIoT ecosystems	Provides resilience, transparency, and accountability

14.7 Industrial use cases and case studies

The applicability of machine learning and deep learning-based security solutions to the Industrial IoT (IIoT) setting is proven by industrial use cases and case studies. In smart manufacturing, intrusion detection systems based on ML process multi-modal sensors, machine logs, and network traffic to detect cyber-physical attacks that may either disrupt production lines or affect product quality. Deep learning models that operate based on vision can also be used to identify unauthorized access and abnormal machine behavior using surveillance and thermal imaging data. Deep learning is also used in IIoT security systems to track grid sensors, substations, and control signals to detect anomalies, identify false data injection attacks, and machine tampering early in the energy and power system. Use cases of predictive maintenance make use of security analytics to identify the true equipment faults and malicious sensor data manipulation. ML-based pipeline sensors and acoustic signal monitoring can be used in oil and gas industries to detect leaks, sabotage, and coordinated cyber intrusions in real time. The examples of smart factories emphasize that edge-based ML models are being adopted with the help of blockchain-based audit trails to guarantee the integrity of data, its traceability, and compliance with regulations. On the same note, autonomous systems and industrial robotics use reinforcement learning to access control and to ensure secure coordination. These practical applications demonstrate that ML and DL can be used to increase situational awareness, decrease response time, and overall resilience of the IIoT infrastructures [24,25].

14.8 Implementation challenges and performance evaluation

Application of machine learning and deep learning-based security systems in Industrial IoT (IIoT) settings has a number of technical and operational challenges. The heterogeneity of IIoT devices and data modalities is one of the biggest problems and makes the integration of data, model design, and interoperability between legacy and modern industrial systems difficult. The device and edge resource constraints restrict the execution of computationally intensive DL models, which require model compression, pruning, and lightweight architectures. The problems in data quality are also noise, imbalance, and scarce labeled attack datasets, which further hinder the reliability of the models and their generalization. The challenges related to security are vulnerability of ML/DL models to adversarial attacks, data poisoning, and model inversion, and challenges in achieving secure updates to models and lifecycle management. Complexity of detection mechanisms is also limited by latency and real-time response requirements in industrial processes. Evaluation of IIoT security solutions needs to be evaluated in a comprehensive way using metrics such as accuracy but also precision, F1 score, false alarm, detection latency, computational overhead, and energy consumption. The evaluation is usually done with real industrial data, testbeds, and simulation environments to measure the resilience to different workloads and attack conditions. Performance indicators that are very important are scalability, resilience, and adaptation to changing threats. The challenges are critical to attaining dependable performance, and deployable IIoT system security that is enabled by ML/DL.

14.9 Future directions and emerging trends

The future trends and directions of securing the Industrial IoT (IIoT) systems are more toward intelligent, adaptive, and reliable machine learning and deep learning solutions. Among the trends is the use of self-education and independent security systems, which are constantly evolving with the changing attack patterns through online and constant learning. Explainable AI is becoming relevant to increase transparency and trust to make human operators interpret and justify ML/DL-based security decision-making in safety-critical industrial settings. Federated and collaborative learning is likely to become more integrated and allow the sharing of threat intelligence across organizations without compromising the privacy of data. Digital twin-based security analytics and graph neural networks are seen as the new potent devices for modeling complex industrial dependencies and simulating the conditions of cyber-physical attacks. Moreover, blockchain and ML/DL will further enhance the decentralization of trust, data provenance security, and policy enforcement. The use of edge-native AI with dedicated hardware accelerators will make security analytics real-time and low-latency, and it will be brought closer to industrial assets. Studies on strong and adversarially robust models will fix such weaknesses as data poisoning and evasion attacks. Lastly, the future IIoT deployments will be influenced by the standardized benchmarks, regulatory compliance, and the human-in-the-loop security frameworks to provide the scalable, resilient, and ethically focused intelligent security solutions.

14.10 Conclusion

This chapter provided a full perspective of the use of machine learning and deep learning models to protect multimodal data in Industrial IoT systems. It pointed out that there are various sources of industrial data and that the threat environment is expanding and posing a challenge to the traditional security mechanisms. The chapter, by reviewing ML-based and DL-based systems of anomaly and intrusion detection, secure system architectures, privacy-preserving systems, and trust management, showed how intelligent security systems, resilience, accuracy, and adaptability of intrusion detection can be improved in complex industrial environments. Real-world applicability of the techniques was demonstrated by practical use cases and case studies, whereas deployment issues and performance evaluation metrics stressed deployment concerns. The emerging trends and future research directions were also talked about in the chapter and explained the significance of explainable, federated, and edge-based intelligence. On the whole, ML and DL provide a strong base to develop secure, scalable, and trustworthy IIoT systems, which can help the industrial automation and digital transformation of the next generation.

References

[1] A. Ghaffari, N. Jelodari, S. Pouralish, N. Derakhshanfard, and B. Arasteh, “Securing internet of things using machine and deep learning methods: a survey,” *Cluster Computing*, vol. 27, no. 7, pp. 9065–9089, 2024.

[2] H. Attar, “Joint IoT/ML platforms for smart societies and environments: a review on multimodal information-based learning for safety and security,”

ACM Journal of Data and Information Quality, vol. 15, no. 3, pp. 1–26, 2023.

[3] J. Shen, M. Morrison, H. Miao, and F. Gu, "Harnessing deep learning for fault detection in Industry 4.0: a multimodal approach," in *2024 IEEE 6th International Conference on Cognitive Machine Intelligence (CogMI)*. IEEE, 2024, pp. 288–294.

[4] John Mulo, Hengshuo Liang, Mian Qian *et al.*, "Navigating challenges and harnessing opportunities: deep learning applications in Internet of Medical Things," *Future Internet*, vol. 17, no. 3, p. 107, 2025.

[5] B. Almadani and S. M. Mostafa, "IIoT based multimodal communication model for agriculture and agro-industries," *IEEE Access*, vol. 9, pp. 10070–10088, 2021.

[6] Shudong Zhou, Yu Liu, Rui Wang *et al.*, "A multimodal predictive channel model based on dual-camera images for IIoT communications," *IEEE Internet of Things Journal*, 2025.

[7] S. Rani, A. Kataria, P. Bhambri, P. K. Pareek, and V. Puri, "Artificial intelligence in personalized health services for better patient care," in *Revolutionizing Healthcare: AI Integration with IoT for Enhanced Patient Outcomes*. Springer, 2024, pp. 89–108.

[8] V. Puri, A. Kataria, S. Rani, and P. K. Pareek, "DLT based smart medical ecosystem," in *2023 International Conference on Network, Multimedia and Information Technology (NMITCON)*. IEEE, 2023, pp. 1–6.

[9] S. Kumar, S. Rani, S. Sharma, and H. Min, "Multimodality fusion aspects of medical diagnosis: a comprehensive review," *Bioengineering*, vol. 11, no. 12, p. 1233, 2024.

[10] D. Mittal, H. Singh, and S. Rani, "Exploring explainable artificial intelligence techniques for hate speech detection," in *International Conference on Innovative Computing and Communication*. Springer, 2024, pp. 545–554.

[11] S. Rani, A. Kataria, S. Kumar, and V. Karar, "A new generation cyber-physical system: a comprehensive review from security perspective," *Computers & Security*, vol. 148, p. 104095, 2025.

[12] A. Kumar, R. Gupta, S. Kumar, K. Dutta, and M. Rani, "Securing IoMT-based healthcare system: issues, challenges, and solutions," *Artificial Intelligence and Cybersecurity in Healthcare*, pp. 17–56, 2025.

[13] D. Alsadie, "Artificial intelligence techniques for securing fog computing environments: trends, challenges, and future directions," *IEEE Access*, 2024.

[14] O. F. Awad, L. R. Hazim, A. A. Jasim, and O. Ata, "Enhancing IIoT security with machine learning and deep learning for intrusion detection," *Malaysian Journal of Computer Science*, vol. 37, no. 2, pp. 139–153, 2024.

[15] A. Frankó, G. Hollósi, D. Ficzere, and P. Varga, "Applied machine learning for IIOT and smart production—methods to improve production quality, safety and sustainability," *Sensors*, vol. 22, no. 23, p. 9148, 2022.

[16] F. Taher, M. Abdel-Salam, M. Elhoseny, and I. M. El-Hasnony, "Reliable machine learning model for IIoT botnet detection," *IEEE Access*, vol. 11, pp. 49319–49336, 2023.

[17] Ahmad Houkan, Ashwin Kumar Sahoo, Sarada Prasad Gochhayat *et al.*, "Enhancing security in industrial IoT networks: machine learning solutions for feature selection and reduction," *IEEE Access*, vol. 12, pp. 160864–160883, 2024.

[18] T. Saba, A. Rehman, T. Sadad, H. Kolivand, and S. A. Bahaj, "Anomaly-based intrusion detection system for IoT networks through deep learning model," *Computers and Electrical Engineering*, vol. 99, p. 107810, 2022.

[19] Muaadh A. Alsoufi, Shukor Razak, Maheyzah Md Siraj *et al.*, "Anomaly-based intrusion detection systems in IoT using deep learning: a systematic literature review," *Applied Sciences*, vol. 11, no. 18, p. 8383, 2021.

[20] I. Ullah and Q. H. Mahmoud, "Design and development of a deep learning-based model for anomaly detection in IoT networks," *IEEE Access*, vol. 9, pp. 103906–103926, 2021.

[21] H. Djigal, J. Xu, L. Liu, and Y. Zhang, "Machine and deep learning for resource allocation in multi-access edge computing: a survey," *IEEE Communications Surveys & Tutorials*, vol. 24, no. 4, pp. 2449–2494, 2022.

[22] Gurpreet Singh Chhabra, Goluguri N. V. Rajareddy, Abhijeet Mahapatra *et al.*, "Deep learning-centric task offloading in IoT-Fog-cloud continuum: a state-of-the-art review, open research issues and future directions," *IEEE Access*, 2025.

[23] X. Wu, Y. Liu, J. Tian, and Y. Li, "Privacy-preserving trust management method based on blockchain for cross-domain industrial IoT," *Knowledge-Based Systems*, vol. 283, p. 111166, 2024.

[24] Shahid Latif, Maha Driss, Wadii Boulila *et al.*, "Deep learning for the industrial internet of things (IIoT): a comprehensive survey of techniques, implementation frameworks, potential applications, and future directions," *Sensors*, vol. 21, no. 22, p. 7518, 2021.

[25] N. Magaia, R. Fonseca, K. Muhammad, A. H. F. N. Segundo, A. V. L. Neto, and V. H. C. De Albuquerque, "Industrial internet-of-things security enhanced with deep learning approaches for smart cities," *IEEE Internet of Things Journal*, vol. 8, no. 8, pp. 6393–6405, 2020.

Chapter 15

Safeguarding educational multimodal data in the IoT with ML and DL

Abstract

The recent swift introduction of Internet of Things (IoT) technologies into the educational sector has turned the conventional learning space into a smart, data-driven ecosystem that produces a huge amount of multimodal data in the form of sensors, wearable devices, cameras, and learning management systems. This chapter discusses how machine learning (ML) and deep learning (DL) methods can be used to protect educational data in this type of IoT-enabled system. It addresses the multimodal educational information of different types, the security requirements, and the changing threat environment, comprising unauthorized access, data breaches, and privacy infringements. The ANOVA of ML and DL approaches to anomaly and intrusion prevention and secure access control are discussed, as are privacy-saving approaches and ethical and regulatory compliance frameworks. Real-life implementations and case studies are used to show practical applications in smart classrooms, virtual labs, and campus management systems. Lastly, the chapter identifies the implementation issues, performance measurement metrics, and future research prospects of creating secure, adaptive, and trustworthy smart environments of education.

Keywords: access control; deep learning; educational IoT; machine learning; multimodal data; privacy preservation

15.1 Introduction to smart education and Educational IoT

Smart education is a paradigm shift in teaching and learning backgrounds by incorporating digital technologies, data-based intelligence, and interconnectedness. Harnessing the power of the Internet of Things (IoT), schools can turn the conventional classroom into a smart learning environment that promotes student-centered learning, real-time monitoring, and interaction among students. Educational IoT (E-IoT) spaces are networks of devices like smart boards, wearable sensors, biometric devices, cameras, microphones, learning management systems, and environmental sensors that are implemented in classrooms, campuses, and virtual learning environments. These systems are interlinked to form large amounts of multimodal information such as textual learning records, audiovisual classroom interactions, behavioral information, physiological cues, and contextual information of time, place, and learning events [1–3]. This data can be used to provide adaptive learning, student performance analytics, automated attendance, and automated campus management. Nevertheless, the growing dependence on interconnected gadgets and data-focused platforms also comes with a lot of security and privacy issues. Educational information, which is sensitive and associated with students, instructors, and the running of the institutions, should be safeguarded against unauthorized access, abuse, and internet threats. As a result, smart learning systems grounded in machine learning and deep learning are becoming critical in providing safe, effective, and reliable smart education systems in the contemporary IoT-based learning settings.

15.2 Educational multimodal data types and security requirements

IoT-based educational environments produce a variety of multimodal data (shown in Figure 15.1), which are used together to facilitate intelligent learning and smart campus functions. Textual data, which covers academic records, assessments, learning management system logs, discussion content, classroom cameras, facial recognition systems, and smart boards; audio data, which includes lectures, discussions, and voice-based interactions; and sensor data, which includes wearables, attendance systems, and environmental monitors of factors such as location, movement, temperature, and occupancy, are all types of this data. Educational analytics is also enhanced with behavioral and contextual information such as

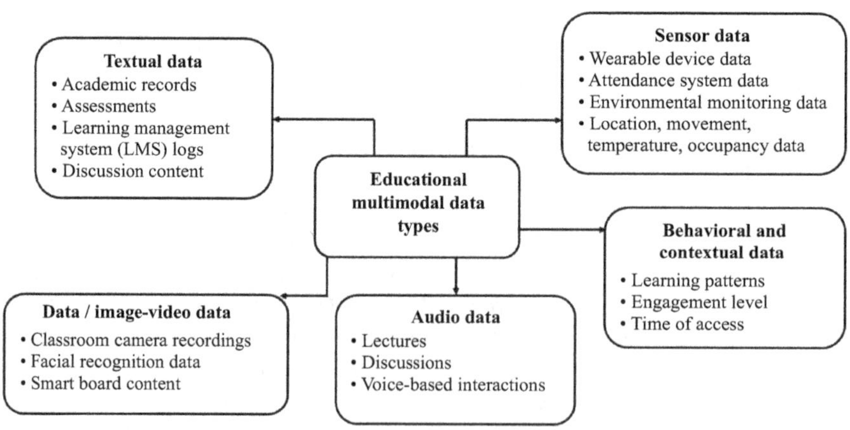

Figure 15.1 Educational multimodal data types

learning patterns, the level of engagement, and time of access. Educational multimodal data is sensitive and therefore comes with high security demands. The information (personal and academic) should not be disclosed to third parties because there should be confidentiality. Integrity also guarantees that there is no interference with grades, attendance records, and learning analytics. Availability is vital to ensure that the learning resources and services are not interrupted. It is also essential to maintain privacy, access control, authentication, and secure data storage as well as adhere to the educational data protection rules. The fulfillment of these security requirements is the key to establishing credible, moral, and robust smart education systems [4–7].

15.3 Threats and privacy challenges in Educational IoT systems

Despite the opportunities of smart learning provided by Educational IoT (E-IoT) systems, there is a spectrum of threats and privacy concerns (summarized in Table 15.1) because of the gathering, data storage, and exchange of sensitive multimodal information. Such threats as unauthorized access, data breaches, identity theft, ransomware, and insider attacks are common and may affect student records, performance data, and other information belonging to institutions. Cyberattacks may interfere with learning platforms, inject malware, spoof networks, or manipulate the assessment process, attendance, and grading tools. The problem of privacy is associated with collecting a lot of personal and behavioral information such as biometrics, video content, geographic positions, and interaction history. Mismanagement or distribution of data may result in profiling, surveillance, or exposing sensitive information of students and faculty. Also, the distributed and heterogeneous character of E-IoT devices makes data management more challenging, which makes it more susceptible to eavesdropping and data leakage as well as unauthorized cross-platform integration. The data confidentiality, integrity, and adherence to regulations such as FERPA or GDPR are essential to establishing trust and keeping the smart educational ecosystem safe and privacy-protected [8–14].

15.4 Machine learning techniques for data security and access control

Intelligent and adaptive solutions to improve data security and access control in Educational IoT (E-IoT) systems can be offered by machine learning (ML) techniques. Algorithms that are used to classify and detect unauthorized access attempts, phishing attacks, or anomalous user behavior include supervised learning algorithms like the support vector machines, decision trees, and random forests, which is based on historical access logs and authentication patterns [15–20]. Clustering and autoencoders are unsupervised methods of learning that detect

Table 15.1 Summarization of threats and privacy challenges in Educational IoT systems

Category	Threat/challenge	Description	Potential impact
Unauthorized access	Unauthorized system entry	Attackers gain access to IoT devices, learning platforms, or databases without permission.	Exposure of student records, institutional data leaks.
Data breaches	Leakage of sensitive information	Large datasets stored in E-IoT systems may be accessed or stolen by attackers.	Loss of confidential academic and personal information.
Identity theft	Misuse of personal identity	Personal credentials or biometric data of students or faculty may be stolen.	Fraudulent activities and impersonation in educational systems.
Ransomware attacks	System lock and data encryption	Attackers encrypt institutional data and demand payment to restore access.	Disruption of academic activities and financial losses.
Insider threats	Malicious or negligent insiders	Authorized users misuse access privileges intentionally or unintentionally.	Manipulation or leakage of institutional and student data.
Malware and network spoofing	Injection of malicious software or fake networks	Attackers introduce malware or create spoofed networks to compromise systems.	System disruption and unauthorized data access.
Manipulation of academic systems	Tampering with digital processes	Attendance systems, grading tools, or assessments can be altered by attackers.	Integrity loss of academic records and evaluation systems.
Privacy concerns	Collection of sensitive personal data	E-IoT collects biometric data, video streams, location data, and behavioral interactions.	Risk of surveillance, profiling, and misuse of personal data.
Data management complexity	Distributed IoT infrastructure	Large number of heterogeneous devices makes security monitoring difficult.	Increased vulnerability to cyberattacks and data leaks.
Eavesdropping and data leakage	Interception of communications	Data transmitted between IoT devices can be intercepted by attackers.	Unauthorized disclosure of sensitive information.
Regulatory compliance	Compliance with privacy regulations	Institutions must comply with standards like **FERPA** (Family Educational Rights and Privacy Act) and **GDPR** (General Data Protection Regulation).	Legal penalties and loss of institutional trust if violated.

anomalies in the normal operation of the system, allowing intrusions, insider attacks, and abnormal access patterns to be detected early, without the need to use labeled data. Reinforcement learning can provide dynamically controlled access to the system by constantly maximizing the authenticity rules and user rights according to the observed system behavior and the surrounding environment. Deep learning models, including convolutional and recurrent neural networks, are used to process high-dimensional multimodal information, like audio, video, and sensor data, to identify anomalies, track classroom interactions, and find suspicious behaviors. Hybrid models integrating the traditional ML with deep learning increase the detection accuracy and decrease the false positives. Also, predictive analytics based on ML can be used to predict possible security breaches and implement access control more flexibly, enhancing real-time resilience. Combining these methods, E-IoT systems can provide context-aware, scalable, and automated security, which will guarantee the confidentiality of sensitive educational data, its integrity, and accessibility to authorized users and facilitate personalized and secure learning settings [21].

15.5 Deep learning approaches for secure learning analytics

Deep learning (DL) solutions provide more sophisticated possibilities to secure learning analytics in Educational IoT (E-IoT) systems (summarized in Table 15.2) due to their ability to analyze high-dimensional and multimodal data efficiently and identify anomalies and integrity of data. Convolutional Neural Networks (CNNs) are trained on visual information from the classrooms' cameras, smart boards, and video lectures to identify illegal access, suspicious behaviors, or manipulation of the teaching materials. The recurrent neural networks (RNNs), especially long short-term memory (LSTM) networks, are learned on the history of student interaction logs, attendance history, and the online activity stream history to detect abnormal behavior, possible insider threats, or fraudulent submissions. Autoencoders and variational autoencoders are used as unsupervised anomaly-detecting tools, and they are used to reconstruct the normal activity patterns and identify anomalies that can be the signs of a cyberattack or policy breach. CNN-based hybrid architectures with RNNs and attention mechanisms can improve performance through the joint analysis of the multimodal educational data in space, time, and context. In addition, DL models can be used to provide secure, privacy-sensitive learning analytics using federated learning, in which the models are trained locally at devices or edge nodes, and only model parameters are exchanged but not raw student data [22,23]. This method will be confidential with the ability to predict, provide personalized learning, and allocate resources in a flexible way. In general, deep learning offers powerful, scalable, and intelligent systems to safeguard sensitive learning information and uphold the integrity of learning analytics.

Table 15.2 DL for secure educational data analytics

Deep learning method	Data type used	Application in E-IoT security	Key benefit
Convolutional Neural Networks (CNNs)	Classroom video streams, smartboard visuals, lecture recordings	Detect unauthorized access, suspicious behavior, and manipulation of teaching materials	Accurate visual monitoring and real-time threat detection
Recurrent Neural Networks (RNNs)	Sequential student activity data, attendance logs, interaction histories	Identify abnormal behavioral patterns and insider threats	Effective analysis of temporal activity patterns
Long Short-Term Memory (LSTM) networks	Long-term student interaction logs and online activity streams	Detect fraudulent submissions and unusual behavioral sequences	Captures long-term dependencies in sequential data
Autoencoders	Normal activity patterns from educational systems	Detect anomalies indicating cyberattacks or policy violations	Unsupervised anomaly detection without labeled data
Variational Auto-encoders (VAEs)	Multimodal behavioral and system data	Identify deviations from normal learning behavior patterns	Improved anomaly detection and data reconstruction
Hybrid CNN–RNN models	Multimodal educational data (video, logs, interaction data)	Joint spatial and temporal analysis for detecting threats	Higher accuracy through multimodal learning
Attention-based deep learning models	Contextual learning analytics data	Focus on critical patterns indicating suspicious activities	Enhanced interpretability and detection performance
Federated learning with DL	Distributed student data across devices or edge nodes	Secure model training without sharing raw data	Preserves privacy and supports decentralized analytics

15.6 Privacy-preserving, ethical, and regulatory considerations

The security of Educational IoT (E-IoT) systems is important because they are vulnerable to privacy-invasive, unethical, and regulatory threats; these systems store sensitive student, faculty, and institutional information. Privacy-saving measures are intended to defend personal and behavioral data and offer learning analytics based on data. Multimodal data analysis in educational institutions can be performed without the risk of revealing identifiable data, which is minimized through the usage of techniques such as data anonymization, pseudonymization, differential privacy, and federated learning, which reduce the likelihood of misuse or breaches. Ethical aspects demand that there be fairness, transparency, and accountability in ML- and DL-based security solutions. Algorithms should not be biased in the evaluation of students, their access, or analytical prediction, and the institutions should explain to the stakeholders the meaning of the automated choices clearly. To ensure trust and avoid unwanted implications in automated systems, human control is imperative. Legal compliance is also core since the educational data may frequently fall under the regulations of FERPA, GDPR, and COPPA, which require a high degree of data protection, access control, and consent management. These legal requirements need secure data storage, communication that is encrypted, audit trails, and controlled sharing protocols. Privacy, ethics, and adherence to regulatory practices are the factors that will make smart education systems trustworthy, responsible, and safe as well as facilitate the advantages of intelligent learning environments [24].

15.7 Applications and case studies in smart education

Smart education applications and case studies illustrate how machine learning (ML) and deep learning (DL) methods could ensure and optimize Educational IoT (E-IoT) systems and improve learning outcomes. ML-based access control and anomaly detection are used in intelligent classrooms to control student engagement, deter unauthorized access, and guarantee the integrity of digital learning content. Smart sensors and wearable devices can be used to monitor physiological and behavioral data to facilitate adaptive learning, automation of attendance, and personal feedback, whereas audiovisual streams can be analyzed by the DL models to recognize abnormalities or possible security risks. The case studies put an emphasis on practical applications like smart campus systems in which blockchain and ML are used to manage academic records, certificates, and credentials with increased security and without the ability to be tampered with. In e-learning, predictive analytics are used to detect at-risk students and intervene with them, and privacy-sensitive methods safeguard sensitive personal data. ML–DL hybrid frameworks have been implemented in virtual laboratories and distance learning to check for cheating, fraudulent submissions, or access to unauthorized resources. These applications demonstrate the twofold advantages of increasing security and facilitating intelligent educational services and offer scalable, adaptable, and reliable solutions to the contemporary learning ecosystems. With multimodal data analysis, institutions can develop secure, effective, and individualized learning experiences by integrating multimodal data analysis with effective security protocols.

15.8 Challenges and future research directions

The application of machine learning (ML)- and deep learning (DL)-based security to Educational IoT (E-IoT) systems has a few issues. Multimodal educational data, such as text, audio, video, and sensor signals, are heterogeneous, and data integration, preprocessing, and the training of models are made more difficult. Small labeled datasets, incomplete or noisy data, and imbalanced classes lower the accuracy and generalization of ML/DL models. The edge devices and wearable sensors have resource constraints, which also limit the implementation of sophisticated deep learning architectures and require lightweight models and efficient inference. There are also privacy issues, ethical issues, and regulatory compliance, which introduce more complexity to the problem, because student and institutional data should be safeguarded against breaches, misuse, and bias. Future research directions are aimed at the creation of privacy, adaptive, and explainable security frameworks. Federated and distributed learning strategies can make it possible to train models collaboratively without exposing raw data, whereas adversarial-resistant models can resist tampering of data and malicious attacks. Implementation of blockchain to assure data provenance, complex anomaly detection with hybrid DL models, and simulations based on digital twins to foresee security are future trends. Also, standardization, ethical principles, and human-in-the-loop will be essential toward establishing trusted, scalable, and resilient smart education ecosystems.

15.9 Conclusions

In this chapter, a detailed description of the process of ensuring the security of multimodal educational data in IoT-based smart learning systems through machine learning (ML) and deep learning (DL) approaches was provided. It also pointed to the variety of educational data, such as textual files, audiovisual feeds, sensor data, and behavioral data, and pointed to the privacy, ethical, and regulatory issues. The chapter has described the ML and DL methods of detecting anomalies, intrusion protection, and access control and how intelligent models can be used to improve security and also promote adaptive learning and individualized education. The methods to preserve privacy, federated learning, and blockchain-enabled trust systems were studied to guarantee confidentiality, integrity, and accountability. Practical implementations in smart classrooms, virtual labs, and management systems on campus were demonstrated on real-life applications and case studies. The chapter was concluded by discussing the implementation issues and the future research directions, such as the lightweight models, explainable AI, and resilient privacy-preserving systems, with the emphasis on the need to develop secure, trustworthy, and intelligent Educational IoT systems.

References

[1] A. Badshah, A. Ghani, A. Daud, A. Jalal, M. Bilal, and J. Crowcroft, "Towards smart education through internet of things: a survey," *ACM Computing Surveys*, vol. 56, no. 2, pp. 1–33, 2023.

[2] M. A. Rahman, L. Alqahtani, A. Albooq, and A. Ainousah, "A survey on security and privacy of large multimodal deep learning models: teaching and learning perspective," in *2024 21st Learning and Technology Conference (L&T)*. IEEE, 2024, pp. 13–18.

[3] P. Nanjundan, L. Thomas, P. Indu, and S. Eslamian, "Challenges and opportunities in multimodal learning research," *Multimodal Learning Using Heterogeneous Data*, pp. 239–246, 2026.

[4] U. B. Qushem, A. Christopoulos, S. S. Oyelere, H. Ogata, and M.-J. Laakso, "Multimodal technologies in precision education: providing new opportunities or adding more challenges?," *Education Sciences*, vol. 11, no. 7, p. 338, 2021.

[5] K. Sharma and M. Giannakos, "Multimodal data capabilities for learning: what can multimodal data tell us about learning?," *British Journal of Educational Technology*, vol. 51, no. 5, pp. 1450–1484, 2020.

[6] Y. Yan, H. Liu, H. Zhang, T. Chau, and J. Li, "Designing a generalist education AI framework for multimodal learning and ethical data governance," *Applied Sciences*, vol. 15, no. 14, p. 7758, 2025.

[7] W. Gan, M. S. Dao, K. Zettsu, and Y. Sun, "IoT-based multimodal analysis for smart education: current status, challenges and opportunities," in *Proceedings of the 3rd ACM Workshop on Intelligent Cross-Data Analysis and Retrieval*, 2022, pp. 32–40.

[8] A. A. Mawgoud, M. H. N. Taha, and N. E. M. Khalifa, "Security threats of social internet of things in the higher education environment," in *Toward Social Internet of Things (SIoT): Enabling Technologies, Architectures and Applications: Emerging Technologies for Connected and Smart Social Objects*. Springer, 2019, pp. 151–171.

[9] M. Adam, M. Hammoudeh, R. Alrawashdeh, and B. Alsulaimy, "A survey on security, privacy, trust, and architectural challenges in IoT systems," *IEEE Access*, vol. 12, pp. 57128–57149, 2024.

[10] Y. Khan, M. B. M. Su'ud, M. M. Alam, S. F. Ahmad, N. A. Salim, and N. Khan, "Architectural threats to security and privacy: a challenge for internet of things (IoT) applications," *Electronics*, vol. 12, no. 1, p. 88, 2022.

[11] N. El-Haggar, L. Amouri, A. Alsumayt, F. H. Alghamedy, and S. S. Aljameel, "The effectiveness and privacy preservation of IoT on ubiquitous learning: modern learning paradigm to enhance higher education," *Applied Sciences*, vol. 13, no. 15, p. 9003, 2023.

[12] L. A. Alexei and A. Alexei, "Analysis of IoT security issues used in Higher Education Institutions," *International Journal of Mathematics and Computer Research*, vol. 5, no. 5, pp. 2277–2286, 2021.

[13] A. Outchakoucht, E.-S. Hamza, and J. P. Leroy, "Dynamic access control policy based on blockchain and machine learning for the internet of things," *International Journal of Advanced Computer Science and Applications*, vol. 8, no. 7, pp. 417–424, 2017.

[14] P. M. Khilar, V. Chaudhari, and R. R. Swain, "Trust-based access control in cloud computing using machine learning," in *Cloud Computing for Geospatial Big Data Analytics: Intelligent Edge, Fog and Mist Computing*. Springer, 2018, pp. 55–79.

[15] S. Rani, A. Kataria, P. Bhambri, P. K. Pareek, and V. Puri, "Artificial intelligence in personalized health services for better patient care," in *Revolutionizing Healthcare: AI Integration with IoT for Enhanced Patient Outcomes*. Springer, 2024, pp. 89–108.

[16] M. Chauhan and S. Rani, "Covid-19: a revolution in the field of education in India," in *Learning How to Learn Using Multimedia*. Springer, 2021, pp. 23–42.

[17] D. Mittal, H. Singh, and S. Rani, "Exploring explainable artificial intelligence techniques for hate speech detection," *in International Conference on Innovative Computing and Communication*. Springer, 2024, pp. 545–554.

[18] S. Kumar, S. Rani, S. Sharma, and H. Min, "Multimodality fusion aspects of medical diagnosis: a comprehensive review," *Bioengineering*, vol. 11, no. 12, p. 1233, 2024.

[19] S. N. Hegde, D. Srinivas, M. Rajan, S. Rani, A. Kataria, and H. Min, "Multi-objective and multi constrained task scheduling framework for computational grids," *Scientific Reports*, vol. 14, no. 1, p. 6521, 2024.

[20] S. Rani, A. Kataria, S. Kumar, and V. Karar, "A new generation cyber-physical system: a comprehensive review from security perspective," *Computers & Security*, vol. 148, p. 104095, 2025.

[21] M. N. Nobi, R. Krishnan, Y. Huang, and R. Sandhu, "Administration of machine learning based access control," in *European Symposium on Research in Computer Security*. Springer, 2022, pp. 189–210.

[22] M. A. Elsayed and M. Zulkernine, "PredictDeep: security analytics as a service for anomaly detection and prediction," *IEEE Access*, vol. 8, pp. 45184–45197, 2020.

[23] Seyed Ali Osia, Ali Shahin Shamsabadi, Sina Sajadmanesh *et al.*, "A hybrid deep learning architecture for privacy-preserving mobile analytics," *IEEE Internet of Things Journal*, vol. 7, no. 5, pp. 4505–4518, 2020.

[24] Shuang Wang, Xiaoqian Jiang, Siddharth Singh *et al.*, "Genome privacy: challenges, technical approaches to mitigate risk, and ethical considerations in the United States," *Annals of the New York Academy of Sciences*, vol. 1387, no. 1, pp. 73–83, 2017.

Chapter 16
Conclusions

Abstract

With the fast digital revolution and ubiquitous connectivity, heterogeneous multimedia data protection has become a major problem of concern to smart systems. The chapter is a conclusion to the book *Machine Learning and Deep Learning-Driven Techniques in Multimodal Data Security in the Internet of Multimedia Things* (IoMT) and summarizes main findings and conclusions about the topic and perspectives of the future. It mentions the relevance of machine learning (ML) and deep learning (DL) methods in solving security challenges in multimodal IoMT settings, including intrusion detection, authentication, anomaly detection, privacy preservation, and trust management. The cross-domain experiences of applications such as smart healthcare, transportation, smart cities, and industrial IoT are summarized. The chapter also covers the recent trends, open research issues, and future outlook with the necessity of scalable, robust, explainable, and ethically responsible AI-based security systems in the next-generation IoMT ecosystems.

Keywords: artificial intelligence; deep learning; Internet of Multimedia Things; machine learning; multimodal data security; privacy preservation

16.1 Overview of the book and key contributions

With the fast digital revolution, the spread of interconnected multimedia devices has transformed the way data is produced, transmitted, and consumed in intelligent surroundings. *Machine Learning and Deep Learning-Driven Techniques for Multimodal Data Security in the Internet of Multimedia Things (IoMT)* presents an in-depth and prospective examination of intelligent security frameworks in such complicated, data-intensive settings. Since IoMT systems combine heterogeneous modalities, such as images, videos, audio, text, and sensor data, data confidentiality, integrity, privacy, and trust have become a pressing issue. The main contribution of the book is that it covers multimodal data security in the entire IoMT lifecycle, including data acquisition and fusion to secure storage, communications, and intelligent decision-making. It chronologically gives machine learning and deep learning methods of intrusion detection, authentication, access control, anomaly detection, privacy preservation, and trust management [1].

Federated learning, blockchain-based security, adversarial defense strategy, and explainable AI are also emerging paradigms that are discussed as scalable and resilient solutions to modern multimedia systems. One of the strengths of the book is that it is application-oriented. The book provides practical examples on how theoretical models can be applied in creating practical security solutions using real-world case studies and domain-specific scenarios, including smart healthcare, intelligent transportation, smart cities, agriculture, and industrial IoT. In addition, it also identifies the research issues of open research regarding the heterogeneity of data, robust models, resource limitations, and ethics. On the whole, this book can be considered an excellent source of information to support the work of researchers, academicians, and practitioners as it helps to identify the place between intelligent learning models and secure multimodal IoMT deployments and shape the way of further research in this field [2].

16.2 Summary of ML and DL techniques for multimodal data security

In the Internet of Multimedia Things (IoMT), heterogeneous data are constantly produced and shared, meaning machine learning (ML) and deep learning (DL) are now key to securing multimodal data. Multimodal data is generated and shared continuously in the Internet of Multimedia Things (IoMT), where images, video, audio, text, and sensor streams are the central products in the Internet of Multimedia Things. Data-driven intelligent techniques are commonly necessary because traditional rule-based security mechanisms are often unsuitable to manage the volume, diversity, and dynamism of such data. Intrusion detection, malware classification, access control, and anomaly detection are some of the commonly used ML methods like support vector machines, decision trees, random forests, k-nearest neighbors, and clustering algorithms. These techniques are based on handcrafted features that are taken out of the multimodal sources and they are appreciated for their interpretability, reduced computational expense, and their applicability to resource-limited IoMT devices. Ensemble-based and statistical learning methods also help in enhancing detection and resisting familiar attack patterns [3]. DL methods build on these features by learning features between raw multimodal data automatically. Convolutional neural networks can be used to protect image and video data by means of biometric authentication, surveillance analytics, and verification of content integrity. Recurrent neural networks and long short-term memory are used on the sequential data, including network traffic and audio streams, to identify the temporal anomalies and the malicious activities. Transformer-based architectures also improve multimodal representation learning through long-range dependencies and cross-modal correlations. In multimodal security, hybrid and advanced frameworks are important. Multimodal fusion models combine information in one or more data modalities to produce more precise and context-sensitive threat detection. Federated learning can facilitate model training in a distributed IoMT when the nodes maintain the privacy of data.

Frameworks based on ML with the aid of blockchain increase the level of trust, traceability, and safe data exchange, whereas adversarial learning methods increase the resistance of models to attacks. On balance, ML and DL methods offer dynamic, scalable, and smart security, which can be considered the basis of effective multimodal data protection in future IoMT systems [4–7].

16.3 Cross-domain insights from IoMT applications

Internet of Multimedia Things (IoMT) applications cut across a wide range of fields including smart healthcare, intelligent transportation, smart cities, industrial automation, agriculture, and surveillance systems. Although the goals and operational settings vary, cross-domain analysis provides a number of general lessons that can be used to create secure and intelligent IoMT systems. A major lesson here is that there is a common problem of processing heterogeneous multimodal data such as images, videos, audio, text, and sensor streams. In the broad areas, situational awareness, accuracy of decisions, and detection of security threats are greatly improved by effective multimodal data fusion models with machine learning and deep learning algorithms. The other relevant lesson is the necessity of universal adaptive and real-time security systems. Low latency and high reliability are also important in fields like healthcare monitoring and traffic management, where lightweight ML models on the edge and more sophisticated DL models on the fog or cloud layers are required. This multilayered intelligence structure is continuously found throughout the applications of the IoMT to balance among performance, scalability, and resource limitations. The cross-cutting issues include privacy and trust, especially in healthcare, smart cities, and surveillance. Such methods as federated learning, differential privacy, and blockchain-based systems are becoming more and more popular in various fields in order to guarantee the protection of data exchange without sensitive data leakage. Also, explainable AI is becoming increasingly relevant in safety-critical systems, where the regulatory requirement to be transparent in making decisions is needed to gain user trust. Lastly, cross-domain lessons emphasize general issues, such as resistance to adversarial attacks, heterogeneous devices, ethical issues with data usage, etc. The experience of lessons taught in one area, e.g., intrusion detection in industrial IoMT, can successfully be applied to other areas, e.g., smart grids or transportation systems. All these common insights reinforce the importance of cross-domain knowledge transfer in creating resilient, secure, and scalable IoMT solutions [8,9].

16.4 Emerging trends and technological implications

The blistering development of the Internet of Multimedia Things (IoMT) is giving rise to new tendencies that greatly affect multimodal data security and intelligent system design. Among the trends is the movement of centralized cloud-based processing to edge and fog intelligence. The closer proximity of machine learning and deep learning models to the source of data will allow real-time threat detection, lower latency, and enhanced privacy, which are essential in applications, including healthcare monitoring, autonomous transportation, and smart surveillance. The other trend is the increased use of privacy-saving learning methods. Secure multi-party computation, federated learning, and differential privacy are some of the techniques becoming popular to ensure sensitive multimedia data is not compromised and, at the same time, allow collaborative model training among distributed IoMT nodes. These strategies have high technological connotations to regulatory adherence, information possession, and confidence among users, particularly in information-sensitive areas. Another significant trend is the development of multimodal deep learning architectures. Transformer models, cross-modal attention models, and foundation models are facilitating the more robust integration of heterogeneous data types, which results in security analytics and context-driven decision-making. Meanwhile, adversarial machine learning has become a subject of interest as a defense, as well as a threat, and has led to the creation of resilient and robust models resistant to spoofing, poisoning, and evasion attacks. Another direction of development is blockchain integration into IoMT security models that provide decentralized trust, unalterable audit trails, and safe data exchange. This is technologically helpful in enhancing the availability of transparent access control and responsibility in large-scale IoMT implementations. Lastly, the growing interest in explainable and trustworthy AI is an indicator of the desire to have interpretable security choices in safety-critical applications. On the whole, these tendencies are transforming the architectures of IoMT and emphasizing the necessity of scalable, secure, and ethical intelligent systems [10].

16.5 Research challenges and open issues

Although there has been a major advance in machine learning and deep learning-based security solutions for the Internet of Multimedia Things (IoMT), a number of research issues and gaps in the field are still present. One of the major problems is the heterogeneity and high dimensionality of multimodal data. The unified and efficient integration of images, video, audio, text, and sensor streams without loss of information or bias in the model is a research problem open to investigation particularly under real-time constraints. Another important problem is scalability and resource constraints. Numerous IoMT devices have constrained computation, memory, and energy, and it is challenging to implement the sophisticated deep learning models at the edge. There is a continuous challenge of designing lightweight, energy-efficient, and adaptable models that ensure high security performance. Moreover, generalization of models to new environments and domains is not as common, with models trained in a specific setting failing in dynamic or hidden attack conditions. The very security and robustness of learning models are significant issues. The adversarial attacks that IoMT systems are susceptible to include data poisoning, inversion of models, and evasion attacks that could affect the reliability of decisions. The creation of strong, self-regulating, and constantly educating security models remains a research problem. Preservation of privacy is also not easy, particularly when data utility is weighed against stringent privacy demands in sensitive applications such as healthcare and surveillance. The problem of interoperability and standardization also makes large-scale IoMT deployment difficult. The absence of standardized security within devices, platforms, and communication protocols does not enable easy integration and confidence management. Lastly, the ethical, legal, and explainability issues need more in-depth research since clear and responsible AI-based security systems are the key to compliance with regulations and the confidence of users. It is important to tackle these issues in order to achieve secure, scalable, and sustainable IoMT ecosystems.

16.6 Future directions and recommendations

The Internet of Multimedia Things (IoMT) research in the future must aim at the development of smart, safe, and scalable systems that can respond to changing threats and heterogeneous conditions. The design of lightweight but powerful machine learning and deep learning models designed to address edge and fog computing is one of the main directions. Real-time security analytics can be supported by model compression, pruning, knowledge distillation, and adaptive inference and meet the resource constraints of the IoMT devices. The other direction of significance is the development of privacy-preserving and collaborative learning methods. Federated learning together with differential privacy, secure aggregation, and blockchain-based trust management can facilitate the safe exchange of data without sensitive multimodal data being disclosed. Cross-domain and transfer learning methods should also be studied by the researchers to enhance generalization of the models and minimize the amount of training data in the case of various applications in IoMT. One of the most important recommendations is to improve the robustness and resilience of a model. The systems of the future must incorporate adversarial defense systems, constant learning, and self-adaptable security models that can identify new and zero-day offenses. Explainable AI should also be used to enhance transparency, accountability, and trust in the user, especially in areas of healthcare and smart transportation that are safety- and regulation-critical. In a system-level approach, standardized architecture and interoperable security protocols are vital to large-scale IoMT implementation. Academia, industry, and standardization bodies can work together to create shared benchmarks, datasets, and metrics of evaluation faster. Lastly, the smart security solutions must be designed with ethical and legal dimensions, allowing fairness, accountability, and adherence to the data protection rules. All these guidelines and prescriptions will give a blueprint of how to construct safe, trustworthy, and sustainable IoMT ecosystems in the future [11].

16.7 Final remarks

The Internet of Multimedia Things (IoMT) is the paradigm shift where devices are intelligent and interconnected to constantly create and share rich multimodal data.

It is now impossible to secure such complicated ecosystems with the help of traditional methods only and it requires the combination of machine learning and deep-learning-based security frameworks. The possibilities of the intelligent models in maximizing confidentiality, integrity, privacy, and trust in multimodal IoMT settings have been addressed in a systematic manner throughout this book. The discussions note that the use of ML and DL, together with emerging technologies like edge computing, federated learning, blockchain, and explainable AI, can provide adaptable and scalable solutions to the changing security threats. Meanwhile, the book also stresses that technological progress should be supported by attentive attitude toward robustness and interoperability, a responsible attitude toward ethics, and compliance with regulations. These are the areas that need to be addressed to have reliable and socially acceptable deployments of IoMT. To sum up, this book highlights the significance of the holistic and interdisciplinary approach to multimodal data security, which unites the theory, application, and future perspectives of research. It will be aimed at being a useful resource to researchers, practitioners, and policymakers as well as motivate further innovation in the design of secure, intelligent, and trustworthy IoMT systems that will be able to support next-generation digital applications.

References

[1] Y. B. Zikria, M. K. Afzal, and S. W. Kim, "Internet of multimedia things (IoMT): opportunities, challenges and solutions," *Sensors*, vol. 20, no. 8, p. 2334, 2020.

[2] E. Curry, D. Salwala, P. Dhingra, F. A. Pontes, and P. Yadav, "Multimodal event processing: a neural-symbolic paradigm for the internet of multimedia things," *IEEE Internet of Things Journal*, vol. 9, no. 15, pp. 13705–13724, 2022.

[3] Haewon Byeon, Vikas Raina, Mukta Sandhu *et al.*, "Artificial intelligence-enabled deep learning model for multimodal biometric fusion," *Multimedia Tools and Applications*, vol. 83, no. 33, pp. 80105–80128, 2024.

[4] Qingzhi Liu, Yuchen Huang, Chenglu Jin *et al.*, "Privacy and integrity protection for IoT multimodal data using machine learning and blockchain," *ACM Transactions on Multimedia Computing, Communications and Applications*, vol. 20, no. 6, pp. 1–18, 2024.

[5] S. Rani, A. Kataria, P. Bhambri, P. K. Pareek, and V. Puri, "Artificial intelligence in personalized health services for better patient care," in *Revolutionizing Healthcare: AI Integration with IoT for Enhanced Patient Outcomes*. Springer, 2024, pp. 89–108.

[6] S. Kumar, S. Rani, S. Sharma, and H. Min, "Multimodality fusion aspects of medical diagnosis: a comprehensive review," *Bioengineering*, vol. 11, no. 12, p. 1233, 2024.

[7] D. Mittal, H. Singh, and S. Rani, "Exploring explainable artificial intelligence techniques for hate speech detection," in *International Conference on Innovative Computing and Communication*. Springer, 2024, pp. 545–554.

[8] K. Anitha, B. M. Kumar, and K. V. Prasad, "Heterogeneous interoperable sensors integrating cognitive knowledge for IoT-based cross-domain applications," *IEEE Sensors Journal*, vol. 25, no. 7, pp. 12119–12127, 2025.

[9] N. Sharma and P. G. Shambharkar, "Multi-attention DeepCRNN: an efficient and explainable intrusion detection framework for Internet of Medical Things environments," *Knowledge and Information Systems*, vol. 67, pp. 5783–5849, 2025.

[10] A. Nauman, Y. A. Qadri, M. Amjad, Y. B. Zikria, M. K. Afzal, and S. W. Kim, "Multimedia Internet of Things: a comprehensive survey," *IEEE Access*, vol. 8, pp. 8202–8250, 2020.

[11] M. Seth, H. Jalo, Å. Högstedt, O. Medin, B. A. Sjöqvist, and S. Candefjord, "Technologies for interoperable Internet of Medical Things platforms to manage medical emergencies in home and prehospital care: scoping review," *Journal of Medical Internet Research*, vol. 27, p. e54470, 2025.

Index

www.ingramcontent.com/pod-product-compliance
Lightning Source LLC
LaVergne TN
LVHW011850200926
848484LV00002B/435